International Intervention in Afghanistan

International Intervention in Afghanistan

MOTIVES AND APPROACHES

Edited by
Arpita Basu Roy
Binoda Kumar Mishra
Aliva Mishra

Maulana Abul Kalam Azad Institute of Asian Studies, Kolkata

Indian Council of World Affairs, New Delhi

SHIPRA

ISBN: 978-81-7541-656-7

First Published in India in 2012

International Intervention in Afghanistan

Published by:
SHIPRA PUBLICATIONS
H.O.: LG 18-19, Pankaj Central Market, Patparganj,
I.P. Ext., Delhi-110092, Tel: 91-11-2223 5152, 2223 6152
Br.Off.: 4617/18, Ansari Road, Darya Ganj,
New Delhi-110002, Tel: 6594 6453, 9810522367
E-mail: info@shiprapublications.com
www.shiprapublications.com

Contents

Dimensions of State and Nation-building

The Government and the Taliban

Regional Concerns

Introduction

The issue of intervention, humanitarian or otherwise has generated one of the most heated discussions in international relations over the past decade. Intervention remains a controversial norm in international relations, largely because of continued opposition from certain members of international society, and concerns about its potentially negative consequences. Both theorists and practitioners have been involved in the debate which revolves around alleged tension between the principle of state sovereignty, a defining pillar of the United Nations (UN) system and international law, and the evolving international norms related to human rights and the use of force. Is humanitarian intervention evolving in a post-9/11 world? Many academic discussions focus on the question of whether there is a legal right of humanitarian intervention, giving insufficient attention to the underlying ethical issues, the politics within international organizations and coalitions, and the practical dilemmas faced by international actors—before, during and after intervention. The post-cold war international scenario witnessed a series of military actions explicitly supported by a humanitarian rationale. In these cases, the apparent conflict between sovereignty and human rights has been addressed in two ways: through an evolution in the notion of sovereignty, from 'sovereignty as authority' (control over territory) to 'sovereignty as responsibility' (respect for a minimum standard of human rights); and through an expanded definition of what constitutes a 'threat to international peace and security' under chapter VII of the United Nations Charter. While the 1990s saw some successful cases of intervention to address humanitarian catastrophes (such as East Timor), the current capability of international organizations to undertake humanitarian interventions remains limited.

In the case of Afghanistan, the military intervention by the US and NATO was not humanitarian in the first place. It was an exercise of the right of self-defence, an action provoked by the terror attacks on New York and Washington DC in September 2001. In the past 9 years, the vision of the international American-led intervention in Afghanistan has moved from that of a successful new paradigm in warfare to a potential quagmire on the scale of Vietnam. Humanitarian concerns came to be attributed to the action as it was played out in Afghanistan, in part as an attempt to win the hearts and minds of the Afghans themselves, as well as to hold together an increasingly shaky international coalition. Indeed, scholars like Simon Chesterman have raised a question in the context of attributing humanitarian objectives to the intervention, i.e. why almost nothing was done for the Afghan population before 11 September 2001. In fact inhumanitarian non-intervention has usually been the rule in international relations. The USA in this case, in effect chose not to participate in the broader activities of the United Nations, the establishment of the interim administration, or the activities of the International Security Assistant Force (ISAF). The decision to escalate or de-escalate the scale of intervention will have a profound effect on the development of the Middle East and South Asia, in addition to the consequences for the Afghan people themselves.

This volume aims at analysing the international intervention in Afghanistan and debate on whether this intervention has actually changed anything for the better. It seeks to question whether the intervention led to the creation of unrealistic expectations on the part of oppressed peoples and whether there were negative effects of the use of force. It questions the rationale for occupation by the intervening power. How and to what extent is this intervention plagued by problems of will and capacity? The intervention was justified through an expanded definition of what constitutes a 'threat to international peace and security' under chapter VII of the United Nations Charter. Has the intervening community been able to successfully counter the threats to international peace and security? How far can such intervention lead to state-building and creation of democratic institutions? The issue of humanitarian intervention has the potential to divide international institutions such as the UN and damage their credibility. Has this intervention posed new challenges for humanitarian organizations, whose neutrality has been compromised in cases such as Kosovo and Afghanistan? What kind of scenario is likely to develop in case of non-intervention in Afghanistan, i.e. in case of withdrawal of the international forces from Afghanistan, both within Afghanistan and in the region?

The volume which is a product of an international seminar on *Rethinking International Intervention in Afghanistan* in 2011, organized by the Maulana Abul Kalam Azad Institute of Asian Studies, Kolkata in collaboration with the Indian Council of World Affairs (ICWA), New Delhi was aimed to bring together academicians, UN officials, journalists and military personnel to engage in interaction related to the following themes. The discussion revolved around the themes which are divided into 5 major sections in the volume:

1. Debating International Intervention in Afghanistan
2. Military Withdrawal: Scenarios and US Strategies
3. Dimensions of State and Nation-building
4. The Government and the Taliban
5. Regional Concerns

The volume attempts to discuss major issues related to the intervention in Afghanistan from these 5 perspectives. The aim was to prepare a capsule on the intervention of 2001, how the processes related to state and institution building shaped up and the future scenarios likely to develop followed by the concerns of the region.

Section one opens up the main debate on intervention. Binoda Kr. Mishra argues that there have been situations in the world that called for intervention for protecting mankind. The nature of the problem in many of them demanded a military approach. It is not that the international community has been swift in all cases. Therefore, if international community seeks legitimacy for its intervention it must also be held guilty for inaction in certain cases. In cases where force has been used, there has been mixed reactions from the international civil society, specifically the academic community in evaluating them. The basic parameters used for evaluating the interventions are: legality, conditionality, desirability, the approach, and the effect of the intervention. The legal aspect of intervention has always been predicated on the attainment of the desired effect of intervention. In a successful intervention, the legality, the approach and other value laden parameters have largely been upheld or in some cases condoned by the international community. International intervention in international relations is permitted on the premise that the intervener would create a better system for human living than the prevailing times. A procedural question is also involved wherein the intervener is bound to operate within laws, created by it/them, that are better than the laws they break for executing the intervention. The paper evaluates the past international interventions in terms of their effects and draws some lessons for rethinking international intervention in Afghanistan.

Shanthie Mariet D'Souza argues that the military intervention in Afghanistan, a fall out of the attacks on US homeland on 11 September 2001, attracted huge international attention towards Afghanistan. Expectations of an early resolution of the conflict, however, have been belied. Ten years of military operations have not been able to turn the tide of war against the Taliban, who remain ensconced in their sanctuaries in Pakistan's tribal areas. Stabilization as well as nation building agenda in Afghanistan, as a result, continues to be the casualty. Presence and diverse range of activity of plethora of actors involved in the reconstruction activities has added to the complexities of Afghanistan. Lack of a unified vision and consequent lack of unity of effort has led to dissipated efforts. Lack of understanding of the nature of state in Afghanistan among the actors trying to shape the country's future has ensured that the ways and means of rebuilding the war ravaged country remains an elusive project. Not surprisingly, the situation in Afghanistan has reached a 'stalemate'. This paper is a stock taking exercise of the international community's role in the reconstruction of security, political, economic, and governance sectors. It attempts to provide an alternative course of action for the international community to augment the Afghan Government's capacity and make the reconstruction process truly Afghan led and owned.

The military campaign of international coalition, started in fall 2001, was considered by many outside Afghanistan as model action against terrorist forces and punishment for their 9/11 attack. Vladimir Boyko argues that the restoration of state and public order in this war-torn country required the development of sustainable/step-by-step social, educational programs and projects. The initial military successes against Taliban, technical/logistical advantages of USA and their allies produced nearly-triumph sentiments, which were damaged by prolonged fighting nationwide and ill-facilitated state-building. Therefore the success in this field was not convincing despite heavy human, financial and prestige losses. He analyses social dimensions of current/ongoing intervention to Afghanistan from comparative perspective. One more purpose is to explore social consequences of international intervention of the first decade of 2000s in Afghanistan: new configuration of social strata and ethnic groups, dynamics of social (group/regional/nation-level) identities, including current perceptions of "other" (neighbours, Muslim *umma* at the whole, the West and specifically USA, Russia, etc.—in terms of *dar ul-harb* and *dar ul-islam*). He argues that the Afghan Diaspora worldwide is one of most significant features, including the efforts of current order-installers to return Afghans to homeland under special bonus programs. One of the reasons of this failure is a weak public involvement in terms of expertise, control and supervision, the lack of massive international cooperation with minor roles of Iran, Russia, and overshadowed tensions between some other influential regional actors. A really workable Afghanistan strategy demands strong social and cultural considerations and references to past experiences re-appraised politically and ethically in a scholarly manner.

In the tenth year of the international intervention in Afghanistan, Afghans remain second class citizens in their own country. This is the primary argument of Aunohita Mojumdar's paper as she argues that the citizen has not been at the heart of efforts directed at building the Afghan state, the Afghan nation or reconstruction of the country. The international military intervention and state-building efforts began in response to the perceived threat to the security interests of the US and its allies post 9/11. They have rarely deviated from that formula. With the change in perception that these interests are best served by a narrower approach that precludes nation-building, the international community is now on the exit path. Realpolitik demands that every nation or group will follow its own interests. However it also works on the principle of a commonality of interests, a shared platform of mutually beneficial interests. In Afghanistan however these benefits have not flowed to the citizen. Though Afghanistan is termed a democracy the citizen has little influence on decision-making or participation in governance. The creation of a state, institutions and processes that are not answerable or accountable to the Afghan citizen has not been of great concern to donor nations. While many of them have been well-intentioned in their efforts in reconstruction of Afghanistan, needs of Afghans have always been subservient to the over-riding strategic interests. She argues that the policies, projects and governance have therefore become tools in a militarized approach for strategic ends. While there have been some benefits that have resulted in a spin-off or trickle-down effect, these have been sparse, sporadic and patchy. The benefits to the bulk of the population have not been commensurate with the resources spent. The current mantra of reconciliation is an apt example of an approach that has little space for the concerns of the citizen. The long term goal of peace, transitional justice and rule of law are being given short shrift in the hurry for political reconciliation with a section of the insurgents. This narrative suits most of the decision-makers: a non-performing government that can eschew governance for political deals; an international community in a hurry to achieve temporary stability in order to exit, and a resurgent intolerant ideology that is sniffing at power. Therefore she feels that ignored for years, the Afghan citizen now faces not just neglect but increasing pressure, being squeezed from all sides, in the midst of spiralling violence and a deteriorating economic situation.

Prospective withdrawal of US-led NATO troops from Afghanistan is on the cards, albeit it is in the recent Lisbon summit that the dateline has been extended to 2014. The Nine-years of military intervention in Afghanistan is now facing a state of exhaustion: neither the foreign forces are able to control and normalize Afghanistan nor are the Taliban elements able to reassert control. In the meantime, the NATO forces are considering building the capacity of Afghan forces, police and other security-related infrastructure to avoid a repetition of hasty Soviet withdrawal in 1989 which led to, first, murderous infighting and, later, control by the Taliban forces. Maqsudul Hasan Nuri's paper attempts to discuss the post-withdrawal scenarios of Afghanistan—if and when it comes about. He analyses several issues: will the exit of foreign forces leave behind a peaceful Afghanistan or will it again erupt into internal violence and regional rivalries and interventions? If foreign forces do not stabilize the country and do not maintain a supporting role for another decade or so, could Afghanistan slip into violence again? However, if some necessary arrangements are made for a possible setting up of a Contact Group (US, Russia, China, India, Iran, Pakistan) to plan stationing of peacekeeping forces drawn from non-regional countries (Africa, East Asia and Latin America) for some time, Afghanistan could be made to stand on its own feet as an independent, sovereign state. Failing this, it might relapse into an arena of 'Great Game' for regional powers which would further destabilize the region. Hence, he argues that it is in the interest of all neighbours of Afghanistan to have a peaceful, stable and moderate state at peace with themselves and the outside world through a consensual, harmonized approach. In order to realize the dividends of NATO intervention— if any—a 'soft exit' of NATO-led forces with necessary safeguards in place is essential. This is to avoid renewed adventurism by regional states to further their own short-term agendas.

Since the military intervention in 2001, the international community has not been able to define their objectives in the long run. Shahmahmood Miakhel argues that the US was not in favour of nation building or state building in Afghanistan. The international community increased military activities in Afghanistan on the basis of threats generated within Afghanistan and from outside not on the basis of long term planning. If level of threats to security of Afghanistan is not reduced, transition of security to Afghanistan National Security Forces (ANSF) which is foreseen in 2014 cannot be addressed; a factionalized ANSF cannot hold security even for a few months without support of international forces. If the international community, especially the US, clearly do not define their objectives in Afghanistan as well as in the region, it is not easy to bring stability to this part of the world. If international forces prematurely depart from Afghanistan on the basis of any bilateral deal, this region will face a bigger turmoil which will have very negative consequences for all because enemies of stability and good governance are more sophisticated now and the danger will not stay in the territory of Afghanistan only. It may expand to South Asia, Central Asia and Middle East in worse form. Of course it may expand to Europe and the rest of the world. Therefore, he argues, it is imperative for international community to engage all national, regional and international stakeholders to find a reasonable solution for the Afghanistan crisis and to have durable peace and stability.

Jagmohan Meher argues that the US is following a two-prong military strategy in Afghanistan. After ten years of protracted war, so far this counterinsurgency strategy has shown little success. Secondly, and more significantly, what has turned out to work well is an approach American officials have talked much less about, i.e. counterterrorism: military-speak for the targeted killings of insurgents from Al-Qaeda and the Taliban. It is argued in some US military circle that this shift could change the nature of the war and potentially hasten a political settlement with the Taliban. Thus, the emerging American model can best be described as counterterrorism, with some counterinsurgency strategy that forces the hands of insurgent leaders. Would this American strategy work in Afghanistan? So far, the answer is in negative. Since 2006, the Taliban have made a dramatic comeback in Afghanistan after being driven from the country in 2002. As security has deteriorated, they have steadily taken control of more and more territory, especially in the southern and eastern parts of the country. Violent attacks constitute the most visible part of their tactics; targets are the ISAF forces, Afghan security forces, and the civilian population. These violent attacks are designed to further recruiting and financing efforts, to provoke reactions from ISAF that further alienate the population, and to weaken the government by demonstrating its inability to provide security. The American 'surge' has met with the Taliban 'surge' with similar force and vigour. The offensive and counter-offensive has resulted in a stalemated situation; but it has failed to create a conducive atmosphere for negotiation which is the ultimate aim of the United States and the Afghan Government. What is the focus of the US military strategy in Afghanistan? And despite several initiatives by the Afghan Government and the international forces, why is the negotiation not taking momentum so far, and unlikely to do so in the current situation? His article revolves around these questions and attempts to look beyond the current entanglement.

A number of indicators for state weakness potentially leading to state failure have been identified: disharmony between communities, inability to control borders and the entirety of the territory, growth of criminal violence, corrupt institutions, and a decaying infrastructure which are common in the post-war societies. Jamal Rehman argues that post-war reconstruction efforts sometimes—but not always—focus on what is commonly called state-building, i.e. establishing an effective, central state that operates under the rule of positive law and in accordance with contemporary standards of transparency and accountability. Post-war reconstruction in Afghanistan is such a case. He argues that in order to preserve peace and security in Afghanistan, it is necessary to give priority to the state-buiiding instead of nation building because the weak state can give an upper hand to the neighbours. Thus, state or nation-building process requires huge efforts in order to be successful. It is often assumed that strong leadership helps a country to mobilize the necessary resources. Nation-building is more successful if the state has had experience in effective self governance and if it has had a viable economy. Nation-building in Germany and Japan was successful principally because both nations had existing functional governmental and economic structures. Having been thoroughly defeated in World War II, both these nations were ripe for the seeds of democracy to take hold. His primary argument is that the lack of democratic experience or economic institutions will remain formidable challenge to nation-building process in Bosnia, Kosovo, and Afghanistan.

The state-building agenda in Afghanistan, which should have gradually built the infrastructural power of the state with which to overcome its weakness, was overshadowed by the short-term stability and international security imperatives. According to Zubair Popalzai, these imperatives placed a number of limitations on the ability of the technocratic core of the weak central government in Kabul and forced them to co-opt warlords. The co-optation strategy, however, was often used as a tacit pact for often-short-term alliances of convenience for personal gain at the expense of institution-building. The concept of state-building as a process whereby operations of the state and its institutions and actors are depersonalized and formalized was thus replaced by building and extending the power and influence individuals, often but not always with military backgrounds. Although developments in Afghanistan are closely tied to regional and international politics and today it is the Taliban that present the greatest threat to the nascent Afghan state, it remained a valid point that the Afghan and foreign actors failed to align themselves around a common set of objectives culminating in the formation of a strong state. Instead, each actor pursued its own military, political and economic interests; subsequent developments further weakened the Afghan state. He looks at the history of the most recent state formation exercise to show how it began with the handover of Afghanistan to militia groups with a history of rivalry and violence among themselves. He also discusses the subsequent seizure of state administration for the centralization and distribution of patronage, the incentives to remain armed and powerful despite undergoing a disarmament process and an apparent break with military practices. He shows that co-optation was used to build and maintain power networks and reflects on the process of building the coercive apparatuses of the state namely the army and police.

In the last three decades, Gulshan Sachdeva argues, Afghanistan has witnessed diverse projects of nation-building and socio-political transformation. The current international project of building democracy and market economy is mandated by the United Nations and being implemented mainly by the western alliance led by the United States. More than 70 nations have committed resources for Afghan reconstruction with US being the biggest donor. In addition, many European and Asian countries have also committed significant resources. A major portion of these resources have gone into building Afghan National Army, Afghan police as well as education, health, community development projects and institutions of governance. As a result of these efforts, large gains have been made in education, health, infrastructure, economic development as well as in women empowerment. This has happened despite difficult and deteriorating security situation in many parts of the country. Many regional countries including India, China and Iran are also actively involved in reconstruction and development. It is realized that despite major challenges, Afghanistan has the potential to play an important role in facilitating regional integration for different economies of South and Central Asia. If proposals concerning regional economic cooperation originating from Afghanistan are implemented by other countries in the region, this could ultimately improve chances of peace not only between India and Pakistan but also in the entire Eurasian region.

State-building is a narrative, although not fully coherent or developed, that has served to coordinate and focus the intervention of international actors in Afghanistan, in collaboration with the emergent Afghan state from 2001, argues Sayed Mohammad Shah. These actors include Afghan politicians, civil servants and national technical advisors, as well as a variety of diplomats and analysts working on behalf of the United Nations or one of the 62 aid-contributing countries and agencies. Many of these actors share some level of commitment to state-building, although they may have different ideas about what a state should be, while simultaneously advocating for the particular sets of interests that they represent. Formal policymaking, especially at the national level, has been one of the most publicly visible means of developing and advancing the state-building agenda. Such processes of policymaking in turn interact with existing organizational cultures and pre-existing, often informal, policy and practice. It is from such interaction that the emerging state is shaped. A number of national-level policymaking processes are described by Shah, seeking to provide insight into the broad patterns and recurring issues that characterize such processes in post-9/11 Afghanistan.

Abdul Rehman Ulfat Mahmoodi argues that implementing good governance in the country in national and sub-national levels is imperative. Good governance should end all dilemmas which exist for the time being in the country and this can be done by appointing civil servants on the basis of merit. But unfortunately, all high ranks are occupied by relations, political or ethnic, and not based on qualifications. The article reviews the relationship between the rule of law, good governance, and sustainable peace development in Afghanistan. It discusses the Afghan legal situation, which is very sophisticated and complicated because part of the system is based on Islam. Another part is based on the *Uorf or Rawaji Qanoon* (Traditional Law). Also a part of the law which has been recently inserted is based on western jurisprudence. He discusses how the statutory law and the constitution contradict each other and reviews how religion, nationalism, and politics in Afghanistan form a cornerstone in this country. The article provides insights into governance challenges and suggests guideposts that may assist government officials, leaders and decision makers to adopt appropriate governance systems and tools as part of post-conflict reconstruction efforts.

At ten years and counting, the US war in Afghanistan is the longest in its history, surpassing even the Vietnam War, and it will shortly surpass the Soviet Union's own extended military campaign there. It has become complicated to the extent that neither the international community nor the Afghan state could bring significant change in the situation in the country despite utilizing all tactics and weapons. Sanaullah Tasal argues that the United States should by no means abandon Afghanistan, but it is time to abandon the current strategy that is not working. Trying to pacify Afghanistan by force of arms will not work. A costly military campaign there is more likely to jeopardize America's vital security interests than to protect them. America and its allies should try to win the hearts and minds of Afghans and should work closely with the Afghans to rebuild their country, politically and economically. He argues that it is necessary that all official and governmental affairs should be organized in accordance with Afghani traditions and national values, and not copy alien ideologies containing non-Islamic and non-Afghani guidelines and policies. This, however, does not mean that Afghans should not learn and utilize technology and science from the West.

On the role of the regional states, Savita Pande in her article argues that Pakistan's foreign policy interests generally, as well as strategic interests specifically, revolves around one fulcrum: India.

Rooted in asymmetricity, partition and historic relations, Pakistan's predominant strategic interest is curbing India's presence and role, regionally and globally, everything else is subordinate. Her paper is an attempt to look into implications of the Global War on Terror on Pakistan's strategic interests in Afghanistan. Thus Pakistan's prime concern in Afghanistan is seeking "strategic depth" against India, a concept mooted and conceptualized in 1980s. The status of "frontline state" acquired twice, first against the Soviets and then against its own creation, the Taliban, has been exploited by it for the purpose. On both occasions the United States provided aid and arms, thus they also count for strategic interests. Sharing a border with Afghanistan has also been both a boon and bane for Pakistan. It was chosen as frontline state precisely because of this proximity, and it has been able to curb India by designing trade agreement with the landlocked state and almost realized its strategic depth dream when the Taliban were in power. However it has been concerned about Pushtun nationalism in the border regions of Khyber Pukhtunkhwah as well as Baluchistan and Durand Line, dividing line set by the British between Pakistan and Afghanistan, but not accepted by Afghanistan ever since Pakistan came into being. Even during Taliban regime the issue of Durand Line could not be resolved in its favour, nor could much be done on Pushtun nationalism front, though Taliban were Pushtun; but their agenda was religion rather than ethnic. Pakistan's strategic interests, she argues, have dynamism of its own, as is reflected in turning against its own creation, the Taliban. In its assistance in global war on terror, it has turned terrorism within by its own policies and actions. Pakistan's strategic interests also have a bearing on its relations, in varying proportions with, Iran, Central Asia and China.

Mariam Safi argues in favour of including the Quetta Shura in the peace process. She says that western countries are ostensibly eager to keep Mullah Muhammad Omar, the Amir-ul-Momineen (Commander of the Faithful) of the Taliban movement out of peace talks with the Afghan Government. But is this a realistic approach, or at the very least, a viable strategy? Looking at the structure of the insurgency it seems highly ambitious to assume that elements within the insurgency will circumvent its Amir and join the negotiation table to end the long and tragic violence that has paralyzed the socio-economic and political development of Afghanistan for three decades. The Strengthening Peace Commission (PTS) established in 2003 and led by Hazrat Sebghatullah Mojaddedi claims to have disarmed 9,000 insurgents since its creation but in reality these numbers are questionable. The failures of PTS were largely a result of an incoherent reintegration strategy, lack of mechanisms for oversight and implementation and insufficient resources. This article evaluates the insurgency's position on reconciliation and reintegration and identifies possible hindrances and solutions as dictated by current members of the Taliban insurgency, former members of the Taliban regime, members of Kandahar's Provincial Council and tribal elders representing various ethnicities and district level Shuras in Kandahar province. Exclusively, this analysis has drawn on interviews with the former Foreign Affairs Minister of the Taliban regime Mullah Wakil Ahmad Mutawakil, prominent Afghan journalist Mujahid Kakar, Kandahar Provincial Council Vice Chairman Aghalali Dastagiri, and tribal elders from the most volatile district in Kandahar, Panjwayi district.

As the idea of national reconciliation regains currency, numerous back channels running through a complex multi-layered and often an overlapping socio-political network, contemporary and old, are apparently active and evolving. It remains to be seen whether the diversity of multiple actors involved, Afghan as well as foreign, are an asset or a challenge to the process. Vishal Chandra's article is an attempt to explore the future prospect of the current Afghan peace and reconciliation process in view of the given time frame for withdrawal of the US and NATO forces from the country and the politics beyond 2014. The supposedly Kabul-led process aimed at armed opposition groups operating from their safe havens inside Pakistan inevitably reminds one of initiatives of early 1990s. The politics and the challenge of the Afghan reconciliation initiatives remain somewhat the same. There are larger policy dilemmas involved while approaching the idea and the conduct of reconciliation process in terms of its legitimacy, timing, sustainability and, more importantly, its wider consequences. At the same time, the futility of 'peace through war' approach too seems to be coming to the fore. The article recognizes the growing momentum and appeal of the idea, as well as scepticism over the process at various levels. It is difficult to fully surmise at the moment if the current reconciliation initiatives could be a way forward in the given in-conflict scenario. There is a strong view that any let up in political or military pressure on transnational militant groups and their backers would exacerbate the conflict with far reaching consequences for regional and global security. However, based on a set of assumptions, the paper tries to explore whether the idea of reconciliation has the potential to transform if not exactly resolve the three-decade old Afghan conflict into a more manageable chaos.

Looking in general at the situation in Central Asian republics, it may be mentioned that Central Asia has been transformed from peripheral region to a region which occupies important position in the political agenda of Eurasia. Vafo Niyatbekov argues that one of the main factors that have determined its new political role is the potential of transportation complex and mainly its transit component. Central Asia holds quite an enormous transportation and communication network and is at the junction of Euro-Asian railways. It has access to the Persian Gulf through Iran, through Afghanistan and Pakistan to the Indian Ocean, through China to Asia-Pacific region. The region possesses quite a great potential to participate in present dynamically formatting international transit. The current development explains the ambition of Central Asia countries to provide effective realization of existing potential. The Central Asian transit of cargo to Afghanistan firstly depends on Russian Federation. In general, Washington is satisfied with transit to Afghanistan through Russian Federation. American authorities are happy to see the realization of agreement with Moscow on air transit of military cargo for NATO military in Afghanistan. The participation of Russian Federation itself in transit process of military cargo is considered to be a significant contribution into NATO efforts in providing security and stability in Afghanistan. The Republic of Tajikistan has considerable appeal as transit territory, offering optimum conditions of passage of goods. Transport communications passing into the country through Republic of Uzbekistan and Republic of Kyrgyzstan and provide alternative routes. This can be followed up through Afghanistan and Pakistan also. Transport arteries crossing through the Republic of Tajikistan allows considering the republic in the near future as the centre of transit traffic.

Regional organizations operating in Afghanistan lack expertise to effectively counter international militant activities. Oybek Makhmudov argues that the 6+3 initiatives of multi regional security organizations, including neighbouring countries would be effective in efficiently solving militant conflicts in Afghanistan. Every organization tries to serve its own national interests. It has been estimated that roughly one half of the small arms currently circulating within Afghanistãn arrived there during the cold war years, most of them from countries involved in the Afghan conflict. For example, the United States delivered at least 400,000 Kalashnikov assault rifles to the Afghan guerrillas in cooperation with the Pakistani ISI. In addition, at the beginning of the 1990s, the ISI still had access to around 3 million Kalashnikov originating from the pipeline operations. The small arms accumulation in Afghanistan came from three main sources: the stocks of foreign governments, small-scale arms manufacturers in the region, and black-market suppliers. The ongoing armed conflicts in Afghanistan could spread to Pakistan that is destabilizing the neighbouring South Asian and Central Asian countries. Operationally, there is some evidence of Al-Qaeda working with the Afghan Taliban. Al-Qaeda itself does not do real operations in Afghanistan; it is not in the position to do so. The most it can hope to be is a kind of force multiplier for the other entities that are already there. In that context it has been ready to provide some support and assistance to Afghan Taliban units in weapons training and providing some material assistance. He also point out at certain factors which provide grounds for concern that Al-Qaeda may expand its activity to Central Asia.

The 11 September terrorist attack on the United States and the subsequent responses since then has been to a large extent responsible for the change of strategic calculations of many countries towards Afghanistan and the region at large. Anwesha Ghosh argues that single event brought to surface a number of trends that were less visible earlier. Perception of threat and sense of national insecurity reached its height during this period which made a country like India feel like she was on the front line of America's war on terror. Age old historical ties, India's experiences with the Taliban regime and their supporters, the strategic challenges that the nexus poses and India's own security perceptions are some of the factors that have shaped India's policy towards Afghanistan. Her article attempts to analyse determining factors of India's interest, her role in Afghanistan's reconstruction endeavour, challenges faced in the context of her past experiences and her strategic stakes in Afghanistan. The argument of the paper is that India's interest and stakes in the country is legitimate and should be considered from a broader geopolitical context. Even after the US withdrawal it is likely that India as a rising regional power would make her presence felt through her development initiative and exercise her capabilities, willingness and legitimacy for a long-term engagement in Afghanistan.

The United States' responses to the 11 September terrorist attack have been to a large extent responsible for the change of strategic calculations of many countries towards Afghanistan and the region at large. Krishnan Srinivasan argues that in the search for a solution, various regional approaches have been mooted, especially since diverse ethnicities in Afghanistan need reconciliation. The ethno-linguistic complexities are immense, with Pashtun, Uzbek, Tajik and Hazara majorities living outside the country and the minority within Afghanistan. The neighbours act out competing and conflicting interests, to say nothing of outsiders like Saudi Arabia with its profound and malignant links with the Taliban. Pakistan wants to exclude any Indian influence in what it regards as its backyard; Iran cannot accept Shias being treated as apostates by Wahabis; China fears Uighur contamination by extremism; Central Asia fears narcotics and terrorism. The US refuses to involve Iran, while any armed action against Iran by USA or Israel will hugely increase radicalism in the Middle East and Central Asia with unpredictable consequences. Pakistan can be a deal-maker or deal-breaker, but a Pakistani brokered peace will not be acceptable to its neighbours or to all the Afghans. There is no such thing as a card-carrying Taliban. *Pashtuns* and *Talibs* are not synonymous and the Taliban are not monolithic. The Talibs are in at least three formations: Mullah Omar's *Quetta Shura*, Haqqani in North Waziristan (strong Arab element and attached to Pakistan's ISI) and the Pakistani Taliban. Each Taliban group has a different leadership with different agendas. The Taliban are therefore more of a 'movement' intending to defeat ISAF/NATO and re-claim Afghanistan. Ethnicity and Islam are not cementing factors. Hekmatyar, the mujahid of anti-Soviet vintage, is a constant spoiler, and the Taliban will not cohere after any settlement and once the NATO troops withdraw. Despite all this, moves for a settlement are constantly afoot. Karzai is moving closer to regarding Pakistan as essential for his continuation, and Rabbani, a former Afghan president, is acting as his intermediary with the *Quetta Shura*, though the US does not want Mullah Omar in the peace and reconciliation process. The process is highly opaque between all the various players.

Arpita Basu Roy

Debating International Intervention in Afghanistan

1

Debating the Question of International Intervention: The Afghanistan Context

Binoda Kumar Mishra

Intervention has always remained an uneasy concept in international relation primarily because it exposes uncomfortable juxtaposition of two basic concepts of contemporary global politics, such as sovereignty and human rights. The academic world is divided in between the two extremes: complete rejection of the concept of intervention; and intervention as right of international community, that has a "responsibility to protect." There have been situations in the world that called for intervention for protecting the mankind. The nature of the problem in many of them demanded a military approach. It is not that the international community has been swift in all cases. Therefore, if international community seeks legitimacy for its intervention it must also be held guilty for inaction in certain cases. In cases where force has been used, there has been mixed reactions from the international civil society, specifically the academic community in evaluating them.

The basic parameters used for evaluating the interventions are legality, conditionality, desirability, the approach, and the effect of the intervention. The legal aspect of intervention has always been predicated on the attainment of the desired effect of intervention. In a successful intervention, the legality, the approach and other value laden parameters have largely been upheld or in some cases condoned by the international community. International intervention in international relations is permitted on the premise that the intervener would create a better system for human living than the prevailing times. A procedural question is also involved wherein the intervener is bound to operate within laws, created by itself/themselves, that are better than the laws they break for executing the intervention. This paper intends to revisit the debate on the question of intervention and place Afghanistan within it to set the context for rethinking international intervention in Afghanistan.

The scope of using military force against the political independence or territorial integrity of member states was eliminated through the UN charter (Article 2(4)).[1] But international community has been witness to military action against the political independence of member countries by the UN itself or by other members of the comity of nations. There being no legal basis within the UN framework, the term "humanitarian intervention" is largely used to justify the use of force against any country. The pretext is protection of human rights of the population of any particular country that is under threat and which calls to the conscience of the international community to intervene. But the debate continues as to whether the international community or a part thereof has the legitimacy to intervene for this purpose. The issue is who has the authority of authorizing intervention and who can be authorized to intervene. It has been seen that interventions in some cases have been undertaken by without the 'so called' authorization of the United Nations. Thus, the date becomes more crucial, as it includes not only the legal question but also the conditions under which the intervention was carried out, how desirable was the action, what was the approach of the intervening party/parties and whether the result of the intervention was in line with the objectives mentioned in rationalizing intervention with or without UN authorization. The legality of interventions for humanitarian purposes was officially not there till the adoption by the General Assembly of the 2005 World Summit Outcome Document. From then on there seemed to be universal acceptance that the Security Council could act coercively under Chapter VII of the Charter to protect people from genocide, war crimes, ethnic cleansing and crimes against humanity.[2] But in some important cases of intervention the intervening party/parties have acted without the mandate of the Security Council. How legitimate are those interventions? A look at the history of international intervention (humanitarian) is warranted to evaluate the merit of the concept to protect humanitarian causes.

At the academic level there are two opposite view points on this question of intervention, even if the intervention is of humanitarian nature. The polarisation of views among the academics is due to the fact that this particular concept exposes the uncomfortable juxtaposition of the two most important concepts of contemporary international relations, i.e. sovereignty and human rights. Most often intervention is legitimized on the ground of 'supreme humanitarian emergency'.[3] This concept also is not uncontested and there are arguments that there is nothing called 'supreme humanitarian emergency'. Opponents of the concept argue that the values against which a situation is termed as 'supreme humanitarian emergency' is always culturally biased.[4] The debate on intervention can be broadly divided into two camps, namely the pluralists and the solidarists. Both the camps draw on various theories and legal formulations to argue their cases. The solidarists are of the opinion that the international community has the right and duty to intervene for humanitarian purposes under certain circumstances. While the pluralists dismiss the notion of 'supreme humanitarian emergency' as the rationale of humanitarian intervention on the ground that it is culturally loaded and may be misused, the solidarists defend the concept of 'supreme humanitarian emergency' as valid and "argue that international society has developed a basic common understanding of what constitutes a supreme humanitarian emergency."[5] The supporters of humanitarian intervention draw their arguments on 'Natural Law'. They argue that "our common human nature generates common moral duties – including, in some versions, a right of humanitarian intervention."[6] The right of the states to intervene is also mentioned by Hugo Grotius who advances the argument that states may exercise their right, based on "natural law notion of the universal community of the humankind."[7] The solidarists further bring in the utilitarian argument that intervention is justified if it saves more than lives than would have been lost without intervention and if intervention helps the cause of greater numbers.

Pluralists on the other hand argue that intervention cannot be a permitted international behaviour as it violates the fundamental norm of the international society—international peace and security rests on reciprocal recognition of sovereign rights by states.[8] This is ironic as it may sound that the pluralists on a different platform challenge the unregulated sovereign power of the state. However, the solidarists respond to the sovereignty argument with the exception to the rule of non-intervention in extreme cases where states try to abuse human rights and take shelter behind the concept of sovereignty to escape just prosecution. Now a just doubt can be cast on some of the interventions actually undertaken. What represents the universal community of humankind? Even if we accept the UN as the representative of this universality, then a good number of interventions have actually been carried out by interested/capable/ stakeholder members of the international community, not always gaining universal acceptance even *post-facto.* This brings in the question of motives behind the interventions that have taken place. Non-intervention in worse humanitarian crises certainly points to the motive factor. Interventions have been selective thus, the influence of other issues like interest/motive cannot be ruled out. Solidarists take cover behind a weak logic of the right of the international community and humanity to intervene for humane purposes. It is not a duty; thus states may exercise their option in deciding whether to intervene or not. As the debate on international (humanitarian) intervention goes on another thing that has come up during the debate on intervention is the consent of the parties that are to be intervened. This means intervention within a particular country would require the consent of that country. The requirement of obtaining the consent of the authorities before humanitarian intervention is limited to non-military intervention only. No authority or regime would allow military intervention in the country unless there is seceding part that needs outside military presence to stabilize politically, as in the case of Indonesia agreeing for international military presence in East Timor. But seeking the consent of someone who effectively has lost legitimacy, and against who the intervention is to be directed, is an ideal situation which may never materialize.

History of International Intervention: Humanitarian Aspect

In the Post-World War II period international intervention was a phenomenon which was never subject to international scrutiny as it was considered part of the super power game; rationale of intervention was obtained with reference to the actions of the other super power. US intervention in Vietnam and Soviet intervention in Afghanistan were prime examples of such intervention. But in the post cold war scenario, the phenomenon of intervention became a matter of international debate. The legitimacy of such action has been the core of the debate. The legitimacy question is imbedded more with the ethical dimension of international behaviour of states than with the legal issues. In a comity of sovereign nations, whether there exists a scope for external intervention in another country is certainly a legal question, but more pressing is the question whether the sovereign country has the right of wishful governance that contravenes the basic principles of governance in the eyes of the international community. The issue is more ethical than legal because there exists no standard measure to evaluate the functioning of the sovereign states within its territory. This is the primary reason of differentiated international reactions to various crises that have evoked international reactions both in action and inaction.

International community or at times its member(s) have undertaken the act of intervention in some cases while choosing not to do so in other cases. Intervention, whenever it has occurred, has been on the pretext of upholding the values of humanity that were purported to be under threat within a sovereign country. While the commission of intervention should have been under scrutiny only on legal grounds, the inaction in similar crisis elsewhere questions the moral rights of the international community to act in the cases it or its members did act. The intervention, whenever it has occurred has taken the cover of humanitarian principles to gain legitimacy. But in close scrutiny, most of the interventions have humanitarian principle at best as an appendage to many other motives of the intervening party or parties. As it happened in the cases of Kuwait, Northern Iraq, Somalia, Bosnia and Kosovo, leaves a lot to be explained about the rationale of intervention. A brief description of some of these cases would provide a context to interpret international intervention.

Bosnia

The first instance of humanitarian intervention took place in Bosnia in the year 1995. But this intervention was preceded by a number of UN resolutions and attempts to stop the crisis from escalating to the level needing military intervention. The intervention that came too late in time achieved nothing in the direction of protecting the human right of the affected population as at the end of the intervention it effectively left those responsible for the crisis in positions of power. "It entrenched ethnic division: explicitly in its constitutional arrangements and in reality for those unable to exercise their right of return to their former homes."[9]

Kosovo

The 1999 NATO intervention in Kosovo was not authorized by the UN or the Security Council. It was undertaken as an action deemed morally expedient considering the humanitarian crisis that was seemingly worsening in Yugoslavia. The statements made by prominent NATO leaders during that time reiterate the humanitarian rationale of the intervention. The US president Bill Clinton, speaking to KFOR troops in Macedonia said:

> It is not free of danger; it will not be free of difficulty. There will be some days you wish you were somewhere else. But never forget we can do it here, and if we can say to the people of the world, whether you live in Africa or Central Europe, or any other place, if somebody comes after innocent civilians and tries to kill them en mass because of their ethnic background or their religion and it is within our power to stop it, we will stop it.[10]

Though it was termed as intervention for humanitarian purposes, on the issue of legality there are three opinions – it was legal, it was illegal and the third that it was illegal, but a potential harbinger of future legality.[11] The fact that the intervention was not mandated by the UN or its Security Council causes legal complications for the action. Nevertheless the intervention took place. While the US and the NATO members kept on harping on the humanitarian purpose of the intervention, critics pointed out other motives behind the US and NATO action: (1) to dismantle Yugoslavia's competing socialist economic system; (2) to gain control of valuable mineral resources; and (3) to command the site of a future energy distribution network. Whatever the motives and the legality of the intervention in Kosovo may be, the end result is that the intervention prevented mass migration of Kosovo Albanians and their feared persecution. The desirability of the intervention may also be justified on the ground that it was intended not to persecute a government for launching atrocity against any other country but the prevent large-scale genocide within the country itself. The UN humanitarian operation in Kosovo ended with some 250,000 Kosovo Albanians displaced within the province. Some 200,000 others had sought safety outside the province over the previous twelve months. The political situation in Kosovo still remains unsolved as its status is yet to be determined and there is yet to be an indigenous governance system in place.

In Africa, Somalia experienced international military intervention for humanitarian purpose during 1993-95. This was a disaster as the US led troop had to make a shameful exit without achieving anything either in military or in political terms. A mob of petty gang leader-tyrants defeated the will of the international community. Though it was a UN mandated intervention and undertaken for no apparent reason other than the stated mandate of stabilizing the country, it failed leading to the American reluctance in getting involved in future humanitarian interventions. This may partially explain inaction of the international community in the case of Rwanda where nearly a million Tutsis were killed in one of the worst ever genocides. The international community could not gather its will together to react during the 100 days madness that clearly was a humanitarian crisis.

There are numerous cases of international intervention that can be mentioned. However, the purpose is not discussing all the interventions but rather point to the fact that all intervention does not have humanitarian purposes consistently as a rationale. Secondly, all interventions do not have the full support of the so called universal community of humanity. While supporters of intervention avoid inaction as a matter of choice (right) not a duty, the pressure on their legitimacy keeps on increasing. No longer the international community or its leading members can avoid responsibility to protect if they wish to retain the right to intervene. Thus, right to intervention was tried to be refashioned as "Responsibility Protect (R2P) that at present is the ruling concept in the context of intervention of military nature for humanitarian purposes.

Intervention in Afghanistan: From Self Defence to Responsibility to Protect

With the above discussed debate on the question of intervention and a brief mention of three interventions of the post cold war period we need to look at the case of Afghanistan as to how far it is an intervention and of what kind. What legal, ethical conditions does the intervention meet to be terms as a humanitarian intervention. Whether it is a fit case of intervention at all? If not, then what is it and what is the expected future of Afghanistan?

The US Defence Secretary, Donald Rumsfeld, argued that the military action was in line with previous US-led interventions in Kuwait, Northern Iraq, Somalia, Bosnia and Kosovo "for the purpose of denying hostile regimes the opportunity to oppress their own people and other people," adding that, "We stand with those Afghans who are being repressed by a regime that abuses the very people it purports to lead."[12] This was in contrast to the one page letter sent, on the day it initiated air strikes against Afghanistan, by John Ngroponte, US Ambassador to the UN, to the President of the UN Security Council invoking the self-defence principle for US action.

> In accordance with Article 51 of the Charter of the United Nations, I wish, on behalf of my Government, to report that the United States of America, together with other States, has initiated action in the exercise of its inherent right of individual and collective self-defence following the armed attacks that were carried out against the United States on 11 September 2001.[13]

These two simultaneous views emerging out of the US regarding its action in Afghanistan points to the fact that the intervention was not a clearly articulated political action. It rather was a response to unprecedented event the US experienced. The intervention in Afghanistan that began with the US air strikes on the Taliban's refusal to hand over the alleged perpetrators of the September 11 attacks on the US soil was clear reprisal in reference to the UN Charter provisions and also considering the process followed. The swift military action against one state that refused to hand over the perpetrators of a crime against the US suggests that humanitarian considerations were hardly in US leaders' minds at the time of considering military action in Afghanistan. But there is no scope for reprisal in the form of military action against any state. The UN General Assembly, in a 1970 resolution construing the Charter, stated, "States have a duty to refrain from acts of reprisal involving the use of force."[14] "Military action against Afghanistan cannot be legally justified on the grounds of punishment, retaliation, or even revenge. Although it is obvious that revenge is playing a big part in the actions of the United States government which re tends to only seek to punish the unpunished crime. But under well recognized principles of law, and especially of criminal law, state power cannot be used to exact revenge."[15] Thus, the US leadership understood that it has to be presented to the international community in way that can be permissible. Invoking the self-defence principle seemed the most plausible explanation that can be both invoked and be defended legally. The then US president asserted US rights of conducting the intervention with the open declaration of capturing Osama bin Laden "dead or alive."[16] The intervention in Afghanistan was a clear act of American readiness to "use decisive and overwhelming force, unilaterally if necessary, to defend America's vital interests"[17] camouflaged as self-defence. The complications of the war in Afghanistan warranted some additional guards against international criticism. The criticism was legal and technical. The self-defence principle is applicable to cases wherein a state reacts to active military action against itself. But in the case of Afghanistan campaign, the US was not facing active military action either from Afghanistan or from forces operating from inside Afghanistan. Even the allegation of terrorist forces operating from Afghanistan posing constant threat to US security, does not stand international judicial scrutiny as both International Court of Justice and the International Law Commission have opined that , "the right of self-defence does not apply with full force in cases involving terrorists operating from a third country."ug[18] The notion of humanitarian intervention needed to be introduced through the backdoor. The Taliban regime of Afghanistan was identified with evils against humanity with aiding terrorist groups as their manifested behaviour needing or justifying intervention. Since the UN could not endorse the US demand of intervention under self-defence on technical grounds, humanitarian principles were imported into the arguments in support of the intervention. This is reflected in the then Defence Secretary Donald Rumsfeld's statement mentioned earlier. However, both self-defence and humanitarian rationales of US intervention falls short of legitimacy in both strict legal and moral terms. If prohibition of use of force by UN Charter and various international judicial pronouncements render the intervention legally untenable, the intervention, soon and only after an attack on the US soil makes the moral stand weak. The moral question again goes back to the same debate of international community's right and duty of intervention. If, as described by the US and the coalition partners, the Taliban regime epitomised evil and unleashed serious human rights violation on Afghans, then why did the US and others including the UN did not consider action much earlier than the 9/11 acts took place? Ancillary questions can be raised as to what was the US interest in ignoring the human disaster that was taking place inside Afghanistan long before the 9/11 incident? Critics go to the extreme extent of alleging that US had planned the Afghan campaign much prior to the 'so called' 9/11 attack.[19] US oil interests in Central Asia and other strategic interests are accounted for such US action. Strictly, one cannot rule out the presence of other motives in any intervention of humanitarian nature; therefore, it may not be considered as an unprecedented dangerous precedence being set up by the US. One may tend to argue that Afghanistan nonetheless was a fit case for intervention for humanitarian purposes and the international community or the US and the coalition partners acted late; but still the intervention can be judged as legitimate considering the appalling conditions Afghans were in under the medieval Taliban rule. There are scholars who argue that a norm of international intervention for humanitarian purpose is evolving and the Afghan campaign adds to the evolution of this international norm. Even Kofi Annan argued for such evolving norm.[20] He argued:

> … if humanitarian intervention is, indeed, an unacceptable assault on sovereignty, how should we respond to a Rwanda, to a Srebrenica – to gross and systematic violations of human rights that offend every precept of our common humanity?[21]

Reviewing the past interventions Nicholas Wheeler argues that there is a trend towards authorizing interventions in humanitarian crisis under the UN and even UN unauthorised campaigns.[22] If the intervention in Afghanistan can be justified on humanitarian ground in line with the evolving norm of international intervention then it must also fulfil the criteria that are prescribed for a legitimate intervention under the concept of responsibility to protect or R2P. The procedure of intervention and the conduct of intervention must show signs of the international community showing the intent of fulfilling a responsibility rather than just exercising the right to intervene. Debating on the question of intervention, the "International Commission of Intervention and State Sovereignty" outlined the criteria that an intervention must fulfil the qualification and succeed as a legitimate intervention according to the emerging norm of international intervention, namely, responsibility to prevent; responsibility to react if prevention fails; the responsibility to rebuild.[23]

So far as responsibility to prevent is concerned, the international community in common and the US in particular clearly failed to prevent the humanitarian crisis that was persisting in Afghanistan under the Taliban. The most significant issue in this is the "root cause prevention."[24] The root cause of the human rights or humanitarian crisis in Afghanistan lay in the past actions of the US in the region and in the country itself. The use of religious fundamentalism as a unifying force against the Soviet intervention and converging US interest of driving the USSR and Pakistani interest of raising a *jihad* against India and use of Afghanistan as a space for Pakistan's strategic depth in the region is at the root of the crisis. This was further exacerbated by US abandoning these radically charged Islamist forces after the then US interest of humiliating the USSR was over. The swamp of fundamentalist forces that were carefully nurtured in Af-Pak region was not regulated by the US and Pakistan got a free hand in using these forces for both its purposes. Secondly, when the US did intervene, despite the legal and moral weak grounds, its basic operational strategy did not emit any allusions toward the intention of addressing the root cause. Instead of addressing the humanitarian crisis at its roots, ironically it chose Pakistan as the partner in this campaign. This not only casts doubt over addressing the root cause under responsibility to prevent but also responsibility to react. The reaction suggested more interest driven approach than any concern for the plight of the Afghans. Even during the military intervention, the intervener has the duty to ensure no or minimum civilian casualty. Though the US promised to minimize civilian casualty and talked about winning the hearts and minds of the Afghans, the ground reality shows to the contrary. The civilian casualty has been on the rise and primarily due to the operations of the US and the coalition forces.[25] Such approach certainly does not indicate fulfilling the mandate of responsibility to protect.

Further, when it comes to responsibility to rebuild, scholars like Robert O. Keohane held that sustained involvement after intervention will be necessary for intervention to be effective.[26]

The primary intervener the US's refusal to contribute ground troops to the UN-mandated International Security Assistance Force (ISAF) and make a sustained contribution to rebuilding Afghanistan speaks volumes about the insensitivity to the responsibility to protect. It proves that the US or the coalition partners were in no mood for a long involvement in Afghanistan. Thankfully, the UN took over this responsibility after an irresponsible intervention. The USS 's plans to withdraw in 2014 is also indicative of its impatience to get out of the country no matter the objectives of humanitarian intervention are complete or not. The intervention has achieved the dubious distinction of being the longest intervention in US's history of interventions but direction seems to be in the opposite of a legitimate humanitarian intervention under the responsibility to protect principle.

Conclusion

The intervention by the US in Afghanistan was initially projected as an action justified on the ground of self-defence. The US realized at the same time that it is impossible to handle the situation in Afghanistan alone and a better rationale was needed to increase the acceptability of the act by the international community and involvement of allies. Thus evolved this idea of intervention in Afghanistan for humanitarian purposes. No matter the legalities and the ethical considerations that may prove the intervention unethical in principle and technically illegal, one can certainly agree that Afghanistan was a fit case needing humanitarian intervention if intervention is a right of the international community under the concept of 'responsibility to protect'.

But considering the way the intervention is being conducted one cannot rule out the certain other motives of various countries involved in Afghanistan. The failure to improve the situation in Afghanistan emerges from the uncomfortable match between the demands of genuine intervention under responsibility to protect and the strategic interests of the dominant and involved stakeholders. Therefore, it is time that the so called "engagement" of the international community with Afghanistan is given a name that closely, if not completely, corresponds to the ground situation. Because, the longer the uncertainty over the nature of 'engagement' persists, the grey areas expand and create scope for unscrupulous interests of other countries gaining ground in the situation and defeat the purpose of intervention in Afghanistan and create a hurdle in the emergence of a clear set of principles to guide genuine interventions for humanitarian purposes in the future. There is a clear consensus that the situation in Afghanistan is a humanitarian disaster. This consensus should form the basis on which future course of action in Afghanistan must be prepared. As per the fundamental elements in executing a humanitarian intervention, the international community is obliged to ensure that the humanitarian principles take precedence over narrow strategic interests of the primary intervener and the free riders.

Notes and References

1. All members shall refrain in their international relations from the threat

or use of force against the territorial integrity or political independence of any state, or in any other manner inconsistent with the purposes of the United Nations. Article 2(4), UN Charter.

2. GA Res. 60/1, 24 October 2005, A/RES/60/1 at paras 138 and 139.
3. The term 'supreme emergency' was coined by Michael Walzer. See Michael Walzer, *Just and Unjust Wars: A Moral Argument with Historical Illustrations*, 2nd edn. (Harmondsworth: Penguin, 1977), 251–255. The term 'supreme humanitarian intervention' was coined by Nicholas J. Wheeler. See Nicholas J. Wheeler, *Saving Strangers: Humanitarian Intervention in International Society* (Oxford: Oxford University Press, 2000).
4. C. Brown, *International Relations Theory: New Normative Approaches* (New York: Columbia University Press, 19920; A. Renteln, *International Human Rights: Universalism versus Relativism* (Newbury Park: Sage, 1990).
5. A.C. Arend and R.J. Beck, *International Law and the Use of Force: Beyond the UN Charter Paradigm* (London: Routledge, 1993); F.R. Teson, *Humanitarian Intervention: An Enquiry into Law and Morality* (Dobbs Ferry: Transnational, 1998). Both the works are cited by A.J. Ballamy, "Humanitarian Intervention and the Three Traditions," *Global Society*, 17/1 (2003), 4.
6. Terry Nardin, "The Moral Basis of Humanitarian Intervention," *Ethics and International Affairs*, 16/1 (2002), 57–70. See also Alan Donagan, *The Theory of Morality* (Chicago: University of Chicago Press, 1977); John Finnis, *Natural Law and Natural Rights* (Oxford: Oxford University Press, 1980). Works cited in J. L. Holzgrefe, "The Humanitarian Intervention Debate," in *Humanitarian Intervention: Ethical, Legal, and Political Dilemmas*, J. L. Holzgrefe and Robert O. Keohane (eds.) (Cambridge: Cambridge University Press, 2003), 25.
7. Joseph Boyle, "Natural Law and International Ethics," in *Traditions of International Ethics*, Terry Nardin and David R. Mapel (eds.) (Cambridge University Press, Cambridge, 1992), 123. Cited in Holzgrefe and Keohane (eds.), *Humanitarian Intervention: Ethical, Legal, and Political Dilemmas*, 9.
8. Ballamy, "Humanitarian Intervention and the Three Traditions," 4.
9. Nicholas Morris, "Humanitarian Intervention in the Balkans," in *Humanitarian Intervention and International Relations*, Jennifer M. Welsh (ed.) (Oxford: Oxford University Press, 2004), 110.
10. President William Jefferson Clinton, Remarks to the KFOR Troops, in U.S. NEWSWIRE, 22 June, 1999. Cited in Bartram S. Brown, "Humanitarian Intervention at a Crossroads," *William and Mary Law Review*, 41/5 (2000), 1691.

11. For the details of all three prognoses see Nigel S. Rodley and Basak Cali, "Kosovo Revisited: Humanitarian Intervention on the Fault Lines of International Law," *Human Rights Law Review*, 7/2 (2007), 275-97.
12. Donald Rumsfeld, "Text of the Defense Secretary's Briefing on the Military Strikes, the Pentagon, 7 October 2001," Associated Press. Available at, http://www.nytimes.com . Cited in David Chandler, *From Kosovo to Kabul and Beyond: Human Rights and International Intervention,* new edition (London, Ann Arbor, MI: Pluto Press, 2006), 1.
13. Letter dated 7 October 2001 form the Permanent Representative of the United States of America to the United Nations addressed to the President of the Security Council, UN Document S120011 946.
14. Declaration on 1)principles of International Law Concerning Friendly Relations and Co-operation Among States in Accordance with the Charter of the United Nations, UN General Assembly Resolution 2625, UN General Assembly Official Records, 25th Session, Supplement No. 28 (Al8028).
15. Roland Weyl, *What's happening to International law in Afghanistan?* www.iadllaw.org/files/WHAT'S HAPPENING TO INTERNATIONAL LAW IN.pdf.
16. President George W. Bush, Remarks by the President to Employees at the Pentagon (17 September 2001), available at, www.whitehouse.gov/news/releases/2001/09/20010917-3.html
17. Karin von Hippel, *Democracy by Force: US Military Intervention in the Post-Cold War World* (Cambridge: Cambridge University Press, 2004), 7.
18. The ICJ and International Law Commission judgements summarized in Leslie M., *Is the U.S. Bombing of Afghanistan Justified as Self-Defense Under International Law?* www.iadllaw.org/files/IS THE U.S. BOMBING OF AFGHANISTAN JUSTIFIED AS.pdf
19. For details of this line of argument, see, Patrick Martin, "US planned war in Afghanistan long before September 11," 20 November 2001, www.wsws.org/articles/2001/nov2001/afgh-n20.shtml
20. Kofi A. Annan, *The Question of Intervention: Statements by the Secretary-General* (New York: United Nations Department of Public Information, 1999a), 44.
21. Kofi Annan, *We the Peoples—the Role of the United Nations in the 21st Century*, (March 2000), 48.
22. Nicholas J. Wheeler, "The Humanitarian Responsibilities of Sovereignty: Explaining the Development of a New Norm of Military Intervention for Humanitarian Purposes in International Society," in Welsh (ed.), *Humanitarian Intervention and International Relations.*

23. *The Responsibility to Protect Report of the International Commission on Intervention and State Sovereignty* (Ottawa: The International Development Research Centre, December 2001)./
24. *The Responsibility to Protect Report of the International Commission on Intervention and State Sovereignty*, 22-23.
25. For a detailed analysis on the civilian casualty and its impact on Afghan campaign, see Binoda Kumar Mishra, "Thinking of Security in the Shadow of Conflict," in Arpita Basu Roy and Binoda Kumar Mishra (eds.), *Reconstructing Afghanistan: Prospects and Limitations* (New Delhi: Shipra Publications for Maulana Abul Kalam Azad Institute of Asian Studies, 2011).

2

International Community in Afghanistan: From a Stalemate to a Definition of Success

Shanthie Mariet D'Souza

The Present Stalemate

Notwithstanding the large international presence and huge pledges to rebuild the country, Afghanistan continues to be wracked by a deadly phase of Taliban-led insurgency[1] targeted at discrediting the legitimacy of the Afghan Government and weakening the resolve of the international community. Nearly nine years after their ouster from Kabul, the Taliban are resurgent and have carried out many lethal strikes against the international and Afghan forces and civilians. The levels of violence and insurgent attacks dramatically increased in 2010, and available data portend a continuation of this trend into 2011. While south and east Afghanistan continue to witness raging insurgency, the more stable north too has lapsed into instability.

While insurgency and counter-insurgency (COIN) are complex subsets of warfare, the nature of COIN is dynamic, as it constantly evolves in response to changes in insurgency. While "insurgency is a struggle to control a contested political space, between a state (or a group of states or occupying powers), and one or more popularly based, non-state challengers," the COIN campaign comprises "military, paramilitary, political, economic, psychological and civic actions taken by a government to defeat insurgency."[2] Over-reliance on military means runs the risk of severely undermining the COIN effort. Thus, synchronization of military and non-military efforts, combined with optimal contributions from different agencies, international organizations, and host nation organizations, are essential for an effective COIN response. More importantly, in a complex multi-actor environment, 'unity of effort' among the various agencies becomes a crucial factor, not merely to neutralize threats from insurgents, but also to build long-lasting institutions to extend the reach of the government to counter future destabilization efforts.

In the wake of spiraling violence and spreading instability in Afghanistan, the international community's COIN strategy seems to be floundering. Absence of a unified COIN strategy, lack of coordination in aid distribution, and minimal measures to shore up the capacities of the Afghan Government remain the principal problems impeding the international effort. The presence of a plethora of actors with multiple layers of interaction among the various donors, the Afghan Government, nongovernmental organizations (NGOs), and international military forces has created a complex web of interaction, further complicating the task of coordination. The resultant divergent perceptions of reconstruction among the aid agencies, differing operational approaches of the American and NATO militaries, and unwillingness of external agencies to coordinate their efforts with the Afghan Government appear to undermine the international COIN efforts towards long-term stabilization of the country. The nature of international intervention has thus exacerbated the internal divisions in Afghanistan. As a result, stability remains an elusive goal.

Security

The increasing levels of violence and deteriorating security situation continues to be a cause of concern. Despite the presence of about 150,000 NATO-led troops, foreign military and civilian casualties are at record levels with 2010 the bloodiest year on record since the Taliban were ousted by US-backed Afghan forces in late 2001. There were a total of 6,716 security incidents in 2010, such as ambushes, roadside bombings, suicide bombings and rocket attacks, The Interior Ministry said 2,043 civilians were killed and 3,570 wounded. The statistics of United Nations indicate 2,412 civilians were killed and 3,803 wounded between January and October 2010—up 20 per cent from 2009. According to Afghan Defence Ministry data 821 Afghan soldiers were killed last year. Foreign forces suffered record deaths in 2010, with 711 troops killed, roughly two thirds of them American.[3] It was by far the deadliest year of the conflict for foreign troops, up from 521 deaths in 2009, previously the worst year of the war.

Security in Afghanistan was initially undermined by the inability of the international forces to hold on to areas cleared of insurgents, particularly in the south and east. Due to the absence of adequate numbers of troops and sufficient resources, the international forces were not able to secure the countryside. The initial ratio of NATO and US troops to the Afghan population was roughly 1: 653, or about 1/10th of the force level required to actually bring about stability when there is no resistance or insurgency.[4] The limited numbers of international forces were too focused on the offensive 'clear and sweep' operations, and rarely sought to hold land, occupy villages and towns, or cultivate relations with locals.

US policy-makers' limited vision of nation-building, short-sighted policies in grappling with the interrelated threats posed by powerful warlords, militias, and the massive drug trade, as well as the inadequacies of security sector reform,[5] only acted as force multipliers for the insurgency.

Fault Lines in the Alliance?

NATO's involvement raised questions about its capabilities in fighting insurgency and rebuilding Afghanistan. NATO's effectiveness in the COIN campaign for the entire duration of its presence in Afghanistan remained severely hampered by the reluctance of its members to provide troops and resources for the Afghan mission, and this "undermined NATO's credibility."[6]

The problem of coordination in the military sphere due to the presence of two major international military coalitions (the US-led OEF and the UN-mandated and NATO-led mission ISAF) violated the principle of 'unity of command' and created operational difficulties. At the same time, the attempts by the Bush administration since 2004 to merge the ISAF and OEF under one command was resisted by the NATO allies, mainly Britain, Germany, and France, due to the differing perceptions on the nature of the two operations and conflicting national agendas.[7]

In addition to problems of burden-sharing and dwindling public support in NATO countries, there were conflicting national agendas and national caveats (national restrictions)[8] at work, imposed by NATO allies on their forces in Afghanistan. This risk avoidance and risk-aversion limited the movement and thereby effectiveness of the NATO forces. Concerns were high on NATO in Afghanistan runs the danger of emerging as a 'two tier' alliance[9] consisting of countries who are fighting the Taliban (counter-insurgency) and others only engaged in the reconstruction effort (stability).

Such variations in the international community's strategy are reflected in the counter-narcotic strategy and the consequent failure to rein in narco-trafficking,[10] which continues to be a major source of funding for the insurgency. The huge array of Taliban-affiliated groups with cross-border networks and support from local commanders and security forces have enabled the easy flow of drugs from Afghanistan into Central Asia, Iran, Pakistan, China, and even India. The Taliban is even manipulating the price of heroin by holding on to their stocks. In December 2010, Antonio Maria Costa, head of the UN office on drugs and crime, in a confidential report indicated that the Taliban and organized crime gangs had withheld 12,400 tonnes of opium from the international market to keep the price of heroin and opium at a profitable level. The opium withheld was worth about $1.25bn (GBP 800m). Each tonne of opium is said to be worth about $100,000 and can be used to produce 100 kg of heroin.[11]

Provincial Reconstruction Teams (PRTs)

Provincial Reconstruction Teams (PRTs) were established with the objective of maintaining a 'light international security footprint' and building the capacity of Afghan institutions to address instability in remote regions.[12] The PRTs work on the principle of classic counter-insurgency, protecting the population from the guerrillas and winning the support of the population in one limited area, in the hope that they can deprive insurgents of support.[13] The lack of personnel and resources, risk avoidance, and national caveats affect the ability of PRTs to spread to rural areas where the insurgency is raging. Presently, PRTs lack the resources to conduct more than three missions a day "outside the wire."[14] Moreover, within PRTs, there is a lack of unified command and PRT projects and programmes are mostly dictated by national agendas and funding priorities of the lead nation with little local participation.

PRTs have been viewed with skepticism by locals and criticized by aid workers for replicating their work, thus 'blurring the lines' between military and development work and placing aid workers in danger, as insurgents see the NGOs as partisan. Also, there is a concern that the PRTs "have neither the capacity nor the intent to confront the security threats and are last to help in times of crisis."[15] With little local participation and oversight of funding and project implementation, PRT projects are stymied by corruption and delays. Importantly, the coordination mechanism for aid distribution through PRTs remains virtually absent. In the absence of agreed goals and benchmarks for the PRT programmes of different countries, it is difficult to assess their usefulness and they are mostly viewed as a 'mixed bag'. PRTs undoubtedly require greater coordination amongst themselves and with the Afghan local community to make their projects more relevant and sustainable.

Political

Creation of a capable and legitimate Afghan Government needs to be the *sine qua non* for the international community's COIN campaign, as it is intrinsically linked to the prospect of long-term security and development. However, the nation-building exercise in Afghanistan had been relegated to the background, particularly by US policy-makers vis-à-vis the counter-terrorism mission in terms of resources, personnel, and political and media attention. Consequently, the primary objective of building a legitimate and capable Afghan government capable of providing security and basic services and gaining credibility has not been addressed.

Presently, the nascent democratic government of Afghanistan led by President Karzai is perceived as "weak, inefficient and corrupt," both by the international community and the Afghan people.[16] The early claims of success in the political sphere were belied as the composition of Afghanistan's parliament has raised serious concerns. In addition to individuals with direct ties to the country's warlords, a number of individuals closely associated with the drug trade were elected to the parliament.[17]

By most media accounts, warlords seem to be accumulating power and the divisions between President Karzai and the Afghan legislature over power-sharing is widening. Moreover, the legal vacuum caused by the absence of the rule of law and the failure of the Disarmament, Demobilization, and Reintegration (DDR) has helped perpetuate a culture of impunity. The problem of reintegration of fighters and providing them useful employment opportunities has largely been unaddressed. Given the spread of the insurgency to the relatively peaceful north and west and spiraling violence, it is evident that Afghanistan's security concerns cannot be addressed by military means alone. The international community needs to develop a coordinated strategy to work with the Afghan Government's national political reconciliation efforts. Engaging the insurgents who are willing to disarm and join the political process needs to be considered.

Economics and Governance

One of the crucial goals of COIN remains separating the populace from the warlords, drug lords, and insurgents, and giving them a viable economic choice. However, despite pledges by the international community in rebuilding, Afghanistan continues to trail at the bottom of every indicator and is heavily dependent on external aid. According to recent World Bank data, Afghanistan presently receives about $3 billion annually in foreign assistance, an increase from $1.3 billion in 2002. President Bush raised humanitarian assistance to Afghanistan from $1.3 billion in 2004 to $1.9 billion in 2008.[18]

The high dependence on foreign aid (although the aid quantum is considered to be insufficient) for a rentier state[19] inevitably creates problems of accountability and taking responsibility for its action or inaction. The international community, through its reliance on alternative delivery mechanisms (NGO/INGO), has not helped the Afghan Government exploit its mineral and agricultural resources, raise its own revenues, and offset its aid dependence. Almost 70 per cent of international assistance is channeled through contracts, subcontracts, embassies, PRTs, or alternative delivery mechanisms, and not through the Afghan Government. Moreover, parallel structures, such as the technical assistance programmes in various line ministries, the PRTs, and private security agencies, have not only consumed substantial amounts of net aid flows but also worked to undermine local ownership as well as the credibility and accountability of the Afghan Government.

During the author's interactions with personnel from the international aid community, the most common argument heard was that the Afghan Government lacks the capacity or is corrupt to be effective in aid delivery. While much of this may be construed as true, the scope for corruption exists due to the manner in which assistance is administered through a series of subcontractors. According to a survey conducted by the Kabul-based internationally funded Integrity Watch Afghanistan (IWA) in May 2008, "64 per cent of respondents considered that the aid was marred by some form of corruption and a majority (60%) considered that more than 40 per cent of aid has been wasted through corruption." Interestingly, "92 per cent of the respondents recommended that the international community should spend aid through the government and 79 per cent agreed that conditionality could be used by donors when giving money to the Afghan government."[20]

The lack of a visible difference in the lives of Afghan people, despite huge aid commitments and pledges, is used by the insurgents to discredit the role of the government and the international community. During a survey conducted by the IWA in 2010, about 50 per cent of respondents said corruption was helping the Taliban expand its influence.[21] Similarly, an earlier study titled "Falling Short" by the Agency Coördinating Body for Afghan Relief (ACBAR), pointed out that since the ouster of the Taliban regime in late 2001 the international community has pledged some $25 billion, out of which only $15 billion has been delivered. The study, while criticizing the "wasteful and ineffective" use of available aid money, also highlights the fact that a 'staggering' 40 per cent of the western funds that are spent on aid projects are returned to the donor countries through fees to contractors and salaries to employees from those countries.[22] This flight of aid capital back to donor countries or 'phantom aid'[23] consists of contracts and salaries of international advisors, aid workers, and consultants. The United States, in fact, has emerged as the biggest source of 'phantom aid', with around 47 per cent of its development aid being spent on overpriced technical assistance.

While coordination in the military sphere is difficult, economic coordination remains a bigger challenge. With the presence of multiple donors (more than 60, including international institutions like the World Bank, the International Monetary Fund, and the Asian Development Bank) with their own respective notions of long-term development, political agendas, bureaucratic procedures, and inertia, the task of coordination remains an arduous one.

Strategic Communications

Given that most COIN campaigns are won or lost in the political and psychological spheres, the importance of information dissemination remains vital. Frank G. Hoffman points out that this 'new' portion of the battle space is being expanded to a more global scale due to the ubiquitous and diffused nature of modern communication techniques.[24] The impact of external forces includes a similar explosion in the number of news organizations, media outlets, and websites offering information and varied imagery. Some analysts are extremely sensitive to the pernicious influence of the media, accusing them of participating in the conflict, or even being a combatant.[25]

The increasingly interconnected nature of communications is altering the pattern of popular mobilization, and the pervasive media presence has radically altered the manner in which insurgents acquire and disseminate strategic intelligence, recruit, and emulate and promote their cause.[26] There is an emerging insurgent mass media[27] with many incidents in Afghanistan and Iraq being recorded for propaganda purposes by insurgent video teams. Likewise, the SITE Intelligence Group Monitoring Service, "by monitoring terrorist and extremist websites and penetrating password-protected Al Qaeda linked sites, provides a state of-the-art intelligence service to both practitioners and analysts to understand the adversary."[28]

The major battle between international forces, the Afghan Government and the Taliban is seemingly being fought in the media. Reports of high numbers of civilian casualties are used by either side to legitimize their actions and to tarnish the image of the opponent. Media images and accounts of unprecedented numbers of civilians killed by international forces has enraged the Afghan public and further de-legitimized the Karzai Government. It has also led to domestic debates in various countries against troop contributions to ISAF's mission. For instance, strong public opinion against continuing engagement in Afghanistan is increasingly evident in Canada, the Netherlands, and Germany.

There exists a need for the counter-insurgent state to engage the media, not as a combatant or opponent, but as "a medium to extend influence or de-legitimize the insurgent."[29] Training the Afghan leadership, proactively controlling 'spin' from incidents, and boosting the 'morale' of the Afghan forces and people are central to operational counter-insurgency. Augmenting local media efforts, including Afghan television broadcasts that promote the nascent democratic government as something worth supporting, particularly in rural areas, will be crucial in changing the perception of the people who increasingly view the Afghan Government as ineffective.

Af-Pak Strategy and the End Game in Afghanistan

President Barack Obama's 'new strategy on Afghanistan', unveiled on 1 December 2009 at the US Military Academy at West Point, linking additional troop deployment to a timetable of drawdown of forces and narrowly defined goals, misses out on the core essentials of counter-insurgency (COIN) campaigns which hinges on time, long-term commitment, institution building and larger political strategy. Ultimately, COIN campaigns are won in the political domain, where military is only one of the many essential elements to achieve the long-term solution.

As the debate on the troop surge raged in the United States following the controversial Afghan presidential elections and waning domestic support for the Afghan war, President Obama announced his decision to send 30,000 troops within the first half of 2010. The most widely and intensely debated aspect of the present strategy is setting the date of draw down of forces. By fixing an arbitrary time frame of summer of 2011, especially when the COIN strategy is just being unveiled, it runs the danger of working to the advantage to the propaganda of the insurgents and their sponsors.

A major problem in outlining a time table for draw down of troops hinges on the need for a phased transition to an Afghan-led security sector, to take over from the US forces. If the objective is to increase ANA's strength to 250,000 and that of the ANP to 150,000, as currently proposed by the Afghan Government, there would remain the problems of mentoring and funding such a huge project. These numbers would be highly unsustainable for an externally aid dependent state. The greater worry, however, lies in the scenario of acceleration of training impinging on quality. Within the specified time frame and with the current level of funds earmarked, the US will not be able to create an army and police capable of independent action. It would alternately rely on the local power brokers (commonly known as warlords). In the absence of clear security and political framework, these instruments of 'community policing' could only promote a culture of impunity.

Although the setting of a date for draw down of forces ends a lot of speculation regarding American intentions in that country, and has provided some clarity to the domestic constituency and allies, it has sent a wrong message to the 'friends and foes' in the region. It has evoked a lot of concern particularly among the Afghans and regional countries. A war strategy review released by US President Barack Obama in December 2010 found US and NATO forces were making headway against the Taliban and Al-Qaeda but serious challenges remain. It said the Taliban's momentum had been arrested in much of Afghanistan and reversed in some areas.

Is There a Definition of Success?

Following President Obama's speech at West Point, announcing troop surge with a tentative date for draw down of forces in the summer of 2011, coupled with talks of withdrawal among NATO countries, concerns abound among the Afghans and regional countries of the international commitment in stabilizing Afghanistan. Though there has been subsequent toning down of the talks of withdrawal since then, there seems to be a rush to bring the Afghan gamble to an end. However, consensus among the NATO allies and the US on the timeline remains elusive as much as defining an 'end state', as witnessed during the NATO Lisbon summit in November 2010. What is really missing in the discourse of 'end state' is the lack of unified vision and therefore, the lack of clarity in defining the end state in Afghanistan. Every actor is interested in imposing an end state on Afghanistan as seen through their national agendas with little understanding or interest in knowing of how the Afghans would like to define their end state.

As the international community seems to be in a rush to bring its ominous gamble in Afghanistan to an end, India has a limited window of opportunity in enabling Afghans play a lead role in their nation building efforts. If the stated goal of transfer of authority, as set out by the Afghan president, were to be actualized by 2014, there are opportunities for international community to deepen its levels of engagement at various levels.[30]

A. *Security*: There is a need of training of the Afghan national security forces and helping build the justice sector. As the process of reintegration gains momentum, setting up an institutional framework for employment generation, amnesty and other such measures will be critical.
B. *Political reform*: Need to work with the Afghan Government towards long term political sector reform in bringing about a parliamentary system with political parties system to build

an inclusive political order. The absence of political parties and its drawbacks is being increasingly felt both by the people and the politicians. The past presidential and parliamentary elections in Afghanistan have indicated the need for electoral reforms.

C. *Reconciliation and Reintegration*: As set out in the London Conference adherence to the red lines stated at the London Conference including respect for the Afghan Constitution, human and women rights would be crucial to prevent subversion from within. Afghanistan's attempt at reconciliation needs to be supported by larger political and constitutional reforms which would necessitate provisions for dialogue, autonomy and special representation of minorities, women and marginalized groups.

D. *Governance*: Immediate need in developing decentralized structures of governance. Promoting grassroots democracy and local self government institutions can emerge as an alternative to the top down approach adopted by the international community. One of the success stories of Afghanistan is the National Solidarity Programme that needs greater funding and support. The participation of the local civilians in identifying and prioritizing aid projects would remain crucial.

E. *Economic:* There is an immediate need for development of alternate livelihood programmes as well as reviving Afghanistan's traditional artisan and agricultural base. India's rich experience with Green Revolution could be usefully replicated in relatively stable northern parts of Afghanistan. Saffron cultivation in poppy growing areas would be useful means of alternate livelihood project. Natural resource exploitation and industrial development in the relatively stable north and west provide opportunities for employment for the youth. Moreover, it would help Afghanistan from graduating from being an externally dependent 'rentier state' to a self sustaining economy.

F. *Employment generation and industrial base*: There is also an urgent need for establishing industries to spur economic independence and generate employment, which would actively engage the youth of the country. Afghanistan, due to its very low tax regime, is swamped by foreign goods mainly from Pakistan, China and Iran. This inhibits the growth of local indigenous industrial base. International community could contribute to establishing small-scale industries like carpet industry along with an ornaments and handicrafts industry to help artisans, weavers and craftsmen. Follow up studies on these projects, assessing their usefulness and linking with the development strategy of the Afghan Government, would be extremely critical.

G. *Social and cultural capital*: As part of counter radicalization campaign, messages of moderate Islam from the Deoband and other moderate Muslim countries would be a good counter to neutralize the radical Wahabi messages. There is also a need to further expand the cultural, sports and educational exchanges.

H. *Strategic communications*: Most of the international media puts out pessimistic stories from Afghanistan. It influences not only domestic public opinion but also works into the Taliban propaganda. It is crucial to build on the strategic communications of putting out positive stories through the radio, television and local print media.

I. *Public diplomacy*: There is a need of active interface and exchange of ides between the academia, non-governmental organizations, media, and youth and women groups as part of Track II initiatives.

J. *Regional cooperation*: There is a need of seamless information sharing, joint patrolling, border regimes and confidence building measures amongst the regional powers. On the economic front, SAARC and SCO could be the vehicles to ensure better economic integration of Afghanistan with the region, which would accrue huge economic benefits and help build the 'peace constituencies' in the region.

These goals, however, will have to be achieved within a limited window of opportunity of 2–3 years (2011–14). The need is to increase Afghan participation by raising stakes and providing incentives. As developments in Af-Pak region impinge on international security, there is an immediate need to bring about a unified effort in defining the end state with Afghans in the lead.

Notes and References

1. The Taliban-led insurgency includes: a loose alliance of Taliban guerrillas, followers of Afghan warlord Gulbuddin Hekmatyar's radical group Hizb-i-Islami, the Haqqani network, Al-Qaeda and its affiliates, narcotic traffickers, bandits, and tribal fighters in the Pakistan-Afghanistan border. This inference was derived from author's interviews, briefings, and discussions with the locals in various Afghan provinces in May–June 2007 and October 2010. For further details on the insurgency, see Seth Jones, "Counterinsurgency in Afghanistan," *RAND Counterinsurgency Study* 4 (RAND Corporation Arlington 2008); Antonio Giustozzi, *Koran, Kalashnikov and Laptop: The Neo-Taliban Insurgency in Afghanistan* (New York: Columbia University Press 2008).
2. Gordon H. McCormick, Steven B. Horton, and Lauren A. Harrison, "Things Fall Apart: The Endgame Dynamics of Internal Wars," *Third World Quarterly,* 28/2 (2007), 322; . David Kilcullen, "Counterinsurgency Redux," *Survival,* 48/4 (2006–2007), 112.
3. For further details on the levels of casualties see monitoring website www.iCasualties.org
4. According to a 2004 estimates, Afghanistan has the lowest international troop-to-population ratio of 1:1,115. In the Kosovo and Bosnia interventions, the ratios were 1:50 and 1:66. See Michael Bhatia, Kevin Lanigan and Philip Wilkinson, "Minimal Investments, Minimal Results: The Failure of Security Policy in Afghanistan," Afghanistan Research and Evaluation Unit (AREU) Briefing Paper (Kabul, June 2004); Barnett Rubin, A. Stoddard, H. Hamidzada, and A. Farhadi, *Building a New Afghanistan: The Value of Success, the Cost of Failure*, Center on International Cooperation, New York University (March 2004), 15.
5. Mark Sedra, "Security Sector Reform in Afghanistan: The Slide towards Expediency," *International Peacekeeping,* 13/1 (2006), 94–110; Richard Rupp, "High Hopes and Limited Prospects: Washington's Security and Nation-Building Aims in Afghanistan," *Cambridge Review of International Affairs,* 19/2 (2006), 291.
6. Karl F. Inderfurth, "A Last Chance", *The Boston Globe*, 8 August 2007, at http://www.iht.com/articles/2007/08/08/opinion/edinder.php (accessed on 10 August 2007); "NATO in Afghanistan: Fault lines in the transatlantic alliance?" IDSA Special Feature, April 02, 2009, http://www.idsa.in/specialfeature/ShanthieMDSouza020409.pdf
7. Britain and Germany wished to preserve ISAF for stabilization, as opposed to combat mission. Britain, leading the ISAF counter-narcotics effort, intended to retain the initiative in the political sphere of 'winning

hearts and minds'. Germany opposed a merger of the commands because German forces in ISAF were trained only for stabilization and not for counter-insurgency operations. The French view was somewhat different and they were concerned that the administration, after having a US commander in place to guide all military activity in Afghanistan, might use NATO as a 'toolbox' to accomplish Washington's broader objectives. Judy Dempsey and David S. Cloud, "Europeans Balking at New Afghan Role," *International Herald Tribune*, 14 September 2005, at http://www.iht.com/articles/2005/09/13/news/nato. php (accessed on 1 July 2007). Also see *Saving Afghanistan: An Appeal and Plan for Urgent Action, The Atlantic Council of the United States*, Issue Brief, Washington, DC, January 2008; V. Krishnappa, Shanthie Mariet D' Souza and Priyanka Singh (eds.), *Saving Afghanistan* (New Delhi: Academic Foundation, 2009).

8. Reportedly, there are 102 restrictions that have been placed on forces by their nations and 50 of these restrictions are considered to be 'operationally significant'. These include "geographical restrictions on locations of units' deployments as well as nature of missions units are allowed to participate and are intended to restrict the affected units from participating in offensive combat operations or other operations that carry a high risk of casualties." See Leo Shane III, "NATO Commander Asks Member Nations to Drop Troop Limits," *Stars and Stripes*, Mideast edition, 25 October 2006, at http://www.estripes.com/article.asp?section=104&article=40041&archive=true (accessed on 27 June 2007); Andrew Feickert, "U.S. and Coalition Military Operations in Afghanistan: Issues for Congress," *CRS Report* RL33503, updated 11 December 2006.

9. Robert Gates, the US defense secretary, on 6 February 2008, warned that NATO risks becoming a 'two-tier' alliance unless some members were willing to send more troops for the campaign to defeat the Taliban in Afghanistan. Demetri Sevastopulo, *Gates Warns of two-tier NATO*, 7 February 2008, at http://www.ft.com/cms/s/0/1e505e66-d54b-11dc-8b56-0000779fd2ac.html (accessed on 4 May 2008).

10. While the United States is not averse to using forceful means like aerial spraying, NATO allies were reluctant to do so mainly for reasons of losing the heart and minds campaign. Forceful eradication like the spraying of herbicides, especially in Helmand, could further undermine support for the government of President Hamid Karzai, alienate the local populace, and provide a support base for the Taliban. In an interview with this author in Kabul, June 2007, former minister of counter narcotics, Eng. Habibullah Qaderi, emphasized the need for a unified and well-coordinated strategy with help from the international community.

11. Rajiv Syal, "Taliban bid to fix heroin prices," *The Hindu*, 21 December 2010, http://www.thehindu.com/news/international/article967344.ece
12. They are integrated civilian–military organizations designed to meet three objectives: improve security, extend the reach of the Afghan Government, and facilitate reconstruction in priority provinces. The PRTs were established in Afghanistan at the end of 2002. Briefing on the role of PRT at ISAF HQ, Kabul, 17 June 2007. Also see *ISAF PRT Handbook*, 3rd edition, (Kabul: ISAF, 3 February 2007). For further details see *Provincial Reconstruction Teams in Afghanistan: An Interagency Assessment*, USAID, June 2006, at http://pdf.usaid.gov/pdf_docs/PNADG252.pdf (accessed 24 June 2007); Feickert, "U.S. and Coalition Military Operations in Afghanistan," n. 28; Kenneth Katzman, "Afghanistan: Post-War Governance, Security and U.S. Policy," *CRS Report,* RL30588.
13. It is a counter-insurgency strategy the British employed with great success during the 1950s, and US Special Forces are taking the same approach in similar bases along the Pakistani border and in central Afghanistan. PRTs are a useful concept of COIN—an 'ink blot' strategy wherein stability created by counter-insurgents in one area can gradually spread to other areas. See Andrea M. Lopez, "Engaging or Withdrawing, Winning or Losing? The Contradictions of Counterinsurgency Policy in Afghanistan and Iraq," *Third World Quarterly,* 28/2 (2007), 247.
14. This inference has been drawn from discussions with Afghan Government officials and Afghan people in Kabul, Herat, and Jalalabad. Also see Ambassador Ronald E. Neumann, *Implementation: A New Approach to Multinational Coordination in Afghanistan*, Policy Analysis Brief, The Stanley Foundation, Muscatine, April 2008.
15. This inference was derived after visits to PRT-funded projects and discussions with NGO personnel and locals in different parts of Afghanistan in June 2007.
16. A former top US military commander in Afghanistan, Lieutenant General Karl Eikenberry, has said that the greatest long-term threat to success in Afghanistan is not the resurgence of the Taliban but "the potential irretrievable loss of legitimacy of the government of Afghanistan." In this regard, he specifically cited several critical areas: corruption, justice, and law enforcement, and said: "We need more urgency to build Afghan Government capacity and help connect it with the Afghan people." General James L. Jones, USMC (Ret.), and Ambassador Thomas R. Pickering, *Revitalizing Our Efforts: Rethinking Our Strategies*, 2nd edition, Center for the Study of the Presidency, Afghanistan Study Group Report, Washington, DC (30 January 2008), 28.

17. Interview with an Afghan member of parliament in Kabul, June 2007 and October 2010. Also see Beth DeGrasse and Emily Hsu, *Afghanistan: Old Problems, New Parliament, New Expectations*, United States Institute of Peace Briefing, October 2005, at http://www.usip.org/pubs/usipeace_briefings/2005/1025_afghanwomen.html (Accessed on 7 March 2007).
18. Joshua Kurlantzick, "The Death of Generosity," *Newsweek*, 9 August 2010, http://www.newsweek.com/2010/08/09/the-death-of-generosity. html
19. For more details on 'rentier state' see Barnett R. Rubin, *The Fragmentation of Afghanistan: State Formation and Collapse in the International System* (New Haven, CT: Yale University Press 2002): 81–105.
20. Yama Torabi and Lorenzo Delesgues, *Afghanistan: Bringing Accountability Back In: From Subjects of Aid to Citizens of the State*, Integrity Watch Afghanistan Report, Kabul, June 2008.
21. Ernesto Londoco, "Survey of Afghans points to rampant corruption in government," *Washington Post*, 8 July 2010, http://www.washington post.com/wpdyn/content/article/2010/07/07/AR2010070705222. html?sid=ST2010070701624
22. Matt Waldman, *Falling Short: Aid Effectiveness in Afghanistan*, ACBAR Advocacy Series, March 2008, at http://www.oxfam.org/files/ACBAR_ aid_effectiveness_paper_0803.pdf (accessed on 23 June 2008).
23. Discussions with Action Aid International staff in Afghanistan in May 2007. For details on the 'phantom aid' see Ann Jones, "How U.S. Dollars Disappear in Afghanistan: Quickly and Thoroughly," 3 September 2006, at http://www.sfgate. com/cgi-bin/article.cgi?file=/c/a/2006/09/03/INGR0KRGMF1.DTL (accessed on 29 July 2007).
24. Frank G. Hoffman, "Mind Maneuvers: The Psychological Element of Counterinsurgency Warfare Can Be the Most Persuasive," *Armed Forces Journal* (April 2007), at http://www.afji.com/2007/04/2550166 (accessed on 18 May 2007).
25. Ralph Peters, "Getting Counterinsurgency Right," *New York Post*, 20 December 2006, at http://www.nypost.com/seven/12202006/postopinion/opedcolumnists/getting_counterinsurgency_right_opedcolumnists_ralph_peters.htm?page=3 (accessed on 21 April 2007).
26. Todd A. Megill, "The Dark Fruit Of Globalization: Hostile Use of the Internet," USAWC Strategy Research Project, US Army War College, Carlisle Barracks, PA, 2005, at http://stinet.dtic.mil/cgibin/GetTRDoc?AD=ADA432655&Location=U2&doc=GetTRDoc.pdf (accessed on 2 August 2007).
27. On modern terrorist organizations' exploitation of the Internet and

modern media, see Bruce Hoffman, *Inside Terrorism*, revised edition (New York: Columbia University Press, 2006), 197–228.

28. Rohan Gunaratna, as quoted in the SITE Institute, at http://www.siteinstitute.org (accessed on 25 May 2007).
29. Interviews with Afghan Government officials, Office of National Security Council, Kabul, 11 June 2007; Ralph Peters, "Progress and Peril: New Counterinsurgency Manual Cheats on the History Exam," *Armed Forces Journal International* 144 (February 2007): 35, at http://www.armedforcesjournal.com/2007/02/2456854 (accessed on 30 August 2008).
30. These views and perceptions were gathered from author's interactions and discussions with senior government officials, governors, policy makers, key interlocutors, academia, media personnel, non-governmental organizations, security personnel and locals during a field visit to Afghanistan in October 2010.

3

International Intervention in Afghanistan 2001-2011: Social Dimensions and Consequences

Vladimir Boyko

As we are hosted by our Indian colleagues, it may be appropriate to quote India's first Prime Minister Jawaharlal Nehru (1889–1964) that "Afghan history is almost part of India's history: indeed, for long Afghanistan was part of India."[1] Probably not all agree with this statement as Ahmad Shah, the founding ruler of the first Afghan full-size state, tribal confederacy known as well as Durrani "empire," invaded India several times. By the middle of 1750s he had annexed the Punjab, Kashmir, Sind, Baluchistan, Balkh, Badakhshan and some territories of Iranian Khorasan. Ahmad Shah's intervention was encouraged much by Sunni Indian Muslim authority Shah Waliullah which was bitterly concerned by the fragmentation of Muslim rule in the Indian subcontinent.[2] Going to more recent interventions by the Afghans, their conquest of northern areas (Afghan Turkistan) in late nineteenth century and *blitz-krieg* of 1919 might be mentioned—the latter motivated by honourable quest for state independence by adventurist, but eventually successful expedition of young amir Amanulah Khan. As my own research has proven, this breakthrough was possible due invaluable service of first [unofficial] Soviet representative in Afghanistan, former Tsarist colonel and commander of Kushk fort Konstantin Slivitsky. He repaired the German radio station in Kabul and supplied the Afghan amir with confidential military information got from the British who had no idea about this Afghan facility and openly exchanged information via radio.[3] In the early 1920s pan-Islamist Afghan leadership was ready to start holy war for Central Asia against Soviets in order to establish Muslim federation/confederation. However the defeat of chief nationalist forces (Basmachi movement) and death of their leader Anwar Pasha (former Ottoman military minister) put an end to this endeavour. These are evidence that Afghans as a nation and Afghan state as historically active player of regional politics in South and Central Asia were not only targets of external interventions, but themselves intervened in the north, west and easterly directions. However, the more recent interventions to Afghan soil cannot be justified on these grounds as these seriously undermined the sovereignty, legal status of Afghanistan and prejudiced the spirit and life of peoples settled here since unmemorable times. When focusing on international intervention of early 2000s, one has to look at it from a broad contextual prism, that is from comparative perspective of two chronologically close expeditions—Soviet invasion and political modernization of late 1970s–'80s and most recent international military expedition, followed by efforts to re-frame Afghanistan in accordance with Greater Middle East geopolitical scheme and liberal values. Each of these interventions was undertaken under quite different domestic and external circumstances and may be accessed in certain socio-political and geopolitical context.

Soviet intervention was caused by internal split of the Afghan regime and numerous appeals of different Afghan leaders to send some troops for securing order across main routes and key cities. Perception of the then political (and in lesser degree military) Soviet leadership on security threat for southern borders of USSR played a role in this decision too. The only statesmen to be informed about it in advance—prior to some top Soviet politicians and military leadership—was Iranian spiritual leader Ayatollah Khomeini. The planned Soviet intervention was explained to him by Soviet ambassador Vinogradov as preventive action which would be undertaken within two months and completed by immediate withdrawal of Soviet expeditionary troops and personnel. Khomeini promised to keep silence; but he changed his mind as Soviet occupation lasted much longer, about 10 years. Internationalization of the Afghan conflict by many state/non-state regional and global actors deepened contradictions of the Afghan political class and society; Soviets in their turn were forced to develop more comprehensive schemes of modernization in the occupied country. More and more economic, military and human resources were involved in this scheme and huge investments were made in some construction, infrastructural and social projects though these did not yield any obvious results. Unfortunately, these projects were implemented in a war-torn country, and coincided with socio-political and economic crisis within the intervening country herself. The USSR in the 1980s faced serious domestic and external challenges, which were accelerated by the Afghan expenditure and eventually resulted in its breakdown. It was this crisis and lack of democracy that left Afghan politics beyond public control and even provoked some strata to take part in intervention to Afghanistan either on obligatory or voluntary basis. The latter reflected a quest of some Soviet folk for *great deal*, even though naïve volunteers (youth, marginalized groups) believed that they could and should help "backward Asians" in struggle for real progress under [tending-to-be-] socialist slogans and patterns. After coming to Afghan earth they realized the inappropriateness of their expectations not only because of rejection of leftist values and patterns (economic and humanitarian assistance was accepted, but not fully appreciated as such—much of goods were stolen before reaching most needed groups), but widespread corruption in all network of Soviet Afghan politics. Current re-appraisal of Soviet presence in Afghanistan in positive, tolerant terms is illuminating proof of the Afghan political consciousness, but in the same time it is evidence of extreme traditional opportunism. Anyway, final assessments and judgments of Soviet intervention will be made later, in the light of later developments, including recent intervention of international coalition led by USA.

The military campaign of international coalition started in the fall of 2001, was considered by many outside Afghanistan as model action against terrorist forces and punishment for their 9/11 attack. But the restoration of state and public order in this war-torn country required the development of sustainable/step-by-step social, educational programs and projects, whose implementation is closely associated with security situation and battlefield outcomes. The initial military successes against Taliban, technical/logistical advantages of USA and their allies produced nearly-triumphant sentiments, which were damaged by prolonged fighting nationwide and ill-facilitated state-building. However, it would be not right to accuse the coalition of narrow-minded approach, taking into account only military goals and means— decision-making/implementation bodies either in USA or other allies were motivated enough to offer a comprehensive strategy of post-conflict development (the *Afghan Compact* is only one, but impressive example of it), but the success in this field is not convincing, despite heavy human, financial and prestige losses.

This paper aims to analyse social dimensions of current/ongoing intervention to Afghanistan from comparative perspective, that is in the light of the related Soviet experiences 1980s: expert framework of the whole Afghanistan-related multidimensional scheme (including intellectual accompaniment of military campaign—ideas, cadres, units, networks), social (together with economic) programs of bilateral and multilateral nature with special focus on educational and purely social (employment, social care, human rights) needs, the dialogue with local government and community (language, means, linkages).

The paper also seeks to explore social consequences of international intervention of the first decade 2000s in Afghanistan: new configuration of social strata and ethnic groups, dynamics of social (group/regional/nation-level) identities, including current perceptions of "other" (neighbours, Muslim umma at the whole, the West and specifically USA, Russia, etc., in terms of *dar ul-harb* and *dar ul-islam*). Special attention will be paid to [new] Afghan Diaspora worldwide as one of most significant phenomena and consequences of the Afghan conflict and international intervention, including the efforts of current order-installers to return Afghans to homeland under special bonus programs and by reconciliation of this turbulent country.

The paper is based on comprehensive research of thematic literature, historical analysis of Soviet and [partially] British intervention cases, as well current international intervention on her joint and country-by-country involvements (USA, Germany, UK, small "players"), with references to fieldwork findings in Afghanistan, outer Asia, Russia and the West.

The main hypothesis is that recent international intervention, being justified in some respect by the threat coming from Afghanistan, is not well-grounded politically and socially/culturally—there is a gap between expectations of the sides involved. However, this is not classical clash of civilizations; rather this is a heavily stagnated conflict, intersected with ill-conceived politics of multilateral forces following multi-faceted and controversial goals, either strategic or operational. Till now it has produced only one more turn of conflict, without much consensus in Afghanistan. One of the reasons of this failure is a weak public involvement in terms of expertise, control and supervision, the lack of international cooperation with minor roles of Iran, Russia, and overshadowed tensions between some other influential regional actors. Really workable Afghanistan strategy demands strong social and cultural considerations and references to past experiences re-appraised scholarly, politically and ethically.

One has paid particular attention to the problem of the Afghan refugees as one of the social features of Afghan conflict and then intervention when I began postgraduate programme at the Institute of Oriental Studies (USSR Academy of Sciences, Moscow) in early 1980s. Information gathered (published in the West or in some regional editions like Pakistani, Indian, Arabian, etc., media and reports) was confidential beyond admitted and affiliated academic community. Thousands of Afghans came to USSR (later Russia) too not only under programs of training and indoctrination; but this failed as Soviet domestic life was full of contradictions and there were breaks between propaganda and reality. Although Afghans easily established themselves in Soviet/ Russian environment psychologically and socially, probably because of some Eurasian similarities, politically they maintained and reproduced peculiarities of home society. It was relevant even to those who were alienated from relatives and homeland for many years, but connected with compatriots throughout Russia and worldwide either virtually or via networks (national cultural societies). More bitter were hostilities at home, more Afghans came to Russia and elsewhere as forced migrants and refugees. Since 1980s Afghans in exile numbered 5–6 million. They formed a specific community, highly diverse legally, politically and socially, but tied together by origin and fate. Globally Afghan community in exile is in general more educated and skilled, with many of them serving now for Afghanistan at home and abroad as professionals. But the large-scale UN programme "returning talent" was not successful as a whole because of changes within this very group and motherland situation. This case is partially comparable with Palestinian Diaspora, which is among most educated, but it cannot be properly involved in development at home because of geopolitical constraints, lack of specific experience and institutional marginalization within Palestinian autonomy. However, Afghans abroad irrespective of their political adherences and geographic location may be held as valuable potential and constituent segment of the Afghan nation. Those still staying in Russia/CIS are particularly sociable and resilient, as they came through challenges of transit developments full of hardships and contradictions, whereas their compatriots who spent long time in liberal wealthy environment are less adaptive and alienated from Afghanistan socially.

One more question centres round how recent/ongoing international intervention influenced social and ethnic composition of the Afghan society. It is not easy to respond to it academically. This is not because of the lack or reliable fieldwork and statistical data (census-like, monitoring, etc.), but because Afghan studies did not occupy the interest of the western academia. When one came to Harvard as Fulbright scholar in 1998 for undertaking project on Northern Afghanistan, there was no one here doing research on Afghanistan; even personnel at the related area centres (like Center of Middle Eastern Studies) preferred to deal with Morocco (North Africa) as there was far more comfortable and safe place. Things were considerably changed after 9/11, but it is hard task to overcome long-time ignorance of this very country and related academic/expert field. One may suppose that Afghan studies should be maintained in UK due her long-time colonial politics towards Afghanistan. Gerard Russell, former British diplomat, is sceptical on the state of Afghan studies either in UK or worldwide: "I do not see a much better situation anywhere else in Europe. Only Russia will definitely have some more people working on it." But this is also not true. One of the main shortcomings of scholarly work during Soviet presence in Afghanistan in 1980s was the lack of comprehensive research on crucial topics such as ethnic identities and dynamics, or other fundamental themes, although Soviets succeeded in training large group of native scholars who complemented findings of their Moscow and Central Asian *ustada* by references to original sources and fieldwork. However, all of them are now out of academia or migrated to the West.

During Soviet occupation one of illuminating cases was extradition of Prof Louis Dupree, the leading US authority in Afghan studies. Islamist governments and *jihadi* commanders never favoured balanced research which would expose their own activities. During most turbulent 1990s only single experts succeeded in continuing their work on Afghanistan. German scholars, especially those under umbrella of international organizations or NGOs were among them; the reputation of their country as "third force" in game of traditional invaders (like British, Soviets and then Americans) gave them exclusive access and travel for research purposes. The most productive research networks on Afghanistan since the start of new international intervention are multinational analytical NGO-like teams: Control Risks, AREU, DeLoitte Consulting, Afghan Analysts Network. There are they producing top class data and analysis (selective censuses, case studies, policy briefs, etc.), including the establishment of knowledge infrastructure: libraries, source/data-banks. Research/ analytical institutions of national/government affiliation (Centre of Strategic Studies at IRA7's Ministry of Foreign Affairs, Centre of Afghanistan Studies at Kabul University founded and developed from Peshawar-based NGO ACBAR nucleus by legendary US enthusiast Nancy Dupree, widow of Prof Louis Dupree, American Institute of Afghan Studies and its Kabul branch, etc.) are actually very few and have their original focus. They are the parts of non-cohesive, but topically distinctive network. Hopefully, this institutionalized and personalized entity will play its role in defining and implementing social politics in Afghanistan on consultative basis.

This goal will not be accomplished without real international cooperation either on state/government or institutional and even personal level. It is important to stress the contribution, completed and prospective, by such countries as India and Pakistan. Pakistan which pays big price for her front-line position is isolated geopolitically and destined to pursue subordinate roles in others grand strategies, whereas India is growing increasingly as an influential regional, in some respects even world, power. President Dmitry Medvedev said recently on the eve of his visit to India that Russian-Indian cooperation should play a significant role in solving the Afghan problem. He added that India also can take part in the summit of "four" on the sidelines of the SCO, involving Afghanistan, Pakistan, Russia and Tajikistan.[4]

Nation-building

In order to evaluate current ethno-social composition as the factor of much-awaited reconciliation and reintegration in Afghanistan, one may notice not only demographic and statistical changes within Afghan society, but dynamics of political and social roles. Whereas most numerable minorities (Tajiks, Hazara and Uzbeks) strengthened their representation in all fields, Pashtun considerably weakened its long-time majority through splits in elite and tribal level, though claiming leading positions in politics and governance. During 30 years of civil conflicts traditionally subordinated or even marginalized national groups gained invaluable self-governance, management and other experiences, although Afghanistan is not yet prepared for federal system as political culture of the vast majority of population and elite still not ready for federalism. It is not surprising; even sophisticated European and American political systems came to existence with the passage of long time (e.g. Russian sovereign democracy is paving her way on stony path of federalism with many impediments and contradictions between centre and periphery). And federalism is not only power-sharing vertically and horizontally, being ideally based on proper socio-economic basis and programs. Conceptualizing past and recent patterns of nation-building in Afghanistan, American scholar S. Hess came to the conclusion that this developments were going on the basis on *patrimonialism* and *neopatrimonialism*—Weberian term(s), identifying political regime, based on traditional authority rather than rational (formal) bureaucracy. He suggested that nation-building in this country was featured since the end of nineteenth century by external patronage and domination/occupation (consecutively by British, Soviets, and Americans) and similarly developed by dozens of years under patron/client regimes [of Taraki-Karmal, Najibullah, and now Karzai]. "Karzai ... as a leader of post-Taliban Afghanistan, has maintained his grip on power through textbook neopatrimonial practices, capitalizing upon his position as President and distributor of American and foreign aid, weapons and cash and the appointer of powerful government offices, to build a body of personal patronage in support of his rule."[5]

Recent intervention in Afghanistan is featured by certain socio-cultural dimension which has been reinforced by well-developed strategic schemes (the Afghan Compact, etc.) and pilot projects for their implementation. Even *jihadi* leaders and warlords coming to power in early 1990s realized the necessity of social programmes, appreciating that a workable political argument might be in the opening of new schools, vocational centres, etc. *Jihadi* emissaries carefully searched in Moscow/Dushanbe/Tashkent publishers' basements for school note-books—the remainder of NDPA indoctrination programmes—often just for political self-promotion. The A.R. Sayaf wing of Hezb-e Islami opened "university-in-exile" in Peshawar suburb; its vice-chancellor was a *jihadi*, whereas his deputy graduated from a Russian provincial university. Even Taliban with their significant lack of civil professionals published some external advices academy of sciences proceedings and made some gestures in education field. The military campaign 2001 of international coalition was variously accepted by the international community; diverse attitudes were shown in USA itself, even by some noted experts who were disappointed by straightforward military approaches far beyond battlefield tactics, such as culture and education. Euphoric feelings of early stage of new war in Afghanistan—this time called as "war against terrorism"—were changed with surprising rebirth of Islamist forces and networks in 2010s. These forces can be hardly assessed as "classical" religious fighters. Despite their references to fundamentals of Islam as the main ideology, these are rather marginalized product of long-time conflicts and open war—orphans grown without family care under supervision of madrasa teachers and military instructors, often alien for them. Taliban main social "body" is not exclusion either in the region or even worldwide—they are an output of socio-political upheavals, new and actually lost generation exploited for dishonourable purposes by local and interventionist forces. As social phenomena it has spread worldwide and is a source of underlined conflicts even in relatively stable countries. Surprising military successes and advent of Islamist youth to power on state and grassroots level was [temporarily] welcomed by ordinary people in Afghanistan and some neighbouring countries/areas.

For exploring the origin and dynamics of opposition to current Afghan regime and its international allies, especially her social nature and background, multi-level approach should be applied, e.g., some pro-Taliban followers were known even among Siberia-based Afghan exiles as close acquaintance with real faces and doings of these new power groupings! Afghan version of Islam is not only as religious but social phenomenon as well and may be estimated as traditional phenomenon; till late 1960s it was hardly connected with its international wings and closely integrated into state [oligarchic] *yahya-khel* machinery. The shift to militant Islam became motivated externally and since middle of 1970s (Panjsher rebellion of 1975) domestically too through fighting against the autocratic M. Daud regime against religious establishment and other opposition forces. By 1990s–early 2000s "Afghanistan's contemporary Islamic movement has cohered around a new Islamic paradigm focusing on the concept of the state and legitimacy of power."[6] In this respect it tends to be politically coloured on the lines of Khomeini's version of Shia Islam with its particular attention to political power above traditional Islamic dogmas.

Conclusion

The latest intervention in Afghanistan began on estimation of interventionist forces themselves as a response for increasing terrorist threat to national security of many countries and global security at the whole in late 1990s–early 2000s. From the scholarly point of view this politics should be analysed from comparative perspective as it is historically preceded by actions of other external players which are similar and at the same time distinctive by motivations, patterns of action, composition of interventionist forces (multilateral, etc). Soviet intervention which lasted 10 years and was one of illuminating cases of international conflict in the twentieth century needs to be re-assessed in the light of more recent campaign headed by USA. Being more legalized internationally, multilateral by representation, it has been, however, viewed by many Afghans and worldwide as formally justified scheme aimed to solve unachievable goals—not only defeat religiously coloured terrorist forces, but re-frame the very nature (either political or socio-cultural) of traditional Asian society and statehood— but too much even for prolonged operation under the slogans to protect the Afghan nation together with the whole civilized world. Being started under applauds of many in the West as a triumphant military campaign, this intervention turned with the passage of time to complicated expenditure with modest outputs and ill-predicted consequences. Leaving judgments of its military achievements and constraints of political stabilization, it may be concluded that restoration of social security and even social survival is still under question for most Afghans. Despite some impressive accomplishments in the field of education, professional [re-]training, growing level of competence by government (at least centrally, but locally as well), there are still many impediments for restoring normal life either nation-wide or on regional and local level. A large stratum of the Afghan society is involved in semi-criminal/criminal activities which have become the only forms of survival (narco-business, kidnapping, smuggling of goods, arms, illegal migration, etc). As a result such preliminary medium-run results of international [US-led] scheme of installing "enduring freedom" in Afghanistan and the rest of Greater Middle East has become a failure, contrasted with initial goals, dates/schedules and scenarios. However, a critical approach to international intervention in Afghanistan by coalition forces should be a straightforward approach, underestimating the scale of threat caused by heavily marginalized groups in states/societies with stagnated conflict/transit stages like Afghanistan and some her neighbours.

Notes and References

1. Jawaharlal Nehru, *Glimpses of World History* (London: Asia Publishing House, 1965), 214.
2. R. Hussain, *Pakistan and the Emergence of Islamic Militancy in Afghanistan* (Aldershot: Ashgate, 2010), 21.
3. V. Boyko, *Government and Opposition in Afghanistan: the Main Features of Political Fighting 1919—1953* (Moscow-Barnaul: The Institute of Oriental Studies of RAS, Altai State Pedagogical Academy, 2010), 34–35.
4. http://en.afghanistan.ru/doc/208.html
5. S. Hess, "Coming in terms with neopatrimonialism: Soviet and American nation-building projects in Afghanistan," *Central Asian Survey,* 29/2 (June 2010), 183.
6. See A. Basu Roy's argument in A. Olesen, Islam *and Politics in Afghanistan* (Richmond: Curzon 1995), 227–55. Also see A. Basu Roy, "The Socio-Cultural Issues in Afghan Nation-Building," *Dialogue,* 11/1 (2009), 51.

4

Rethinking International Intervention in Afghanistan

Aunohita Mojumdar

The State and the Citizens

In the introductory concept note for this seminar MAKAIAS points out that "the issue of intervention, humanitarian or otherwise has generated one of the most heated discussions in international relations over the past decade." And so it should. The issue deservedly draws in the widest range of people from humanitarians to strategists from human rights activists to policy makers. Much less debated is the issue of the end to that intervention or the withdrawal of the intervening power or powers from the country in question. Yet, as Afghanistan shows us, the 'exit strategy' as currently envisaged, is no less and perhaps even more important for the country which has suffered or benefited from that intervention

In fact given the increasing debate over intervention it is time to coin a new word that describes those who have been intervened with: '*intervenees*' perhaps?

In the tenth year since the US-led western intervention in Afghanistan, there are new buzzwords to contend with. 'Afghanization', 'Transition' and 'Reconciliation' are amongst the most popular of them. As concepts they sound both conciliatory and forward-looking. What, after all, could be better than handing over the responsibility of governance to Afghans themselves? (Afghanization). What could be better than having warring Afghan groups sort out their own problems? (Reconciliation). And what could be better than having Afghans take charge of their own security, putting Afghan forces on the streets and valleys rather than foreign forces (Transition). Yet, that is not quite how it is happening. The Afghan citizen is the consistent absentee from the centre of policies, programmes and projects made in his or her name. The international military intervention and state-building efforts began in response to the perceived threat to the security interests of the US and its allies post 9/11. They have rarely deviated from that formula.

It is not just the fact that Afghans have not benefited as much as they should have. But many Afghans are poorer, less secure and less vested in the democratic process as a result of many of these policies that are cast very narrowly for specific strategic interests. Now, with the international intervention moving to transition and the international community perched on the brink of exiting Afghanistan, the approach is narrowing further and squeezing the Afghans even more out of the small spaces of livelihood and liberties that they had wrested.

This is not to say that nothing has happened since 2001. For most people in Afghanistan, with the exception of those caught in the military operations in the most volatile areas of the country in the east and the south, life is better than 2001. However how fair is it to compare Afghanistan in 2011 to Afghanistan in 2001? Surely, progress beyond 2001 was a relevant comparison in 2002, 2003 and 2004. But 2011? The reason why the international community continues to draw a comparison to 2001 is very clear. That is the only way that some progress can be claimed with some authenticity. In fact a comparison of 2011 with 2005 and 2006 would reveal something shocking. It would not only show how little progress there had been in the past five to six years, but it would also make it clear that there had been big reverses in several areas and sectors in that time period making 2011 worse than 2005 or 2006.

The most obvious issue is that of deteriorating security. There are more Afghans being killed every day in Afghanistan, not just in the south and the east, but also in the north and the west, compared to five or six years ago. The graph of violence has been steadily on the rise. While it is true that the international military is inflicting losses on the insurgent groups, the insurgency has shown an ability to recover, reequip and re-staff itself with little loss of momentum or kinetic energy to use the military jargon.

Assessments of course are subjective. So let us stick to facts, encapsulated most recently in the quarterly report of the UN Secretary General Ban ki Moon on Afghanistan. According to the report released in December 2010 the number of security incidents in the period under review—the last quarter of the year—was 66 per cent higher than during the same period in 2009. The report states that though a high number of mid-level anti-government elements continue to be killed or arrested, anti-government elements were able to sustain high levels of activity in areas into which they had recently expanded, particularly in the north and the north-east, where the international military presence is less dense.

The Secretary General said civilians continued to bear the brunt of the intensified armed conflict and casualties; both deaths and injuries increased by 20 per cent in the first 10 months of 2010 compared with the same period in 2009. As the Taliban footprint continues to grow, the international community is more and more confined with larger and larger areas of the country being considered too unsafe for their travel.

So how does the international community deal with this dismal situation? Well, the US annual review of the Af-Pak strategy shows us the way. It claims "notable operational gains," says that "the strategy is showing progress across all three assessed areas of Al-Qaeda, Pakistan and Afghanistan," that there is "significant progress in disrupting and dismantling the Pakistan-based leadership and cadre of Al-Qaeda over the past year" and that it "has reduced overall Taliban influence and arrested the momentum they had achieved in recent years in key parts of the country (Afghanistan)." For those living and working in Afghanistan it seemed as if the assessment was of a parallel universe which we were not privy to.

The US Joint Chiefs of Staff Chairman Admiral Mike Mullen who was in Kabul to release the review justified the assessment saying "If I were to use Kandahar and Helmand as examples, we're starting to see there the nation's beginnings of governance at the very local level–sub-district level." These two provinces have indeed been the focus of much of the violence—the insurgents have displayed a remarkable ability to adapt themselves, moving from one province to another as the pressure builds up, creating new bases or returning once military operations cease as they have been doing over the past five years. The flexibility in their military tactics has been well-recorded and success of military operations in two provinces is no indicator of progress either in the long term or even in the overall situation in the country. The bottom line is that insurgency controls a much wider area and section of the population than it did earlier and there are no indicators as yet that this trend is being reversed.

Does the American administration really believe the situation in Afghanistan is stable enough to allow the western troops to start a drawdown beginning in July 2011? To test that proposition one need look no further than the urgent and desperate meetings that the international community held right after President Hamid Karzai announced a ban on the private security companies that provide security to the diplomatic community, international forces as well as private contractors implementing the aid projects in Afghanistan. Most private contractors threatened to pull out of Afghanistan if they were not allowed to use the private security companies, saying they had no faith in the ability of the Afghan National Security Forces to ensure their security. Yet, it is these Afghan forces who are expected to take over the task of security of the nation, the task which the international forces have failed so far.

While the aim of training, equipping and readying the Afghan forces for an eventual transition is a laudable one, the speed at which this is sought to be done is not. An army built in a hurry and without adequate command and control structures is a potential problem and not a solution except if the solution is seen through the narrow prism of the domestic political interests of the troop-contributing nations.

In fact, the strategic interests of donor countries are so narrow that they often come into conflict with each other, until the only common denominator is the least desirable one. After billions of dollars have been spent in the attempts to disarm the militias—mostly through the processes of DDR and DIAG—the international community is now setting up community militias as a short-cut to even allowing the Afghan National Forces to grow to strength. Not only have community militias been proven counter-productive historically, but they have been introduced under various guises since the auxiliary police of 2007; each attempt has been equally unsuccessful. The last such attempt, in the guise of 'Afghanization', has sought to use tribal structures as the building blocs for this policing. Recently it led to intra-tribal implosions as with the Shinwari tribe in the Achin district of Nangarhar after the US forces paid and armed a section of the tribe in an attempt to counter the insurgents.

One does not have to search far for the reasons for this short sighted view. The US administration under President Obama has been clear about its core goals, which is to "disrupt, dismantle, and eventually defeat Al-Qaeda in the region and to prevent its return to either country." To quote the American President, "From the start,

I've been very clear about our core goal. It's not to defeat every last threat to the security of Afghanistan, because, ultimately, it is Afghans who must secure their country."

While the idea of the Afghan forces securing their country sounds logical, it needs to be remembered that they are being asked to take on a deteriorating security situation in a theatre of war shaped by the international forces over the past nine years, where the aim of securing Afghans has been secondary to the political objectives of the western coalition. There is a significant difference between a war fought to defeat every last threat to a population located thousands of miles away from the battlefield and one fought to protect the population in the war zone, and the US President makes it clear which one he is fighting.

Security clearly is the visible frontier of the conflict. The less reported near invisible violence is that of impoverishment. According to a UN document released in December, the "number of people lacking the minimum daily kilocalorie intake has steadily increased since 2005." This fact may not stun Indians. Figures on malnutrition and poverty in India are shocking. However there is something astounding in the fact that the number of malnourished people in Afghanistan is growing after nine years of concerted efforts by the international community administering aid with billions of dollars.

The UN figure is cited from the recent Consolidated Humanitarian Appeal for Afghanistan launched by the UN last month. The amount sought for emergency aid, was $678 million. It was lower than what had been sought last year despite a "dramatic increase in humanitarian need for its (Afghanistan's) chronically vulnerable rural population"—the UN's words—to try and "market" the appeal better to the donors. Last year's appeal was funded only up to 66 per cent by international donors. Only 1per cent of the amount sought for emergency educational needs was provided under the Humanitarian Appeal. Who would benefit from the full funding of this Humanitarian Appeal? Amongst them would be half of Afghanistan's children under five who are underweight, 16.7 per cent of whom face acute malnutrition. Amongst them pregnant mothers who die at the rate of 1400 per 100,000, the second highest maternal mortality rate in the world.

The failure to fund the appeal is not due to a shortage of money. The entire amount sought for the emergency humanitarian needs is too small compared to what the international community spends in a year on Afghanistan, approximately 8–10 billion. What prevents providing the aid for the most urgent needs and the most vulnerable population? The answer lies in the political and strategic objectives of the donors.

It is true that larger and larger parts of the country are becoming inaccessible, making it more difficult for a substantive section of the aid community to go to those areas. But is the aid then going to the areas where it could actually do some good? No, it is not. The lion's share of the money is being spent in the insecure provinces where it cannot be absorbed easily, while stable areas are being deprived.

Donors, private contractors who implement projects funded by aid, the UN are all increasingly circumscribed by the increasing insecurity, their movements restricted. So is anyone considering giving greater resources to those organizations which are able to travel in the insecure areas because of their well-established links with the community? No, they are not. In fact non-profit NGOs who have been working in Afghanistan for decades complain that they are being squeezed out because they refuse to fulfil the political and military objectives of the donor countries.

How does this deprivation work on the ground? Non-profit humanitarian aid agencies define themselves by their core tents of "humanity, impartiality, and neutrality." But this posture is clearly not something that the donors are willing to invest in. Most of the money being spent in Afghanistan is donor-driven, not needs-driven. That is, a donor determines the geographical locations as well as the sector that it wishes to invest in for the next funding cycle. Once they decide what they want to spend on, they find beneficiaries to fit the profile.

The alternative method, that of determining what a community needs and wants, and then finding a donor to fund that project, meets with much less success. Even in areas where the needs match with the funding, some aid agencies have turned down projects because the donor requires them to carry out tasks such as post-battlefield clean-up. That means that, for example, after international troops have bombed a place to bits, the NGO is required to come in and apply band-aid. Most reputed NGO who pride themselves on their neutrality refuse to do that since it clearly associates them with the military force and their operations.

If this is sounding too much NGO driven, let us look at the development priorities as identified by the donor themselves. In London in 2006, the donor community and the Afghan Government signed off on the ANDS (Afghan National Development Strategy), the initiation of a blueprint that would identify the needs of Afghanistan so that donors could better direct their resources towards those needs. The final blueprint was adopted in 2008 at the Paris Conference. The ANDS is by no means a perfect document but it is the best outline of Afghan needs with a sectoral approach as well as multi-sectoral cross-cutting needs identified by the Afghan and international community working together. In 2010 January however yet another conference was held in London to identify the priorities of Afghanistan. In July 2010 there was another one in Kabul to give greater substance to those priorities. The donors described the conference as a great success since it established priorities.

Though the principle of routing money through the Afghan Government had been endorsed clearly in Paris 2007, it was established once again this year with great celebration. Was there a real donor commitment to this principle? Difficult to say. In March 2010 the UN Secretary General Ban ki Moon referred to the London Conference and pointed out that "the participants in the London Conference supported the ambition of that goal, *but did not explicitly commit themselves to it*" (emphasis added). By June, the Secretary-General was looking afresh at the same facts: in his quarterly report released then, he referred to "*The London Conference commitment to progressively channel financing for development* through the central budget remains critical for a country in which almost 80 per cent of development assistance does not flow through the Government budget" (emphasis added). Same facts, different reading.

So was the Kabul Conference the final blueprint for the priorities, sharpened and focussed beyond the 2005–06 efforts? Not really. The document issued at the end of the conference identifies dates by which the Afghan Government will actually come up with concrete plans. So how does the international community celebrate the fact that priorities are still being established five years since the Paris conference did the same? By re-branding the event as the advent of "Afghanization." The only expression of some self-doubt came from the World Bank, whose Managing Director Ngozi Okonjo-Iweala said: "I propose that we think long and hard before having more conferences until we are sure of seeing more results." It was perhaps not a coincidence that the only pragmatic note of the conference was struck by a woman.

Indeed there are more children in school and more refugees who have returned since 2005. However more children are dropping out of school. As many as 400,000 children in southern Afghanistan are at risk of being deprived of their schooling; the dropout rate from schools is on the rise. Six million refugees have indeed returned home. Lost is the story that the more recent arrivals are being pushed out or that the return of refugees has been found to be the single largest cause of household shock in the most recent National Risk and Vulnerability Analysis (NRVA), far outweighing the shock from terrorism or insurgency related violence.

Given the dismal performance of the international community in Afghanistan the logical question to ask would be why the solution does not lie in the departure of the international community, the transition to full Afghan control, since the international community is making things worse rather than better? That is because the exit will make things worse since their exit strategy carries as much political baggage as the intervention. If the period of intervention was one of narrow strategic decisions, the period of exit, or transition, is one of greater narrowness, with the concerns of Afghan citizens being pushed further into a corner.

In the name of Afghanization, the international community has put in place structures of power that have proven quite clearly to be predatory; it has put in place policies that further impoverish the most vulnerable sections of the population and it has put in place political plans that will further wring out Afghans, divesting them of the small freedoms and political spaces that they had claimed since 2001.

It is a travesty for the international community to talk of Afghanization and Afghan-led processes after having put in power specific individuals and armed groups over the past nine years. Individuals now at the helm of power have been empowered with money as well as arms in order to meet the short term needs of the international community. Most of those in positions of power today are not leaders of the people who have been empowered through an organic process of representative politics with their roots in popular support. Many of them are those whose predatory politics created the space, acceptability and tolerance for the Taliban and its brand of politics in the early nineties. This is not just civil society activists, liberal academics or the human rights community saying this. The Afghan President who accused coalition troops of hiring "thugs and warlords" and "people with no limits to misbehaviour."

Incidentally, a significant section of Afghans influential in decision-making in their country benefit directly from the spoils of war, with the international community paying them whether it is for hiring militias for use in the war against terror, such as the Kandahar strike force working under the US Special Forces which turned the guns against the national police eliminating the head of the police in Kandahar Matiullah Qateh and the head of the criminal investigations unit in Kandahar; or the leasing of land worth billions of dollars from the warlords or buying goods and services at hugely inflated prices. The truth is, in 2001 many of the former militia commanders and warlords were not influential people who had to be dealt with; they were out of power former had-beens who were resurrected, empowered and installed by the warped policies of the international community. While one might argue that the best of leader in all countries may rise above their immediate financial gains, it is clear that the operational practices of the international community has created a clear conflict of interest between the Afghan population and a significant section of its leaders who stand to lose, personally and monetarily if there is peace in Afghanistan.

More significantly, while the international community has signed off on a political process that is described broadly as democracy and can therefore alleviate their collective conscience, the process that has been in place in Afghanistan bears little resemblance to any of the existing and robust democracies whether in the West or in South Asia. Why? Political parties are banned from participation in the elections; the provinces have virtually no power despite having elected bodies. In Afghanistan, which is widely recognized as being a country over which Kabul has exerted varying degrees of limited control, the most centralized system of governance was adopted. The argument in favour of this system was the fact that Afghanistan needed a strong centre in the immediate aftermath of the international intervention. Even if one agreed with that perspective, it is clear that the government in the centre is too weak to provide the kind of strong governance that the particular model requires. The result is centralization without the outreach of the government; the centralization of patronage, not power. Citizens have little or no ability to influence the government and its policies, let alone the donors who wield control over the vast majority of the resources, amounting to between 75-80 per cent. The concept of Afghanization is therefore a travesty of the principle.

The process of parliamentary elections currently underway is a microcosm of what is wrong with the process of both the international intervention as well as exit strategy. In 2009, widespread accounts of fraud in the presidential elections soured relations between the international community and President Karzai. At that time most of the donor nations said they would not fund the next elections without electoral reforms. However they not only funded the 2010 elections, but did so after the president had passed a controversial electoral law that further weakened the electoral institutions. Instead of creating an independent appointing mechanism for the Independent Election Commission, currently hand-picked by the President, the President also assumed the powers for appointment of the Electoral Complaints Commission, which was earlier independent. The current and ongoing tussle over the elections demonstrates how, in the name of non-interference, the donors have allowed the nascent electoral system in Afghanistan to be further subverted.

The international community should not, of course, intervene in the process of elections, but it could have used its considerable leverage, including financial leverage, to strengthen the electoral institutions as well as processes. However in the name of Afghanization, the election process has not been left to a tug of war between political institutions rather than serving the Afghan citizens as it should.

Rather than taking the share of blame for the failure of implementing steps that could support democracy, the international community has washed its hands off by saying Afghanistan is not Switzerland or that Afghans must find their own way. Behind the scenes they express concern about whether democracy is suited to Afghanistan. International analysts questioning Afghanistan's suitability to the democratic process forget that the 'tribal' and 'ethnic' solutions they proffer in its stead were rooted in the principles of democracy long before some of the western countries. Participatory decision making through the *jirga* and representative decision making through the *shuras* have been in use in Afghanistan. The tenets of a democratic state will extend the extent of participation, for example including the voice of women through the vote, or creating councils equipped to deal with contemporary problems with contemporary solutions.

If elections are a microcosm of international intervention and retreat, then 'Reconciliation' is the exit plan. On paper the objective of reconciliation sounds like a good one. The arguments for it include the fact that the international community is not winning the military fight, hence the "no military solution" argument; the fact that Afghans need to come to a mutually accommodative solution, "the solution must be Afghan led" argument; and the fact that Afghanistan is not a western country, "Afghans must find an Afghan solution" argument. A careful look at the current political scenario however shows that whatever the nature of the beast, the process is neither peace-making nor reconciliation in the broader sense, but a move towards cutting a political deal with some of the major insurgent groups.

First of all, it is clear that not all the insurgent groups are on board regarding the policy of reconciliation. Even if one discounts the consistent position of the Taliban leadership expressed not just through statements but in their increasingly virulent actions against the Afghan state, not even the most optimistic spin doctor of the reconciliation process claims that all the armed opposition groups will participate in the process. The best case scenario therefore is to hope that some of the armed groups will reconcile and become part of the power structure, making the Afghan state stronger as well as leaving a smaller group of the disaffected armed insurgents for the state apparatus to deal with. The front-runner in this process is of course the Hizb e Islam faction led by Gulbuddin Hekmatyar who has been sniffing at power for the past five years.

However even if we assume that the best case scenario will be realized, the political process that it envisages leaves out not just a significant section of the armed insurgents but also the unarmed opposition groups.

The body appointed to take the reconciliation process forward, the High Peace Council, is dominated by former *jihadi* leaders and current commanders. Certainly the former *jihadi* leaders must be on board in any peace process; they are part and parcel of the fabric of the social and political template and many of them now hold influential positions. However what they are not are neutral actors with credibility that cuts across the political spectrum. They are very much seen as a part and parcel of the political establishment and beneficiaries of its largesse and cannot be the neutral arbiters who are necessary to take the peace process forward.

The gains made since 2001 at establishing a minimum level of rule of law and rights are in the process of being reversed. Red lines and adherence to the constitution are being mentioned as a guarantee of the minimum fundamental rights. Gains have been made in terms of strengthening some of the laws, for example, the introduction of the law for the elimination of violence against women and the efforts to implement the Child Rights Convention through changes in the Juvenile Justice Code. However in terms of the implementation the reality on the ground suggests a slow retreat of the small gains made in the respect of political, civil and human rights. The short shrift given to the issue of transitional justice is an example.

Prosecution for crimes of war, reparation for losses and acknowledgement of the suffering were principles identified by the Afghan Independent Human Rights Commission as a means of reconciling citizens and bringing a sense of closure to the past. However the first part, of prosecution, worried some of the former combatants so much that they established a law that provides blanket amnesty to all participants in the conflict. Not only does the amnesty give pardon for all crimes, but it also gives pardon in perpetuity. There is no cut-off date. In 2007 this was opposed by the international community for violating of the principles of justice and human rights. However it has now been adopted without a murmur of protest from the international community. The UN itself put peace before transitional justice not only delinking peace and justice but also suggesting that the two were mutually exclusive at this point in time. It is true that prosecuting war criminals may be an extremely difficult task in today's Afghanistan but what the Amnesty law does is to take away the hope of justice from Afghan citizens, something that is not just depressing but also dangerous in the long run. One might also argue that from a clearly practical point of view an amnesty in perpetuity is a clear disincentive for peace. However short term goals are the order of the day.

The narrative of reconciliation suits most of the decision-makers: a non-performing government that can eschew governance for political deals; an international community in a hurry to achieve temporary stability in order to exit, and a resurgent intolerant ideology that is sniffing at power.

Realpolitik demands that every nation or group will follow its own interests. However it also works on the principle of a commonality of interests, a shared platform of mutually beneficial interests. In Afghanistan, however, the citizen has little influence on decision-making or participation in governance. The creation of a state, institutions and processes that are not answerable or accountable to the Afghan citizen has not been of concern to donor nations. While they would like to see less corruption, the mechanisms they have put in place breed corruption. While many would like to see better governance, the aid policies put in place do not make the beneficiaries the central concern. While they would like Afghans to be more supportive of the government and the war against terror, they have put justice on the backburner. While many of the donors have been well-intentioned in their efforts in reconstruction of Afghanistan, the needs of Afghans have always been subservient to the over-riding strategic interests, even if that interest is merely limited to not challenging the decisions that the dominant donor, the US, has taken in its own strategic interests.

In the tenth year of the international intervention in Afghanistan, Afghans remain second class citizens in their own country. This is primarily because the citizen has not been at the heart of efforts directed at building the Afghan state, the Afghan nation or reconstruction of the country. Ignored for years, the Afghan citizen now faces not just neglect but increasing pressure, being squeezed from all sides, in the midst of spiralling violence and a deteriorating economic situation.

Military Withdrawal: Scenarios and US Strategies

5

Military Withdrawal: Prospective Scenarios for Afghanistan and the Region

Maqsudul Hasan Nuri

Is the fifth Afghan war coming to a closure? Nearly 49 nations, including the 28-member NATO coalition, presently form part of the 150,000 foreign forces now deployed in Afghanistan. Since 2006 there has been a rise in militancy of Taliban and allied elements in Afghanistan. President Barack Obama in his speech to the West Point military cadets in December 2009 remarked that western troops would start exiting from Afghanistan by July 2011. The 19-20 November 2010 Lisbon meeting set 2014 as the time limit for final withdrawal of US/NATO troops although they could start coming back as early after July 2011 if conditions permit. 2014 was termed as an "aspirational dateline" and the drawing down of forces was "condition based" and not "calendar driven" synchronizing with ISAF pullout. On 15 December 2010, on the occasion of the first review of US strategy for Afghanistan President Obama has reiterated the resolve to pull out the US troops by the above date.[1]

In fact, the "conceptual withdrawal" has been discussed for the last year or so finding another narrative to justify disengagement over any best possible settlement under the circumstances.[2] However, the dateline was qualified by conditions on the ground: strength of Afghan insurgency and nature of future responsibilities to be taken up by Afghan forces.

That conflicting messages continue to emanate about the withdrawal dates is perhaps due to different audiences at home and abroad and to keep government options open. For example, V.P. Joe Biden said that the end of December 2014 is a "drop dead date," while NATO Secretary General Gen cautioned that NATO troops will stay as long as necessary and "will not transition if our partners are not ready."[3]

The Date Debate

The ambiguity in setting dates is partly due to policy division in the US policy circles (Pentagon and Congress). Thus, it is widely debated if the 'surge' is going to be successful in 'degrading' Taliban insurgency, whether Pakistan launches operations in North Western Waziristan and how soon and effective the Afghan National Army (ANA) will be in assuming its post withdrawal functions.

There is a significant difference of opinion between the US military and political leaders about ending the war. Within the intelligence agencies there is pessimism and citing reasons such as Karzai administration's corruption and reluctance by Pakistan to take stronger action against militants in border areas.[4] Likewise, the Congress is highly skeptical about current government policies and wants extrication of US forces sooner than later.[5] While the US military wants the fight to finish with clear victory, the political leaders are desirous to bring forces home due to an 'unending war' and avoid any Vietnam-like quagmire.

On giving specific dates there are differing views. According to the detractors, it should not have been announced insofar as it emboldens Taliban forces by betraying the impression that Americans are leaving, "the end is near" and Taliban victory over US defeat certain. Moreover, it undermines US credibility as a remaining superpower for its allies and friends, the fecklessness of NATO as a military alliance and sends a message of supporting the Taliban elements which it once so despised and wanted to eliminate. Also, it creates difficulties for the military commanders and sends signals to regional neighbours that the US is soon 'quitting' the region. No wonder military commanders like former Lt. Gen McChryrstal objected and thought it as an unwise policy where military decisions were subordinated to political expediencies.

The supporters take a positive view saying the deadlines tend to focus efforts and speed up the process of assuming responsibilities by Afghanistan and Pakistan; to help promote reconciliation amongst varying groups who may delink the Taliban from Al-Qaeda; disassociate mid-level commanders from top Taliban ideologues and start negotiations to share power.

In all insurgencies, local support, time factor, terrain and sanctuaries normally favour the insurgents. As a common Taliban saying goes, the western forces may have the watch but they have the time on their side. It is a fact that Afghan insurgency is more intransigent and deep rooted than, say, Iraq. In case of Iraq, the Sunni population opposing the allied forces comprised one-fifth of population while four-fifth of the majority was of Sunni and Kurd elements—generally supportive to US forces. In case of Afghanistan, the Pushtuns comprise nearly 43 per cent of the population and were the ruling elite for centuries. Besides, Iraq has a centralized government and is bolstered by nearly $60 billion annual revenues from oil. Afghanistan, on the other hand, is impoverished and relies for war effort on drugs trade and strong tribal traditions. Its rugged, unguarded and meandering border of 2,500 km with Pakistan worked against Soviets forces and contributed to their defeat, besides the role of the mujahedeen and external support.[6]

Yet some kind of major withdrawal of US/NATO forces has to come about one day as it cannot remain an 'infinite war'. Given the upcoming 2012 US Presidential elections, the weariness in the public,[7] heavy economic costs and problems facing western coalition and, over and above, the Afghan war exceeding 10 years (more than Vietnam), turning it into a 'no-win' situation—the compulsions are adding up to wind up the war effort without losing face.

In terms of cost, the US is spending annually $70 billion on Afghanistan. US and ISAF casualties have risen to 2,229 since 2001—over half since January 2009. Nearly 600 have died in 2010 alone as compared to 630 in January 2009.[8] The attacks on coalition forces have risen by 50 per cent and although the Taliban have not been able to capture any major city their influence has spread to 33 out of the 34 provinces, especially in nine south and southeastern provinces.[9]

Perspectives of Actors Involved

The US Perspective

Here it is in order to examine what the American surge strategy aims to achieve. It is withdrawal without conceding military defeat. Based on rather successful results achieved in Iraq, General Petreus thinks that the same methodology could be applied in the Afghan situation to 'disrupt, dismantle and defeat' Taliban forces, delink them from Al-Qaeda, create internal dissensions and woo the middle level leadership to facilitate negotiations, to keep the European allies in tow and demonstrate US will and commitment to its allies and friends in the region.

Ironically, 'surge' and 'exit' are contradictory policies. However, this strategy has been applied with some modicum of success in Iraq in weakening the insurgent forces before starting negotiations. A prime driver in setting the draw down dates seems to be Obama's bid for presidential election in November 2012. After all, Obama's major election campaign focused on peace and disengagement from costly wars in Afghanistan and Iraq. Also, it satisfies Republican and Democrats groups in the US. It keeps the option open that if things do not go as planned these reinforcements could even stay longer after the 2014 cutoff date. In addition, it puts pressure on Afghans and Pakistani governments to exert more effort in weakening Taliban. For Pakistan the demand is to launch military operations in North Waziristan against Taliban if withdrawal is to commence by July 2011. For this the US has granted Pakistan an aid package of $4.2 billion.[10]

The Great Debate

Views of the Pentagon and State Department may differ, but it now seems that the Obama Administration is seriously thinking of negotiating with Taliban forces as the war is getting open ended and unwinnable. It desires Taliban to disassociate from Al-Qaeda which is seen as global threat and perhaps to share power in any future political dispensation. In this regard, it hopes that Pakistan may help create some divisions amongst moderate and hardliners with which to negotiate.

Significant US presence might continue as the US has made a major investment in the region; in the 28 November Lisbon conference it declared that there is not going to be any letup in its commitment to Afghanistan. Also it did not ask any of regional countries for help giving the impression that NATO's occupation of Afghanistan under different guise or address may seem endless.[11]

Taliban Forces

The Taliban has set the following major demands: US military withdrawal, release of captured and detailed Taliban prisoners, removal of Taliban as terrorist entity through the UNSC resolution, ending sanctions, amending the constitution and direct negotiations with the US, major share in future Afghan Government and start of negotiations in some neutral countries like Japan, Turkey or Gulf.

Withdrawal of US troops, on the other hand, is contingent on factors such as disengagement from Al-Qaeda, protection of human rights and women in Afghanistan Constitution and a coalition government comprising all ethnic groups. The US thinks that there is a tight relationship with Al-Qaeda and this linkage should be broken by Pakistan either by carrying out a military action or through veiled threats. Ultimately, the US may strike a strong bargain with making constitutional amendments by synchronizing troop's withdrawal with ceasefire, albeit power sharing questions might pose some difficulties.[12]

The Karzai Government

On its part, the Karzai Government seems to be convinced that US cannot win in Afghanistan. The sentiment against presence of foreign forces and the urge for peace is especially strong in south and southeastern Afghanistan, which has been worst hit by violence. That is why he is favouring dialogue with Afghan Taliban. But his conditions for peace hinge upon lying down of arms by Taliban, a ceasefire (but not surrender), protection of Afghan Constitution and delinking from Al-Qaeda and his immunity after the new government comes into power. It is thought that 2014 was suggested by Karzai and he would like US presence to stay longer to protect his government notwithstanding demands for exit for public consumption. That is why he is relying on Pakistan for a dialogue with Afghan Taliban so that a suitable power-sharing arrangement can be worked out in such a manner that the democratic structure of Afghanistan is maintained.

Pakistan

Pakistan's interest lies in having a stable western and southwestern border adjoining Afghanistan, a peaceful Afghanistan in essence, ending of US forays in the border regions and phased withdrawal of US troops, prevention of undue Indian interference in that country especially to Baloch insurgents. It also wants the gains of the post 9/11 to be retained and some semblance of troops to remain there. Its support for Haqqani and Hizb e Islamic and other like minded groups is based on the premise that once Taliban get power in their region and foreign forces leave they will tend to become more responsible and amenable. Pakistan is of the view that Taliban resistance is nationalistic while that of Al-Qaeda is transnational and that in order to survive they will have to depend upon outside world community for assistance. The replication of the earlier Taliban rule is unlikely as new generation of leadership and experience and the exhaustion level reached has demonstrated.

An opposing view however postulates strongly that these Taliban groups are unreliable and they would revert to their radical ideology and will not forsake their linkages with Al-Qaeda. It is also added that even if it breaks with Al-Qaeda, many splinter local groups are springing up with Al-Qaeda's support in border region and interior of Pakistan.[13]

Regional Reactions

All countries would like some presence of the US, though a phased withdrawal is preferred. None of them want a resurgent Taliban in control (Russia, China and CARs in particular would not like Taliban controlled power elite in government). While Pakistan would like a component of Taliban sharing power in a representative government, India will not be too happy and neither would be Iran with total Taliban control. India would also safeguard its investments in the region and earlier connections with the Afghan state.

Ultimately, it is the prerogative of the Afghan nation to choose its friends and have balanced relations with all. Pakistan's concept of 'strategic depth' is also misnomer as it should aim at have a stable, peaceful Afghanistan which is not overtly hostile to Pakistan.

US/NATO Withdrawal from Afghanistan: Likely Scenarios

What are the ultimate post exit scenarios in Afghanistan, if and when the NATO/ISAF withdrawal takes place after 2014 as "drop dead date." As always, these range from the alarmist to optimistic to realistic.

Scenario 1: Total Withdrawal (Alarmist)

Should the US beat a hasty withdrawal, the implications for the country and region could be dire. A major civil war with foreign intervention could ensue, reenacting the scene of 1989–94. All the gains of NATO/US, if any, will be lost. Moreover, the US global image will plummet further as a capricious and unreliable partner. This might further embolden Taliban groups who shall try to reclaim total power and rule Afghanistan.

The capacity building and training of Afghan National Army (ANA) has to proceed fast from its present level of 171,000 men and police to 134,000.[14] The more ambitious US goals for the police and army are to cumulatively grow from 260,000 to 306,000 by October 2010 and to nearly 350,000 by 2013.[15] Yet they are likely to be poorly trained and there are shortages of adequate trainers. Besides, the desertion rate of troops is nearly 40 per cent. Drawn largely from anti-Taliban elements, i.e. Tajik, Uzbek and Hazara communities, they make the nearly 43 per cent Pushtuns more insecure.

There is also possibility that FATA, Haqqani Group JuD, LeT will join *jihad* to assist the Taliban. This will bolster the TTP to strive for gaining power in Pakistan too and lead to renewed militancy and a further inflow of refugees. Already two million are staying back in Pakistan and are still hesitant to go to their country. This scenario is also in the interest of regional powers. Likewise radical Islamists in China, Pakistan, Russia, Central Asia and elsewhere will get emboldened and terrorism might get a second life. This is the most dismal and disappointing scenario for the region and the world at large. Additionally, foreign intervention may start supporting different groups. The new found resources of gold and copper in Afghanistan could fuel resource wars as in parts of Africa and Asia.[16] At the same time, under the US security cover Hamid Karzai could also find some political immunity if he stays in power or even otherwise.

Scenario 2: Partial US/NATO Withdrawal

This is a more realistic possibility/scenario. It postulates that there is not going to be a total, precipitous withdrawal by US and ISAF and that US token troops will man bases, with some troops and trainers stationed in Afghanistan. The number may be around 50, 000 or so with 1000 trainers to stay beyond 2015."[17] Pullout strategy of NATO forces has to be gradual along with strengthening of Afghan forces; out of 34 Afghanistan provinces (300 districts) where violence is concentrated in 9 of the southern and eastern provinces two third could be handed over without serious risk.[18] The least troubled area is in west Herat where drawing down may start in another six months beginning from July 2011. Likewise, the second largest contingent of British troops (some 9,500) plan to be out of Afghanistan by 2015. In fact, Sir David Richards, British C-in-C remarked that they are "planning for a 30-40 year scenario"[19] or even "stay as long as it takes."[20] These forces could start declining by late 2011/early 2012 in certain areas and then reduced to 20,000-30,000 as stationed as part of an agreement on Status of Forces.[21]

It is believed by some Afghan security analysts that at the very least five major bases will be maintained by the US after the withdrawal.[22] A large embassy in Kabul is being built by "the largest construction engineering group" of Kansas, US with a contract of $511 million.[23] According to the US ambassador, it is "already the largest... in the world" with "more than 1,100 brave and dedicated civilians... from 16 agencies and working next to their military counterparts in 30 provinces" and yet it seems it is still not big enough.[24] This is in addition to expansion of consular facilities planned in Mazar-i-Sharif and Herat. These are considered necessary to secure the gains and in view of the past experience of hasty, ill-planned withdrawal of Soviet troops in February 1989. This led to a debilitating Afghan civil war, the consequent rise of Taliban from 1994–2001 and then its ouster through US intervention in 2001.

Moreover, stationing of US troops makes sense as it would like to protect its geopolitical interests in the region: Central Asia, China, borderlands of Pakistan and Iran to the west. Under this scenario the winning of hearts and minds strategies will continue through economic development and assistance programmes. Also, the aim is to gain time to build ANF and police to the level that they could ensure internal stability and deal with terrorism. It is planned to expand troops from 240,000 to 305,000 by 2011 and 40,000 by late 2012. As of today, unfortunately no Afghan single unit is trained enough to fight independently against militancy and violence.

Scenario 3: Representative/Pluralistic Afghanistan

In the words of an analyst, the future outlook in Afghanistan is going to be in between a "Central Asian Valhalla"[25] or Somalia." In fact, a decentralized democracy could be relatively positive and likely scenario. It presupposes that after 20 years of US occupation and thirty years of debilitating civil war the Afghan society would settle down to some reconciliatory mode and share power with other ethnic groups. Quetta Shura, Haqqani Group and Hezb-e Islami shall be brought into the negotiation process with Karzai Government. However there are apprehensions that Karzai Government being weak, corrupt and affected by drug trade would not be able to handle the crises.

Nevertheless, looking at Afghan history it seems that this is achievable and possible. For instance, from the Afghan War II (1880) to Daud coup (1973) Afghans went through a relatively stable and peaceful period of nation building. The central government gave relative autonomy to local groups for peace and order; but whenever forceful change was brought about from top through Amanullah (1929) and Soviet backed government (pre-1979) the peripheral areas revolted against the central authority. Likewise, the Soviet invasion broke down the authority and led to the end of Pushtun control. Under this foreign policy while the economic and other vital functions would remain with Kabul, the local autonomy would be concentrated in the hands of different ethnic leaders with preference for self government. This meshes with experiences in post conflict states in Ethiopia and Somalia.

Taliban resistance to democracy, defiance of central authority, role of power brokers and corrupt warlord's with vested elements are some of the major challenges that deserve attention. Decentralization also has some benefits, in which smaller projects that can conveniently involve local population in administrative affairs, the weakening of Taliban and other groups and demonstrating the transparency in local leadership can best be considered. Mixed sovereignty could give the provinces more powers in matters of elections and governance, and of course allow moderate level of corruption. Foreign policy will be the domain of centre, but inter-provincial commerce and mining rights could be devolved to the provinces without crossing some red lines, including disallowing the hosting of terrorists in their territories, no infringement on water and mineral rights of others, any large scale pilferage of narcotics, exploitation of state resources, etc.

There are some disadvantages in this scenario. It may be considered a retreat from nine years experiment with the rule of law, reemergence of certain warlords, human rights and women rights violation, costly conflict and the occasional use of force by the central government, need for continued US engagement and aid flows. Nigeria with weak centre and strong region of Biafra can be the best example in this regard in terms of fragmentation of a state for many years.

This also opens possibilities for Pakistan to play a vital role in future dispensation by bringing in those Afghan Taliban who are termed as 'moderate' or 'good' Taliban. Pakistan's position has always been that with Afghanistan having 43 per cent Pushtun population and nearly 9 provinces along the 15, 00 miles border being Pushtun-dominated areas forming the largest ethnic majority, no government can be stable without their involvement. They comprise a major province of Khyber Puktunwa in Pakistan and have been part of the ruling Afghan elite. Also, there is the hope that if and when they get their rightful shares to govern their areas they might get appeased and be less aggressive. That is the reason why Pakistan has been promoting the Afghan Taliban thinking that it will have to live with them as an immediate neighbour.

This point of view is now being realized by Karzai Government and lately by the Obama administration. However, there is also a counter view that these Taliban forces may get more power hungry and try to topple the Northern Alliance once they come into power. This will, of course, have to be preconditioned before the foreign forces withdrew. Pakistan would like to guard its interest as its threat perceptions focus on India, and it considers any rise of influence in Afghanistan as more alarming. The above scenario guards the interest of all who would like to see a stable Afghanistan in the years to come, with an emphasis on democracy and development.

Will Pakistan support them again and get the ire of the world? Pakistan also feels that because of sizable Pushtun population they cannot be excluded from power. Their struggle is against occupation and war of resistance than Al-Qaeda which has worldwide aims. If the Taliban disconnect and limit their designs to Afghanistan than the US too may be amenable.

Some opine that the differences between 'good' and 'bad' Taliban are fallacious and say that these very Taliban could be unpredictable and might eventually train their guns on Pakistan once they come to power. There are many gaps in communication regarding their ideas of development and use of power. They might get busy in internal consolidation and thus choose to look inward; Pakistani Taliban will also be weakened to a great extent in the process.

This is a kind of ideal scenario. Any place for Taliban will have to be negotiated on the grounds of delinking from Al-Qaeda, respect for constitution — albeit with some amendments — protection of human and women rights and a non-aggressive policy with a promise of economic assistance. The facilitation of foreign aid in special areas focused for development and the reconstruction zones can be started by bringing veterans into service and through other means.[26]

Pakistan would ideally wish this arrangement to materialize. Perhaps TAPI and regional cooperation with CARs could start. Pakistan would like US presence as a stabilizing factor as it thinks

Americans are easier to deal with than Karzai Government. Their presence is needed, on one hand, to keep India and Russia out of the loop, and on the other hand, to keep Iran quiescent.[27]

Scenario 4: Fragmentation along Ethnic Lines

This is an unacceptable model for regional and other states. Whether troops withdraw or not, some think that Balkanization of Afghanistan could take place under various ethnic/political groupings *like what had happened in* Yugoslavia: Northern Alliance in northern and western Afghanistan and Pushtun-dominated Taliban forces in south and southeast.

This is a scenario which could entail bloodshed and again unleash refugees into neighbouring countries where these ethnic communities are living together. This will be a possibility in case of a failure of the state which will then have far reaching implications on the region, especially on Pakistan. Free operation of Taliban in south and eastern Afghanistan, like Iraqi Kurds, or PKK guerrillas will certainly lead to battles among the security forces. Atomized civil war condition in present day Somalia and pre-Taliban period with increasing lawlessness provided an opening for Al-Shahab and Al-Qaeda terrorist groups to set up their bases.

Some contend that a control could result, if not separate, states with loose arrangement of ethnic groups. After all, they contend, Afghanistan under monarchy lived under warlords in relative harmony with the state playing a minimal role. The interest in stable, unified Afghanistan remains paramount for the entire region, but some observers think that unless regional and ethnic groups are decentralized this will not work.[28]

But Balkanization with separate states could set a dangerous precedent for other ethnic communities in Afghanistan's neighbourhood. The scenario assumes that in case of fragmented states the Taliban would be content and preoccupied with their power centre and not expand to areas beyond like their rule (1994-2001); secondly, Al-Qaeda will not be allowed to return to Afghanistan as Taliban have suffered due to Soviet, US military interventions; thirdly, dependent upon international aid they will mellow down and interact with international community, and fourthly, with Al-Qaeda more of a liability Taliban would ask them to leave with the latter moving out to regions outside Afghanistan such as Pakistan's tribal regions, Yemen, Somali or some other areas.[29]

Scenario 5: Taliban-Controlled Afghanistan

In an unlikely scenario, total Taliban-controlled Afghanistan will suit neither the interest of any major power nor Afghanistan's neighbours and will strongly be resisted by all Afghan communities, non-Afghan ethnic groups and regional countries, including the left behind US/NATO military forces.

Should this scenario come to pass, Pakistan would again be the worst victim. Many believe that 'good' and 'bad' Taliban are misnomers: once in power they might join hands with TTP due to ideological affinity. Moreover, the Pakistan Taliban will stand strengthened and vindicated to set up a future Islamic caliphate. The country will be inundated with refugees, illegal drugs and weapons, and the ideological ambitions of TE will be whetted in supporting radical Islamist movements in neighbouring Muslim communities in Central Asia, China and Russia.

Unofficially, some doubt the notion that they will be helpful to Pakistan as "strategic assets." It is not true as the TTP refused to hand over Osama bin Laden to Pakistan despite Pakistan's many requests. They may not totally delink themselves from Al-Qaeda too. Already the mujahedeen war and Taliban regime have created problems of refugees, violence, cross border traffic and drug trade in Pakistan. Therefore, some writers warn that in order to abort Indian influence in Afghanistan Pakistan must not support its 'good Taliban' as they have no respect of international borders, norms and conventions and will strongly infiltrate Pakistani society by supporting certain *jihadi* groups.[30]

Scenario 6: Continued Occupation of US-ISAF

The following is a very unlikely scenario but is based on the premise that war is like an 'addiction' and that NATO wants to self-arrogate a permanent role. The Afghan military engagement is the first of its nature out of Europe. The military-industrial complex is raking huge profits and unless mass demonstrations in US and Europe force their governments their troops cannot come back. Moreover, the possibilities of exploitation of minerals and rush for profits will give impetus to the "New Great Game." However, this scenario has few takers in view of the problems faced by US/NATO forces, mounting casualties and the rising costs of occupation. As the overall advantage of a quick eventual pullout overweigh against any continued retention of occupation the latter may not be a likely outcome.

Scenario 7: Centralized Dictatorship

An unlikely scenario is for a centralized dictatorship through the rise of a military dictator to rule Afghanistan where power is dispersed in ethnic, military and economic centres. In this case, Afghanistan could descend into civil war and destabilize the region. A coup or military grab may be militarily possible but is not likely to yield any modicum of stability for the Afghan state in the long-run.

Scenario 8: Punitive Strikes against Pakistan leading to prolonged stay in Afghanistan

Another dire scenario postulates that in the strategic review it was hinted that Pakistan rather than Afghanistan continues to be the source of problem because of sanctuaries on its territory. Hence, it is thought that as security situation keeps on deteriorating for the foreign forces, the scapegoat will be Pakistan[31] with US/NATO forces expanding their operations into tribal regions and beyond into Pakistan territory. Already, CIA-directed *Predator* and *Reaper* drone attack activities, as of 17 December 2010, have grown to nearly 113 strikes which are more than double the number in 2009 and more than total raids conducted in the previous six years.[32] These are backed by a clandestine CIA-run paramilitary force of 3,000 Afghans carrying out sensitive cross-military operations in Pakistan.[33] This could rake up tensions and lead to possible clashes between Pakistan and US forces. The withdrawal plan may get stymied and Allied forces could extend their stay in Afghanistan for many years beyond 2014. Some analysts think that Pakistan's nuclear weapons, its 'dual policies' and US sheer frustration to control Afghan insurgency may force them to launch punitive operations in 'hot pursuit' of militants with attendant internal destabilization for Pakistan.

Conclusions

That the US and NATO forces will *ultimately execute a drawdown is most likely beyond question.* However, the question is: when and how? In other words, whether the timelines will be adhered to or the stipulated deadlines lead to some overhaul in policy, another 'tweak', or a piecemeal approach.[34]

In the ultimate analysis, much will depend upon the results achieved by the US forces' 'surge,' training and preparedness acquired by the

Afghan army, police and civil administration, and existing military conditions on ground. Most probably, the US forces are likely to stay in Afghanistan like Iraq (30,000-50,000.) As they have made major investments in men and material, continued military and economic presence will continue for geopolitical reasons in the form of troops, trainers, advisers, security companies and investment companies.

Meanwhile, talks are on to arrive at some 'compromise formula' at a neutral place which could act as face saving for Taliban and US/NATO forces. All parties agree that Pakistan has a major role to play in the region besides other regional powers and the US. This is amply visible in President Obama's review strategy of 15 December 2010.

Afghanistan has suffered two major interventions by superpowers for about ten years each and has been in turmoil for the last three decades. The Soviets exited after suffering human and material cost while the US may follow suit. In the case of Soviet Union there was the proximity factor and heavy armour, air force was employed to fight against the then mujahedeen. The US is also inducting some tanks as part of the surge strategy. While the Soviets wanted to turn Afghanistan into a socialist state the US under the cover of the UN employed NATO forces to root out transnational actor Al-Qaeda which was considered responsible for 9/11 attacks on the US mainland. The erstwhile Soviet Union followed a solo exercise whereas in the latter it is supported by 27 NATO allies and other 10 non-NATO nations. The death count in case of NATO forces is much less than that of nearly one million sustained by the Afghans with 10,000 Soviet civilians and combatants.[35]

Both ultimately failed to secure the long porous Afghan-Pak borders. The Soviets went on a destructive spree and made little efforts at developmental work while the US-led coalition have attempted something in education, reconstruction, administration and constitutional and other reforms. Both invasions were deeply resented in the Muslim world. However, the US effort in Afghan case became divided with the Iraq military invasion in 2003. The interventionist powers realized their mistakes — the Soviets of remaking Afghan society in the socialist image and the Americans of turning a traditional, tribal Islamic society into a western democracy.

The early December 2010 Wikileaks have put pressure on western governments. However a scenario of an early exit will be contingent on normal course of events for any untoward incident such as

Al-Qaeda inspired attack on Europe or the US, or an attack on Iran, could complicate matters thus either derailing or delaying planned evacuation of foreign forces.

The post withdrawal Afghanistan may continue to simmer with ethnic violence for some time but the intensity may subside. Estranged communities might take revenge and launch vendettas not uncommon to Afghan tradition and history. If transition is not smooth India-Pakistan and Saudi-Iran rivalries could erupt with greater force.

Wars cannot go on indefinitely and have to end over time. The transition management after the US/NATO troops' drawdown is therefore crucial.[36] In this context, the US and Afghanistan's regional neighbours bear heavy responsibility to put back the Afghan nation on its feet. After all, it was the military interveners who were the creators of present woes of the benighted country.

Should this eventuate, post-NATO Afghanistan could turn out to be a win-win situation for all and become a hub for regional cooperation. A Contact Group consisting of US, Russia, China, along with regional nations, should strive to establish mechanisms for a neutral Afghan state with *possible* peacekeeping forces from the Afghan non-neighbours but Islamic countries. These could later facilitate US/NATO withdrawal and set the course for promoting a stable, peaceful Afghanistan.

Notes and References

1. Anwar Iqbal, "US review terms Pakistan ties uneven. Al Qaeda 'diminished'. Gains against Taliban reversible'. Obama repeats 'do more mantra.'" *Dawn*, 17 December 2010, 1.
2. Andrew Small, "The Consequences of a Conceptual Withdrawal in Afghanistan," <http://www.spegal.de/international/world/0.1518.70928.20 html>
3. Quoted in Maleeha Lodhi, *The News*, 29 November 2010, 7.
4. "US intelligence pessimistic about Afghan war success," *Dawn*, Karachi [Islamabad edition], 17 December 2010, 12.
5. "US intelligence pessimistic about Afghan war success," *Dawn*.
6. Patrick Cockburn, "NATO and Afghan war," *Daily Times*, 21 November 2010, A8.
7. For example, an ABC News survey Obama strategy review posted 60 per cent against the war—an increase of 7 per cent rise since July. Moreover, 54 per cent supported withdrawal by mid-July—up by 15

per cent. See "Support for war drops: survey" *Dawn,* 17 December 2010, 12.

8. See Iman Hasan, "Chaos in Washington, where we go from here," Special report from Kabul, *The News*, 29 November 2010, 9; Sardar Ahmad, "Talks with Taliban key to ending Afghan war," *Dawn*, 16 October 2010, 10.
9. Hasan, "Chaos in Washington, where we gc from here."
10. See editorial, "The great exception," *Daily Times*, 26 October 2010, A 6.
11. See Ambassador (retd) Zafar Hilaly, "The Lisbon effect," *Daily Times*, 26 November 2010, A 6.
12. See A.G. Noorani, "Diplomacy and the Taliban," *Dawn*, 27 November 2010.
13. See CPP News, "Pakistan and the U.S. Exit from Afghanistan," 28 September 2010.
14. Patrick Cockburn, "NATO and Afghan war," *Daily Times*, 28 September 2010, A8.
15. See "Assessing an Afghanistan withdrawal" <http://www.thenational.ae/news/worldwide/south-Asia... >
16. On this theme, see Sanaullah Baloch, "Exploitation of mineral wealth," *Dawn*, 25 November 2010, 3; also see Ikram Seghal, "21st century 'Great game'," *The News,* 25 November 2010, 6.
17. Cited in Seghal, "21st century 'Great game'."
18. See APP, "Withdrawal from Herat in July: Pullout from Kandahar, Helmand, not before 2012: US," *Dawn*, 9 November 9 2010, 10.
19. "Withdrawal from Herat in July."
20. "Withdrawal from Herat in July."
21. Michael O'Hanlon, "The Afghan debate," *Dawn*, 4 October 2010, 7. Also see "No need for US troops after 2011, says Iraqi PM," *Daily Times*, 28 November 2010, A 9.
22. Small, "The Consequences of a Conceptual Withdrawal in Afghanistan."
23. See e.g., Tom Engelhardt, "Kabul gets its own stimulus package," *Daily Times*, 21 November 2010, A 8.
24. Likewise, the projected cost of embassies in Islamabad and Baghdad is $736 million and $590 million respectively. The latter is so far the biggest US embassy in the world equaling the area of Vatican City with 1000 "diplomatic" personnel. Engelhardt, "Kabul gets its own stimulus package."
25. As cited in Stephen Biddle, Forini Christia, and J. Alexander, "Defining Success in Afghanistan: What can the United Sates Accept?" *Foreign Affairs* (July–August 2010), 1.

26. Posted by Ed Corcoran, "Afghanistan: No Exit," *Sitrep*, 26 October 2010, <GlobalSecurity.org>
27. Hilaly, "Power games in Afghanistan," *Daily Times*, 15 October 2010, A 6.
28. Hilaly, "If this is our war," *The News*, 29 November 2010, 6.
29. Mark. K. Katz, "Opponents of a US/NATO withdrawal fear the return of Taliban…a common threat," ISN Security Watch <http://www.isn.ethz.ch/isn/Current-Affairs/Secuirty Watch/Detail/Denial/?ing ...">
30. On this see Azizullah Khan, "From good to bad Taliban," *Daily Times*, 17 December 2010, A 7.
31. This is hinted in an editorial, "Strategy review," *Dawn*, 19 December 2010, 7.
32. "Obama's other 'surge': US drone war in Pakistan," *Daily Times*, 25 December 2010, A2.
33. While the US terms it success insofar as it has killed 897 top Al-Qaeda/Taliban leaders Pakistanis say it has led to many unverified civilian casualties and consequently greater resentment against US/NATO forces. "Obama's other 'surge'."
34. "Obama's other 'surge'."
35. See Hanlon, "The Afghan Debate."
36. On this see Air Commodore (Retd) Khalid Iqbal, Paper delivered at Afghan seminar arranged by USIS and Department of Defence and Strategic Studies, Quaid i Azam University, Islamabad, September 2010.

6

Military Withdrawal: Prospective Scenario for the Region

Shahmahmood Miakhel

> *"American policymakers must recognize that COIN is not and cannot be a substitute for policy and principles, and until they decide what it is they want to accomplish and why, even the best and most humane intentions will do little more than delay the inevitable and ignominious retreat to come."*[1]

Historical Background

The Central-Asian region in general and Afghanistan in particular are in a very difficult juncture of history. In the past three decades, Afghanistan has faced severe turmoil: the invasion by the Soviet Union (1979–89), civil war (1992–96), the Taliban regime and Al-Qaeda's influence over the regime (1996–2001), and the military intervention by coalition forces since 2001. But unfortunately none has learnt from the past history and has repeated the same mistakes.

If we look at the recent past, a living history for those Afghans who witnessed it, the Soviet Union gradually increased their influence and forces in Afghanistan without a clear vision of what to achieve in the long run. The Soviet Union invaded Afghanistan on 27 December 1979 with a prime goal of defeating the mujahideen resistance and saving the collapse of the communist regime. But the invasion of the Soviet Union was seen by the Afghan people and the international community as violation of the UN Charter, and faced fierce resistance from all quarters in Afghanistan. The Russians claimed that they had been invited to the country at the behest of President Amin's government and that they were in no way invaders of the country. They claimed that their task was to support a legitimate government and that the mujahideen were no more than terrorists.[2] This argument, however, did not have any base because the Soviet forces killed Hafizullah Amin, the very man they claimed to have invited them. Although the Soviet forces tried to subdue and eliminate the mujahideen resistance quickly, the resistance became even stronger as it began to receive an open-ended support from both the West and the Islamic countries. In addition to the sacrifices of the Afghan nation, the Soviet Union did not succeed in Afghanistan, because from the very outset the People Democratic Party of Afghanistan (PDPA) fragmented and weakened due to the internal rivalries among its leadership.

Firstly, Noor Mohammad Taraki, communist Leader of Khalq Faction of PDPA, was killed by his deputy prime minister Hafizullah Amin on 14 September 1979.[3] The Soviet Union killed Hafizullah Amin, invaded his forces on 27 December 1979 and replaced him with Babrak Karmal, leader of Parcham faction of PDPA, who had been living in exile. Due to his ineffective rule, Babrak Karmal was pressured by the Soviet Union to resign and was replaced by Dr. Najibullah on 4 May 1986.[4] Dr. Najullah was head of the intelligence agency (KHAD) at the time.

Dr. Najibullah launched national reconciliation (Ashtee-e-Milli) plan in 1986 but failed to convince the people of Afghanistan to support the government. Eventually, Dr. Najibullah was overthrown in April 1992 by the mujahideen groups. Subsequently, Prof. Sibghatullah Mujadedi, leader of the National Liberation Front, under an accord in Peshawar with the mujahideen groups which was mediated by the then Prime Minister of Pakistan, Nawaz Sharif, took over as the first mujahideen ruler for only two months.[5] Mujadedi was replaced by Prof. Burhanudin Rabbabi, leader of another faction of mujahideen groups named Jamiat-e-Islami. Consequently, civil war started between different factions of the mujahideen and continued till 1996, when Taliban took over Kabul. Even though a small resistance against Taliban regime was continued by the Northern Alliance under the leadership of Commander Ahmad Shah Masood in the North-East of Afghanistan, the Taliban were able to consolidate their power over about 95per cent of Afghanistan. After the tragic incident of 11 September 2001, the Taliban regime was removed by coalition forces in December 2001 and President Hamid Karzai was appointed, under the Bonn Agreement, as head of the Interim Government of Afghanistan.[6]

Soviet Union Withdrawal from Afghanistan under the Geneva Accord

The Geneva Accord of April between the governments of Afghanistan and Pakistan was signed in 1988 in order to find an exit strategy for the forces of Soviet Union from Afghanistan. The Accord was negotiated between the governments of Afghanistan and Pakistan in indirect talks through the United Nations. While the United States and USSR were signatories to guarantee implementation of this accord,[7] the Afghan mujahideen or resistance groups were not made part of this deal. The Special UN envoy, Diego Cordovez, who mediated this accord, visited refugee camp of Kacha Gari[8] near Peshawar city of Pakistan after signing of the Geneva Accord in 1988. The objective of his visit was to inform Afghan refugees about Geneva Accord and get their opinion. When Diego Cordovez delivered his speech in a big gathering of Afghan refugees, my father Sayed Mahmood Hasrat, on behalf of the Afghan refugees, thanked Diego Cordovez for his visit to the refugee camp to share his views about Geneva Accord and told him: "It would be better if you could visit us before the signing of this agreement and had sought the views of the Afghan refugees. But unfortunately, you seek our views after signing of the Geneva Accord, and it has no meaning now. This accord could not help to solve the problems of Afghans because the refugees could not return to their homeland and the war in Afghanistan could not be stopped."[9] In response to my father, Deigo Cordovez responded that he agreed with him, but when he visited different capitals and meet Americans, Pakistanis and the mujahideen leaders, all of them were of the view that the Afghan problems would be solved if the Soviet Union forces withdrew from Afghanistan. He added that Geneva Accord only paved the way for withdrawal of the Soviet Union forces and could not solve the Afghan problems.

Diego Cordovez was right in saying that the Geneva Accord paved the way for withdrawal of the Soviet Union forces but did not solve the problems of Afghan people by bringing stability in the country. Afghanistan plunged into civil war and the Afghans were the ones who suffered the most after the withdrawal of the Soviet forces.

Soviet Union's Dilemma in Afghanistan

The above events point to the fact that the Soviet Union tried to support a weak government which did not have public support and replaced one with another. The Soviet Union's occupation lasted till 15 February 1989 but left behind a weak government which did not enjoy any support amongst Afghans. Most experts of Afghanistan believed at the time that if the Soviets left, the Afghan Government would collapse very soon in the span of weeks, not even months. But this did not happen immediately thanks to the fragmentation of mujahideen groups! The communist era government lasted for three years and eventually collapsed in April 1992.

Ever since the resistance movement in Afghanistan began during the '80s, most Afghans left their homelands because of the atrocities of the communist regime that not only branded as reactionary elements all those who were not members of PDPA but also counted them as enemies of the April revolution (Saur Revolution). Although ideology was insignificant in the beginning of the mujahideen resistance, it became important because of the systematic interference by various Islamic groups and countries alike. Even the West tried to promote Islamic ideology as a contending force against the communist ideology in Afghanistan.[10]

When the last regime of PDPA collapsed in April 1992, the mujahideen factions, which were supported by close and distant neighbours of Afghanistan, started fighting among themselves for control of power in Kabul. During this period, the capital was destroyed and tens of thousands of civilians were killed in civil war. Unfortunately, the world was silent during this period about the atrocities in Afghanistan. Afghanistan was left at the mercy of Afghan neighbours. Proxy war went on until Taliban emerged in 1984 to consolidate their power in Kandahar with the support of Pakistan and Al-Qaeda networks.[11]

When the Taliban emerged as a powerful force to rescue the people of Afghanistan from the tyranny and atrocities of warlords and criminal networks, Afghans welcomed them; but unfortunately the Taliban regime did not have an agenda to govern Afghanistan on the basis of internationally recognized norms and standards. Eventually, Afghanistan became safe haven for terrorist organization of Al-Qaeda till the tragic events of 11 September 2001 in the United States of America.

NATO and the US Dilemma in Afghanistan

Even though the US administration and NATO repeatedly mentioned that they would not leave Afghanistan without a stable government, as they did in 1990s, the open source information clearly suggests that they have dilemma with the current government of Afghanistan, especially with President Hamid Karzai as reliable partner.[12]

One could say with confidence that the current government in Afghanistan is much weaker than the last communist regime of Afghanistan in 1989 when the Soviet forces withdrew. This is because the communist regime was supported by a largest ideological political party of PDPA in Afghanistan and because the regime inherited a better government infrastructure and system. Mostly, the PDPA members were not corrupt and were very loyal to the regime and their ideology. Also, the communist regime was not faced with an extremely sophisticated ideological enemy such as Al-Taliban and Al-Qaeda which use IEDs (improvise explosive devices) and suicide bombers to blow themselves and others. The US and NATO, like the Soviet Union, did not have plan to stay in Afghanistan for 10 years. They simply increased their activities gradually and do not have reliable regional partners.

While The Afghan security institutions are weak, the Afghan Government set-up remains a conglomeration of factional politics. In the worst case scenario, if the current trend of instability in Afghanistan continues and the international forces leave Afghanistan by 2011 or 2014, the current regime, I believe, cannot stay in power for even a week and civil war would erupt again. This is the main reason why despite all the problems and criticisms, support for international presence and NATO forces in Afghanistan is stronger.[13]

Brief Account of Afghan National Army and National Police since 2001

After military intervention of coalition forces and overthrow of Taliban regime in the end of 2001, the international community was not able to define their objectives in the long-run; particularly the US was not in favour of nation building, state building or institutional building in Afghanistan. Very recently President Obama on 16 December 2010 in his annual progress review of US strategy in Afghanistan said:

> It's important to remember why we remain in Afghanistan. It was Afghanistan where al Qaeda plotted the 9/11 attacks that murdered 3,000 innocent people. It is the tribal regions along

> the Afghan-Pakistan border from which terrorists have launched more attacks against our homeland and our allies. And if an even wider insurgency were to engulf Afghanistan, that would give al Qaeda even more space to plan these attacks. And that's why, from the start, I've been very clear about our core goal. It's not to defeat every last threat to the security of Afghanistan, because, ultimately, it is Afghans who must secure their country. And it's not nation-building, because it is Afghans who must build their nation. Rather, we are focused on disrupting, dismantling and defeating al Qaeda in Afghanistan and Pakistan, and preventing its capacity to threaten America and our allies in the future.[14]

The landmark speech of President Obama clearly indicates that the international community or NATO forces are not in Afghanistan for nation building, state building or institution building. Even though President Bush talked about Marshall Plan[15] for Afghanistan, but in reality he did not have any long-term plan and commitment towards nation building, state building or institution building. Since 2001, the international community increased military presence and other activities in Afghanistan on the basis of threats they faced each year, clearly indicating that they did not have a sustained interest in building security institutions that can meet the needs of Afghanistan. For example, in the beginning the international community only supported the formation of limited forces of 50,000 national police and 12,000 border police.[16] This number of border and national police for a country like Afghanistan with about 30 million populations, a country larger than Iraq, mostly mountainous and emerging from more than three decades of war, was not realistic and too small. They did not want to support a large police force because the donor countries argued that it would not be sustainable for Afghanistan to pay for expenses of police in the long run. The international community, especially the US, considered building Afghan National Police as part of nation building, not as a component to fight war against terrorism. The US, therefore, focused more on building Afghan National Army. Even the number of Afghan National Army was not well calculated against the internal and the external threat existing to the security of Afghanistan.

In Tokyo conference, the strength of the Afghan National Army was approved by the international community to number 70,000.[17] The Afghan National Police, which was counted by the Afghan

Government as main component to fight insurgency, were ill equipped, ill trained and ill paid. In 2003, the Afghan police were paid 30 dollars a month,[18] while Afghan National Army was paid 70 dollars a month. Later on, the salary of police rose to equivalent of Afghan National Army. The actual assistance to police was received by the Government of Afghanistan only in 2006, four years after collapse of Taliban regime, and at a time when the insurgency was already well spread in the southern and south-eastern parts of the country. At that time, with the above pay scale, it was very difficult to have recruitment of qualified and motivated people for Afghan National Police and Afghan National Army. It was only very recently that the salary of patrolmen of ANP and ANA soldiers increased to about 220 US$ per month.

My discussion in September 2003 with former Interior Minister of Afghanistan Ali Ahmad Jalali revealed that when he accompanied the former US Secretary of Defence Donald Rumsfeld to Gardez city of Paktia province during his trip to Afghanistan,[19] Mr. Rumsfeld asked Minister Jalali to convince him to support development of police to help in counter-terrorism strategy. Unfortunately, Mr. Rumsfeld did not envision that the role of the police is very important in counter-insurgency which could help counter-terrorism. I believe that Mr. Rumsfeld would think that support for police was part of nation/state building and he was not in favour of it. As threats have increased, now the ceiling of Afghan National Police and Afghan National Army will be further increased by October 2011 to 134,000 and 171,600 respectively.[20] Still, I believe that the ANA and ANP are ill-trained and ill-equipped to meet current challenges of security in the country. The way in which the cost of ANA and ANP can be covered in the long run is another important question to address. I believe that if ANA and ANP are not paid on time for a couple of months, it will disintegrate very soon again.

Transition to Afghan Forces by 2014

According to the speech of President Obama on 16 December 2010, the US will start reducing their forces from Afghanistan in July 2011 and end combat operation by 2014. Some members of NATO such as Dutch forces have already left Afghanistan in August 2010,[21] and Canada is committed to ending combat operation by 2011.[22] There are two fundamental questions that should be answered. First, are the Afghan National Security Forces (ANSF) ready to take charge of overall security of Afghanistan by 2014? Second, if the Afghan National Security Forces will not be able to meet security challenges by 2014, what would be next?

I believe that if the level of threats posed to the security of Afghanistan by external and internal actors is not reduced, it would be impossible for the Afghan security forces to maintain minimum stability in the country, even by 2014. In order to keep minimum stability in the country, the following points are imperative/ prerequisite to achieve this goal:

1. The levels of threats from internal actors, such as warlords, drug mafia, organized criminals and war mafia should be reduced.
2. The level of threats from external sources such as sanctuaries and financial support to Al-Qaeda and armed opposition to the Afghan Government should be stopped.
3. In order to get support of the people of Afghanistan, governance and rule of law should be improved.
4. The international community, the US in particular, should pledge long-term commitment to cover the cost of ANSF, because with the current internal revenue sources the Afghan Government will not be able to cover ANSF expenses, even with the reduced price tag of Afghan standards, for a very long time.

Given the above prerequisites, it seems that the ANSF are far from ready to meet security needs of the Afghan people, to keep them safe from state and anti-state actors in their houses and to ensure that they carry their day-to-day life normally. A six-year archive of classified military documents made public by WikiLeaks offer an unvarnished, ground-level picture of the war in Afghanistan that is in many respects grimmer than the official portrayal.[23]

The reasons include the following:

1. Warlords, drug mafia, organized criminal networks infested in the political, executive and economic institutions of Afghanistan, and it needs very strong political will, at least to keep them out from the state institutions. I am not talking about their prosecution now. At present, I do not see such a kind of political will existing among the current Afghan

leadership to address this critical issue. The main driver of insurgency in Afghanistan is the existence of criminal networks in the state institutions. Even President Karzai in his inaugural speech in Peace Consultative Jirga in June 2010 mentioned that some people joined with insurgency because of misdeeds of government officials and some joined because of military operation of coalition forces. All surveys so far pointed out that the people of Afghanistan do not support Taliban but in the same time people do not trust and rely on the government security institutions for their safety.

2. With the current setting by the Afghan Government and business of governance, it is not possible to improve governance in the country. The main actors who can make a difference do not see their interest in improving governance in Afghanistan. If governance improved and rule of law can be applied equally in the country, they would be the main losers.[24]
3. So far, there is no sign that external support to armed oppositions of the Government of Afghanistan is waning or it might end very soon under the current volatile situation. Especially Pakistan will not give up option B till it does see a reliable and stable government in Afghanistan for her strategic policy in the region.

   The Afghan National Army and Afghan National Police are not able to cope with current threat of security without the support of International Security Assistance Force (ISAF), and air support seems very critical in this regard. Afghan National Police and Afghan National Army are still factional army and factional police. If there is no supervision by ISAF forces, they will support political agenda of factional leaders rather than national agenda. ANA and ANP can be disintegrated very quickly and may have coups one after another.[25]
4. The long-term commitment by international community to support ANSF will depend on the conditions in the rest of the world, and it is not a guarantee.

Conclusion

In view of the above, I believe that the international community, the US in particular, will still have differences of opinion about their operations and objectives in Afghanistan. Some among the US administration argue that with the current weak partnership with the Afghan Government, it is not possible to win the war in Afghanistan militarily. The US ambassador to Afghanistan mentioned in a leaked cable that President Karzai is not a reliable partner.[26] It has to be weighed whether it is better to make a deal with the Taliban or Afghanistan's neighbour to achieve their main objectives. But at the same time, Vice President of the United States Joe Biden believes strongly that "...despite uneven progress in Afghanistan, next summer's planned withdrawal would be more than a token reduction and that the US would be out of the country by 2014 come hell or high water."[27] Others in the Obama administration have said repeatedly that July would mark the beginning of the troop withdrawals and that their size would depend on military conditions.[28]

The above statements give an impression that there is still ambiguity about the US and NATO objectives, commitment and long-term military presence in Afghanistan as well as in the region. ISAF and US forces transition to the Afghan National Security Forces is not certain to be achieved by 2014 in the absence of the proven capability of ANSF. If NATO forces end military operation in Afghanistan abruptly, without considering on the ground realities, capability of the Afghan National Security Forces, it may cause a big chaos and lead to collapse of Afghan Government.

If international forces depart prematurely from Afghanistan on the basis of some bilateral deal, this region will face a bigger turmoil, will have a profound negative consequences for all countries of the region because enemies of stability and good governance are more sophisticated now than in 1990s. The danger will not be confined to the territory of Afghanistan alone; it may expand to South Asia, Central Asia and Middle East. Of course, in the worst form, it may expand to Europe and the rest of the world as well. Afghanistan might once again become a battle ground for proxy wars, which would pave the way for Al-Qaeda to re-emerge and to have bases in this region. They may threaten the security of Afghanistan, the region and rest of the world. Of course, the Afghans will suffer utmost as they suffered after the Soviet Union's withdrawal on the basis of Geneva Accord in 1988. As various other writers and analysts have also pointed out, there is no short cut to stability in Afghanistan.[29] It is, therefore, imperative for international community to engage all national, regional and international stakeholders to find a reasonable political solution for Afghanistan crisis in order to have durable peace and stability. Ignoring ground realities in this contentious region may have wider implications the world over.

Notes and References

1. David Edwards, "Counter Insurgency as Cultural System," *Small Wars* (December 2010). http://smallwarsjournal.com/blog/2010/12/counterinsurgency-as-a-cultura/ (last accessed on 3 January 2011).
2. http://www.guidetorussia.com/russia-afghanistan.asp (accessed on 20 December 2010).
3. http://www.afghanistan-culture.com/noor-mohammad-taraki.html (accessed on 20 December 2010).
4. http://en.wikipedia.org/wiki/Mohammad_Najibullah (accessed on 20 December 2010).
5. http://www.issi.org.pk/journal/2000_files/no_2_3/article/6a.htm (accessed on 21 December 2010).
6. http://en.wikipedia.org/wiki/Hamid_Karzai (last accessed on 20 December 2010).
7. http://books.google.com/books?id=Ko1O1ZuuVJkC&pg=PA5&lpg=PA5&dq=UN+special+envoy+Diego+Cordovez+role+in+Geneva+acc ord+in+1988&source=bl&ots=RdONvNTI-z&sig=jJiPSFO4liiJ93gGPOCsE92VYZ8&hl=en&ei=GTnyTPCOOYywhQeL39S2DA&sa=X&oi=book_result&ct=result&resnum=2&ved=0C BsQ6AEwAQ# (last accessed on 28 November 2010).
8. At that time our family used to live in Kacha Gari refugee camp and I used to work as local reporter for the Voice of American Pashto service.
9. Shahmahmood Miakhel, *In the light of Truth. Personal account of Mujahideen Uprising* (Kabul: Pir Printing Press 2006) (in Pashto).
10. The author of this paper wrote a personal account of Mujahideen uprising in Khas Kunar district of Kunar province and refugee life. See Shahmahmood Miakhel, *Da Waqiyatuno Pa Hindara Kee* (In Light of Truth) (Kabul: Pir Printing Press 2006) (in Pashto).
11. For more details of civil war in Kabul, see Shahmahmood Miakhel, "Challenges and dilemmas of reconstruction and institution-building: social, economic and political factors," paper read at seminar on *Indigenization of the Afghan Reconstruction: Challenges and Opportunities*, Maulana Abdul Kalam Azad Institute for Asian Studies, 18-19 March 2009, in New Delhi, India.
12. http://www.time.com/time/specials/packages/article/0,28804,2036683_

2037118_2037101,00.html (accessed on 20 December 2010).

13. BBC Survey 2010. http://www.bbc.co.uk/news/world-south-asia-11910134 (accessed on 21 December 2010).
14. President Barak Obama's speech on the Afghanistan and Pakistan Annual Review, White House Press release on 16 December 2010.
15. http://www.nytimes.com/2002/04/19/opinion/afghanistan-s-marshall-plan.html (accessed on 3 January 2011).
16. http://www.crisisgroup.org/~/media/Files/asia/south- asia/afghanistan/138_reforming_afghanistan_s_police.ashx (accessed on 19 December 2010).
17. http://www.mofa.go.jp/region/middle_e/afghanistan/pv0302/ddr_state.html (accessed on 19 December 2010).
18. The author of this paper was Senior Advisor and Deputy Minister of Interior from 2003–05 in Afghanistan.
19. I had this discussion with Minister Jalali on 4 December 2010, in Kabul.
20. http://www.aco.nato.int/page265721841.aspx (accessed on 19 December 2010).
21. http://news.bbc.co.uk/2/hi/8526933.stm (accessed on on 20 December 2010).
22. http://www.reuters.com/article/idUSLDE6AD0GK20101116 (accessed on 20 December 2010).
23. http://www.nytimes.com/2010/07/26/world/asia/26warlogs.html (accessed on 19 December 2010.
24. For more details on this topic, see Andrew Wilder, *Winning Hearts and Minds? Examining the Relationship between Aid and Security in Afghanistan, Pakistan and the Horn of Africa.* http://www.tufts.edu/central/research/ResearchNews/Researchers/wilder.htm (accessed on 3 January 2011).
25. Antonio Giustozzi, "Auxiliary Force or National Army? Afghanistan's 'ANA' and the Counter-Insurgency Effort, 2002–2006," *Small Wars and Insurgencies,* 18/1, 45–67, Crisis States Research Centre, LSE (March 2007); Andrew Wilder, *Cops or Robbers? The struggle to reform the Afghan National Police*, http://www.areu.org.af/index.php?option=com_docman&task=doc_details&gid=523&Itemid=99999999&lang=fa (accessed on 20 December 2010); Susanne Schmeidle and Lisa Rimli, *Private Security Companies and Afghan Population that no one guards the guardian*, http://www.swisspeace.ch/typo3/fileadmin/user_upload/pdf/PSC.pdf (accessed on 20 December 2010).
26. http://www.time.com/time/specials/packages/article/0,28804,2036683_2037118_2037101,00.html (accessed on 20 December 2010).
27. http://www.time.com/time/politics/article/0,8599,2037861,00.html?

xid=rss-politics (accessed on 20 December 2010).

28. http://www.time.com/time/politics/article/0,8599,2037861,00.html?xid= rss-politics (accessed on 20 December 2010).
29. Stephen Carter and Kate Clark, *No Shortcut to Stability, Justice, Politics and Insurgency in Afghanistan* (London: Chatham House, 2010).

7

American Military Strategy in Afghanistan: The Surge and Beyond

Jagmohan Meher

"Nawa: Proof of COIN (Counter insurgency) Concept." This is the title of a PowerPoint slide of Gen David H. Petraeus, displayed before the senior members of President Obama's national security team in early December 2010.[1] Through his presentation, Gen. Petraeus, the top US and NATO commander in Afghanistan tries to validate his contention that a comprehensive counterinsurgency strategy can reverse Taliban momentum and stabilize Afghanistan after nine years of war. He cites Nawa district of Helmand province in the southern Afghanistan as a success story and argues that the district, once a bastion of the Taliban, has been transformed into a safe haven with the arrival of a 1000-strong surge battalion of US marine in July 2009. He also points out that the security situation in and around Kandahar, the country's second largest city, has improved because of the operations conducted by newly arrived US soldiers. The top commander emphasizes that secret missions by Special Operations Forces since June 2010 have resulted in the death or capture of hundreds of mid-level Taliban leaders, resulting in growing demoralization among insurgent commanders and expresses optimism about a 20,000-man village defence programme that is expanding law enforcement into areas police do not control. The General is convinced that the success story of Nawa can be replicated in the other Taliban-controlled districts and Afghanistan can be stabilized.[2]

It may be noted that Gen Petraeus is claiming success in the Afghan battlefields at a time when approximately 100,000 American soldiers (along with about 40,000 NATO forces) are fighting an elusive adversary in a country with a long tradition of humbling foreign armies. The timeline is also crucial in view of the fact that the war is currently costing over 100 billion dollars a year to the US taxpayers and it has become the longest war in American history in summer 2010, when it crossed the time span of the Vietnam conflict. And President Obama has described the deteriorating situation in the region (Pakistan and Afghanistan) as presenting "truly an international challenge of the highest order,"[3] whereas there is growing disenchantment in the Capitol Hill with one House of Representatives member arguing that the Afghan war "represents an epic failure, a national embarrassment, and a moral blight."[4] Most significantly, Petraeus' mandate includes the United States' commitment to starting a drawdown of its troops beginning July 2011. Under such compelling circumstances, when Gen. Petraeus talks tough of an upward curb in the US Afghan mission, it is indeed imperative to study the American military strategy, its contents and tenor, and above all, its scope to provide inroads towards a successful conclusion of the US and the international presence in a secured and stable Afghanistan.

So what is the focus of the US military strategy in Afghanistan? What are the different components of its battlefield tactics? How will the current surge policy allow the United States to turn the operation over to the Afghan Government, the ultimate goal of the American strategy? Why the current US strategy will not help bring about a long term Afghan stability? What are the most feasible first moves the US could make to get out of the present Afghan mess?

The present study revolves around these questions and attempts to look beyond the current entanglement. In order to understand the US military strategy in Afghanistan, the study explores the various ingredients of the surge policy including the transition plan and tries to figure out the US military's false optimism. It examines two important variables as pre-conditions for a stable and secure Afghanistan: (1) increasing the strength of the Afghan National Army and Afghan National Police; and (2) containing Pakistani strategic obsession in Afghanistan. However, as the study finds lots of resemblances in terms of military strategy of the Soviet invasion of the country in the 1980s in the present US set up, it suggests that the US and international forces should leave the country at the earliest and widen the scope for the Afghans to rule their country themselves.

The Surge

"Surge" in American military-strategic lexicon implies increasing the number of boots or escalation of troop level on the battlefield to check a growing insurgency and to maintain law and order in a disturbed area. The objective of such a policy is not different in Afghanistan. From a "light footprint" in 2002 to a 100,000 troop's large-scale counterinsurgency operation in 2011, American military strategy in Afghanistan has come a long way.[5] The idea of a 'surge' policy in Afghanistan goes back to the closing months of the former Bush administration. With the "military success" in Iraq through such a policy, some Bush administration officials became tempted to replicate the same formula in Afghanistan which was increasingly going out of hand despite US and NATO military presence in the country. Before he left the White House, President Bush had announced to send 5,000 additional troops to Afghanistan to check the resurgent Taliban. President Obama, from the very beginning, was in favour of "enough troops and enough resources" for Afghanistan war. On 17 February 2009, he ordered 17,000 more American troops saying the increase was "necessary to stabilize a deteriorating situation in Afghanistan, which has not received the strategic attention, direction and resources it urgently requires."[6] Subsequently, Obama also agreed to a further increase of 30,000 more troops making the total strength to approximately 100,000 American soldiers in the war-torn country.

The current policy of escalation in Afghanistan is distinct in many aspects as the US war efforts progresses in a country that is known as "the graveyard of empires" through ages. The "surge" strategy was chosen after lengthy debates in which some officials, including Vice President Joe Biden, favoured narrowing the US mission to attacks against Al-Qaeda and its affiliates in Afghanistan and Pakistan. They envisaged alternatives to a large-scale foreign troop presence on a long-term basis and argued that Al-Qaeda can be checked using intensive intelligence, predator drones, cruise missiles, raids by Special Operations Commandos and even payments to warlords to deny haven to the terrorist organization.[7] Others, including the military and the department of defence, successfully argued for a more expanded counterinsurgency strategy, with major governance and development components, in addition to providing security for Afghan civilians. But one significant aspect of America's Afghan surge within the military itself is the shift in military strategy from Gen. Stanley A. McCrystal to Gen. David H. Petraeus as Afghanistan's top military commander.

Gen McChrystal's main goal was to halt the progress of the Taliban, to reverse it in key areas, and to regain the initiative. His strategy de-emphasizes the counterterrorism strategy and institutes a counterinsurgency strategy. This means reducing efforts on going after the Taliban combatants and increasing efforts to provide security to the population. The General was clear that security alone is but a means to an end. Once he said, "The point of security is to enable governance ... My metric is not the enemy killed, not ground taken; its how much governance we've got."[8] Even on 'shock and awe' US strategy, McChrystal said, "You can shock and awe human beings but it does not last."[9] At the heart of his strategy were three principles: protect the Afghan people, build an Afghan state and make friends with whomever you can, including insurgents.[10] Killing the Taliban was among the least important things that were expected of NATO soldiers.

Gen Petraeus, on the other hand, is the author of the COIN (Counterinsurgency) manual and known as an expert on modern war strategy in the United States, and hence, many believe, he can do whatever he wants. Petraeus seems to be one step ahead of McChrystal in the sense that it is he who encouraged and allowed frequent use of Special Operation Forces, use of intense force, night time air-strikes and several other oppressive measures. That is why the main component of the US war strategy at present can be outlined in terms of its troop level, Special Operation Forces, introduction of high technology weapons and Tanks, use of intense force, etc., before the American transition plan is put forth in a proper perspective.

100,000 American Troops

After his appointment as the Commander-in-chief of the US and NATO forces in Afghanistan, General McChrystal wanted an in-depth review of the Afghanistan situation. In his initial assessment of the country sent to President Obama early in September 2009, he described "an Afghanistan on the brink of collapse and an America at the edge of defeat." To reverse the course of the war, McChrystal presented Obama with what could be the most momentous foreign-policy decision of his presidency: escalate or fail. McChrystal had asked for 40,000 additional American troops and an accelerated effort to train Afghan troops and police and build an Afghan state. He was so clear in his mind about the troop surge that he once suggested that if President Obama cannot bring himself to step up the fight, then he might as well give up.[11]

The magnitude of the choice presented by McChrystal is difficult to overstate. For what he was proposing is not a temporary, Iraq-style surge — a rapid influx of American troops followed by a withdrawal. His plan was a blueprint for an extensive American commitment to build a modern state in Afghanistan, where one has never existed, and to bring order to a place famous for the empires it has exhausted. Even under the best of circumstances, this effort would most likely last many more years, cost hundreds of billions of dollars and entail the deaths of many more American and Afghan lives. However, the softer side of McChrystal's strategy had two main thrusts: training Afghan soldiers and police and persuading insurgents to change sides. It is here where the best chances of long-term success in Afghanistan may lie.

On 1 December 2009, addressing an audience of cadets at the US Military Academy at West Point, many of whom would have been sent to the war in the next year, President Obama made two remarkable announcement on the Afghan war. First is a momentous decision to send 30,000 additional US troops to Afghanistan by summer (i.e. by July 2010), and secondly, to begin withdrawing forces in July 2011.[12] The President cited his solemn responsibility as commander in chief to protect the United States from the attacks of the Islamic terrorists as he outlined a sharp escalation that makes him the main architect of the eight-year-old war. He sought to prepare the country for the heavier fighting and higher casualties that are likely to result from his strategy in the months ahead. He made his case to the nation that Islamist extremism in the region remains an enduring threat to the security of Americans. He warned bluntly that "huge challenges remain" before US forces begin leaving Afghanistan.[13] Adding 30,000 more troops to the roughly 70,000 that were already in Afghanistan, the troop level went up to 100,000 most of what Gen. McChrystal had requested. The US President said he plans to break the Taliban's momentum, secure key population centres, speed up training of Afghan security forces and then hand over control to Afghan authorities. Although he said that he expected to be able to start drawing down American forces in July 2011, he made no promise about when all American combat troops would be gone, saying only that the decision would be based on conditions on the ground.[14]

Special Operation Forces

After taking over as the US and NATO Commander-in-Chief in Afghanistan, Gen. David H. Petraeus looked for ways to show quick results. Soon the US Special Operations troops stepped up a campaign to kill or capture insurgent leaders. As he made capture-and-kill missions a central component of his counterinsurgency strategy, within months, thousands of insurgent leaders and lower-level fighters were killed or captured which was considered as rare gains in this otherwise protracted insurgency of over nine years.[15] The operations have been most effective in and around the southern city of Kandahar and in eastern Afghanistan, where roadside bomb attacks have decreased and the Taliban control is weakening.

Success in this direction would strengthen the contention made by Vice President Biden and his supporters who are skeptical of the current military strategy in Afghanistan. They argue that Special Operations troops, with their small footprint and skill at tracking and killing the enemy, can be more effective than conventional forces in the difficult conflict the US faces in that country. As stated above, Biden has argued for shrinking the US effort and relying largely on Special Operations troops and air-strikes to disrupt the Taliban and Al-Qaeda. However, President Obama and his military commanders are in favour of using large numbers of US troops as part of a far-reaching counterinsurgency effort, and that has been the main stay of US military strategy in Afghanistan so far.

Gen Petraeus has argued that Special Operations troops are just one tool, albeit a highly effective one, in fighting an insurgency. Nevertheless, the tempo of Special Operations raids has greatly increased on the ground; resulting in what the United States military says is a six-fold increase in captures and killings of Taliban commanders. It has also resulted in an increase in night raids that most of the times lead to civilian casualties.[16]

Largest CIA Station

CIA plays a very strong role in Afghanistan with the largest Central Intelligence Agency station since the Vietnam war located in Kabul. CIA operatives also command an Afghan paramilitary force in thousands and most part of clandestine war in Pakistan through armed drones is carried out by them. It has been reported that the Afghan militias backed by the CIA have carried out a number of secret missions into Pakistan's tribal areas. These operations in Pakistan by Afghan operatives, known as Counterterrorism Pursuit Teams, which used to be solely intelligence-gathering operations, are now on the offensive against the militants.[17] The year 2010 witnessed stepped up air assaults in the tribal areas with an unprecedented number of CIA drone strikes. During the last quarter of the year, the spy agency carried out more than 50 drone attacks in North Waziristan and elsewhere.[18] There have also been special operations by the Afghans working under the direction of the CIA—a militia called the Paktika Defense Force—who cross the border into Pakistan to kill or capture Taliban/Al-Qaeda leaders or to merely gather intelligence. The Paktika Defense Force is one of six CIA-trained Afghan militias that serve as a special operations force against insurgents throughout Afghanistan. The other militias operate around the cities of Kandahar, Kabul and Jalalabad as well as in the rural provinces of Khost and Kunar.[19] American officials claim that the CIA-backed force has proven effective so far.

The Iraq Model

The new Afghanistan strategy draws heavily on lessons learned from George Bush's "surge" and strategy shift in Iraq in 2007, which Obama had opposed. But, now as President of the United States, he tries to step on Bush's shoes. The President has said that "there may be comparable opportunities in Afghanistan to employ the strategies used in Iraq;" although he warned the Afghan crisis there was possibly even more complex.[20] In addition to the influx of troops and the training of the Afghan Army, the US Generals are implementing other lessons from the Iraq build-up, like empowering local security forces to stand up to Taliban militants in their communities and enhancing the training of national forces by embedding American troops with Afghan counterparts and later pairing American and Afghan units to fight side by side.[21]

Introducing Tanks

In a shift that signals a further escalation in the aggressive tactics that have been employed by American forces to attack the Taliban and Al-Qaeda, the United States has decided to deploy heavily armoured tanks in the nine-year old battlefield of the Afghanistan war. The deployment of a company of M1 Abrams tanks, which will be fielded by the Marines in the country's southwest, will allow ground forces to target insurgents from a greater distance—and with more of a lethal punch—than is possible from any other US military vehicle. The 68-ton tanks are propelled by a jet engine and equipped with a 120 mm main gun that can destroy a house more than a mile away.[22]

The tanks will be used initially in parts of northern Helmand province, where the Marines have been engaged in intense combat against resilient Taliban cells that typically are armed with assault rifles, rocket-propelled grenades and homemade bombs. US officials argue that the tank round is far more accurate than firing artillery, and it can be launched much faster than having to wait for a fighter jet or a helicopter to shoot a missile or drop a satellite-guided bomb. Experts believe that "Tanks give you immediate, protected firepower and mobility to address a threat that's beyond the range of machine guns."[23]

Testing New Weapon System

Several new technology weapon systems have been introduced and tested in the Afghanistan war in last few years. One such latest game-changing "revolutionary" rifle is called XM25, which have the capacity to figure out an enemy, even when he is hidden behind building or other barriers. The XM25[24] counter defilade target engagement system is reportedly a high-tech rifle that can be programmed so that its 25 mm ammunition does not necessarily explode on impact, but it can be set to detonate either in front of or behind a target, meaning it literally will go through a wall before it explodes and kills the enemy. It has a range of roughly 2,300ft, which enables it to fire at targets well past the range of the rifles and carbines that most soldiers use these days. Experts believe that this "game-changer," provided to the US soldiers in Afghanistan only in November 2010, will lead to new ways of fighting on the battlefield.

Another cutting-edge technology that is being tested and introduced in Afghanistan war theatre is a revolutionary airborne surveillance system called Gorgon Stare, which would be able to transmit live video images of physical movement across an entire town.[25] The system, made up of nine video cameras mounted on a remotely piloted aircraft, can transmit live images to soldiers on the ground or to analysts tracking enemy movements. It can send up to 65 different images to different users; by contrast, Air Force drones today shoot video from a single camera over a "soda straw" area the size of a building or two. Gorgon Stare would be looking at a whole city, so there would be no way for the adversary to know what the American troops were looking at. Practically, they would be looking at everything and that their capability to strike strategic targets would be enhanced manifold.

"Clear, hold, build and transfer" Strategy

With the announcement of Afghanistan transition plan by President Obama in December 2009, the traditional counterinsurgency mantra of "clear, hold and build" became "clear, hold, build and transfer." "Clear" implies reversal of the Taliban momentum; "hold" involves controlling of the territory by preventing the insurgents from returning; "build" entails rebuilding the area through economic development and to establish the writ of the law, and "transfer" means to handover the area to the trained Afghan National Security Forces. Thus, the strategy requires control of territory and a separation of insurgents from the population. Troops clear an area, remain there, and implement an ambitious development programme intended to gain the support of the population. This strategy is quite significant in view of the fact that the war in Afghanistan is being waged one village and valley at a time. Officially, the Afghan National Police have a presence in each of the country's 365 districts, but many local police units are outgunned, under-trained, or corrupt. The administration's "clear, hold, build and transfer" strategy is meant to win over Afghans in those sensitive areas. It is based on the counterinsurgency principle of protecting the population and to win confidence and support, before isolating remaining insurgents to be killed or captured.

Forming Local Forces

In a crucial stop gap arrangement to combat rising violence in the south and the east, and frustration with the slow pace of training permanent professional security forces—the bottom-line condition for the American military to begin pulling back—the United States military and the Afghan Government agreed to form local armed forces to combat the Taliban.[26] The programme borrows from the largely successful Awakening groups that General Petraeus created in Iraq,[27] though the two programs would not be identical. Unlike the Iraqi units, the Afghan forces would not be composed of insurgents who had switched sides. They would be similar as a lightly armed, trained and, significantly, paid force under the Afghan Interior Ministry. They would be armed and equipped and trained to defend their communities; thus their job is purely defensive by nature. Historically, community defence has deep cultural roots in Afghanistan, where local men form village watch groups to keep out foes. Both the Karzai administration and the American military are describing it as a short-term remedy to the problem of a lack of police officers and soldiers in many areas of the country.[28]

Counterinsurgency or Counterterrorism

The United States is following a two-prong military strategy in Afghanistan.[29] One is the conventional tactics of chasing the Taliban and Al-Qaeda militants, and trying to evacuate and hold territory, and win allegiance of the Afghan people. But, after nine years of protracted war, it is understood that this counterinsurgency strategy has shown little success. The other and more significantly, what has turned out to "work well" is an approach American officials have talked much less about, i.e. counterterrorism: military-speak for the targeted killings of insurgents from Al-Qaeda and the Taliban. US military officials are hopeful that this shift could change the nature of the war and potentially hasten a political settlement with the Taliban. This view seems to be in conformity with the recent American intelligence reporting which has revealed growing examples of Taliban fighters who are fearful of moving into higher-level command positions because of these lethal operations.[30] Thus, with the current military surge, the emerging American model can best be described as counterterrorism, with some contents of counterinsurgency strategy.

Use of Intense Force

Gen David H. Petraeus, who is widely regarded as the father of the military's modern counterinsurgency doctrine,[31] believes in the use of intense force, at times, to wipe out opponents and create conditions for population-centric operations. A less-recognized aspect of the troop surge he commanded in Iraq in 2007 involved a significant increase in raids and air-strikes. Since his arrival in Kabul, Petraeus has permitted—and in some cases encouraged—the use of tougher measures like the use of air and artillery strikes.

Situation in the battlefield indicate that US troop operations since September 2010 have been more intense and have had a harder edge than at any point since the initial 2001 drive to oust the Taliban government. The pace of Special Operations missions to kill or capture Taliban leaders have more than tripled and the US and NATO aircraft unleashed more bombs and missiles in October 2010—1,000 total—than in any single month since 2001.[32] American commanders say their plan in the next few years is to kill large numbers of insurgents in the border region: the military refers to it as "degrading the

Taliban."[33] Senior US military officials involved in running the war contend that all these aggressive measures have dealt a staggering blow to the insurgency.[34] These gains, in turn, would put Gen. Petraeus in a much stronger position vindicating his contention that his military strategy is working in Afghanistan. But at the same time, it is certain that with the increased tempo of Special Operations raids, which includes increased night raids as well, civilian casualties are also bound to increase.

The Transition Plan

In November 2010, the US-led coalition in Afghanistan formally adopted a transition plan designed to turn over control of the war to Afghan security forces by 2014 but continue heavy financial and military support for the indefinite future. The plan emerged as "NATO-Afghanistan Partnership," essentially guaranteed that as foreign forces wind down their combat role over the next four years they will not abandon Karzai's government in its struggle against the Taliban.[35] President Obama has declared that the US troop withdrawal would begin in July 2011 and that Gen. Petraeus had begun "planning and mapping" areas where security conditions would allow a drawdown. Through a four-year transition plan, initial transition areas are to be decided by NATO, then approved and announced by Karzai. But NATO officials have emphasized that transition do not necessarily mean withdrawal, because coalition forces taken out of one area of Afghanistan would be transferred elsewhere inside the country. Each nation makes its own decision on when to withdraw troops.[36] As far as the US is concerned, the size and pace of the US drawdown would be determined by "conditions on the ground."[37] Ostensibly, the Obama administration is negotiating a long-term bilateral strategic agreement with Afghanistan that would promise indefinite US security, economic, cultural and development support. The agreement also aims at establishing permanent military bases in Afghanistan, enabling its troops to stay in the country beyond the 2014 deadline.[38] The US-Afghan accord would be separate from the NATO-Afghan deal which was intended to guarantee continued training and equipment for Afghan security forces after 2014. Time and again, various US officials have reiterated their pledge to their Afghan interlocutors about the United States' long-term commitment to help the war-torn nation beyond the 2014 target.[39]

The US will have to determine the number of troops to be withdrawn by July 2011 in order to fulfil a pledge Obama made when he announced a troop increase in December 2009. But the question here is what would be the US strategy once the drawdown begins? President Obama has said that a US counterterrorism capability would be maintained in Afghanistan after the 2014 deadline. He has emphasized, "Until we have confidence that Al-Qaeda is no longer operating and no longer a threat . . . We don't want to find ourselves in a situation where they've waited us out and they have reconsolidated."[40] It means that there will be greater reliance on counterterrorism elements of the strategy, including Special Forces operations, drone strikes and enhanced intelligence capabilities to keep Al-Qaeda under pressure. It is also possible that the US might sponsor peace talks between the Afghan Government and Taliban on some kind of a power sharing formula in Kabul.

It appears that the US administration is switching its gear towards a phased four-year plan to wind down American and allied fighting in Afghanistan. In many respects, the concept follows the precedent set in Iraq, where a similar troop surge and strategy shift under President George W. Bush in 2007 enabled American-led coalition forces to eventually hand over security duties to the Iraqis region by region. By the summer of 2010, the US was able to pull out two-thirds of its troops from Iraq and declare America's combat mission there over. Any such transition risks declaring Afghan units combat-ready before they really are, and that any transition would be based on local conditions, not a dictate from Washington, and would be a process, not an event, and hence a "ground-up," strategy.[41] By the end of 2014, American and NATO combat forces could be withdrawn if conditions warrant, although tens of thousands very likely will remain for training, mentoring and other assistance, just as 50,000 American troops are still in Iraq. The plan's success depends in part on building an Afghan army and police force genuinely able to defend their country. As a part of the withdrawal strategy, the Afghan National Army is to be built up to the point that the Afghans can at least contain an insurgency still supported by Pakistan. The combined forces today have about 264,000 men, with a goal of 350,000 by 2013. Yet attrition has been a problem for years, with many soldiers and police officers simply walking away, some winding up with the insurgents.

Americans naturally prefer to focus on the handoff, not the fight. Even the name of the command overseeing training for Afghans optimistically signals that goal: "Combined Security Transition Command–Afghanistan." But before the US get into the 'transition' business, it has to win the war; otherwise, there will be nothing to transition to.

Will the current American military strategy work?

False Optimism

It is partially true that the arrival of thousands of additional US and coalition troops in the Taliban's stronghold has prompted insurgents to back away and embrace smaller scale strikes leading to some temporary tactical successes on the battlefield. But there is little indication that the direction of the war has changed as claimed by some US military commanders. If there is a sign that momentum has shifted, it is yet to be seen. Hence, the optimism shown by the American Generals so far appears to be based on political consideration rather than any concrete military gain on the battlefields. Their claims are merely "strategic communication" cynically designed for the consumption in European capitals in order to bolster western public opinion.

- The US military seems to be in a false perception that a surge of forces could undercut the insurgency in six months, since many of the Taliban were ready to negotiate and could be persuaded to swap sides. Within weeks of large-scale escalation of Special Operations and air-strikes, they argued that they have seen isolated indications of slumping morale among some Taliban units, including reluctance among some mid-level commanders to replace superiors who were captured or killed, apparently out of fear that they might meet the same fate. But, paradoxically, Taliban commanders believe that the use of tanks and high-tech weapons by the United States after such a long-drawn-out war is a sign of desperation and that insurgent attacks are up more than 60 per cent in 2010 compared to the previous year. The estimated number of Taliban has increased some ten-fold since the aftermath of their defeat by coalition forces in 2001. Taliban troops now roam large areas in northern and eastern Afghanistan, far beyond the traditional Pashtun provinces of the south.[42]

- A December 2010 key assessment report called "The Afghanistan and Pakistan Annual Review" claims that the Taliban momentum has been arrested in much of the war-torn country and reversed in some key areas. But at the same time the report admits, "These gains remain fragile and reversible" and that "challenge remains" to make these gains "durable and sustainable."[43] Moreover, insurgent attacks and US casualties always drop in the winter as many Taliban fighters go to sanctuaries in Pakistan, producing hopeful trends on the US military's PowerPoint slides. According to a civilian adviser to the NATO command in Kabul, "winter is the season of external optimism in Afghanistan."[44]
- The "clear, hold, build and transfer model" of the US policy has clearly failed so far. One insightful conversation between President Obama and his former Afghan commander Gen. McChrystal remains relevant even after unveiling of Gen. Petraeus' ruthless policy of use of intense force. Before his departure, Gen. McChrystal, in one of his briefings to the President, said the Afghan army and police were not ready to hold territory that the United States had cleared and that this was bogging down the model of clear, hold, build and transfer that were central for the drawdown to begin in July 2011. Obama asked about the operation in Marja where the coalition troops were holding that territory since an offensive in February 2010, "Are we on timeline?" "Yes sir," the General replied. The President: "Where would you put us on the clear, hold, build and transfer model in the places south of Marja?" Gen McChrystal: "We're holding. Our forces are fixed there." The President: "What about the 25,000 US troops in eastern Afghanistan who are there for years? Where they are on the clear, hold, build and transfer model?" Gen McChrystal: "They are still holding, sir." The President: "Any of them close to transferring?" Gen McChrystal: "Not a single one, sir." The model had become: clear, hold, hold, hold, hold and hold.[45] Thus, the clear, hold, build and transfer model has ended half way with only "clear and hold," that too in very few areas.
- Among the officially stated goals of Washington, reintegration of the supposedly "moderate" Taliban and strengthening of the Afghan armed forces are the most

important. Yet in nine years of war, no significant group of Taliban has opted for reintegration (a few individuals have come in, only to return to the Taliban when it again was in their interest). Similarly, coalition military personnel know that there is not a single Afghan army brigade that can hold against Taliban troops. In fact, the ANA is still many years away from achieving the professional standards necessary to manage security on its own.

- The United States' military claims to have killed thousands of Taliban in recent months, mostly foot soldiers and mid-level commanders through its "awe, shock and firepower," and considers it as "main success" of the current surge policy. But it is only pertinent to remember that such military 'success' of the former Soviet Union was thwarted by the Afghans in the 1980s. Moreover, it appears that such commanders and soldiers are immediately replaced by the younger generation fighters well trained and motivated in their religious schools.
- More troops in Afghanistan have been a historic mistake. It is leading to radicalization of Pashtuns who also admire the Taliban's personal honesty and religious piety. That is one reason why the US surge will not intimidate local Taliban commanders and tribal chieftains to negotiate peace deals, especially at a time when they know that the United States will start its withdrawal by July 2011.
- An intense military campaign aimed at crippling the Taliban has so far failed to inflict more than fleeting setbacks on the insurgency or put meaningful pressure on its leaders to seek peace. Escalated air-strikes and special operations raids have sporadically disrupted Taliban movements and damaged local cells.[46] But the insurgents seem to be confident and maintaining its resilience to outlive the American escalation. Moreover, civilian casualties entailing from such air-strikes and special operations have been a very critical and sensitive issue in Afghanistan's stabilization and reconstruction process.[47]
- Creating government structures such as local armed forces may not help in the stabilization process. Such a force might go down as a reminiscent of the period of communist rule in the 1980s, when Muhammad Najibullah, then the president,

created local armed forces to help bolster the government's fight against rebels, a move that alienated many Afghans and strengthened insurgency.

Roads Ahead

The solution to Afghanistan is not and never has been a military one. So, the foreign troops must be withdrawn at the earliest. And, in order to do that the US/NATO have to focus their strategy on two most significant determining factors which are inextricably linked to the geopolitics of the Afghanistan war: the Pakistani factor and the making of the Afghan National Security Forces.

The Pakistani Factor

By all accounts, Pakistan remains the wild card that complicates all predictions on Afghanistan. Recent intelligence reports offer only dim view of the Afghan war focusing the reason as unwillingness of Pakistan to shut down militant sanctuaries in its lawless tribal region. American military commanders on the ground say, "Insurgents freely cross from Pakistan into Afghanistan to plant bombs and fight American troops and they return to Pakistan for rest and re-supply."[48] Pakistanis think that their bad behaviour will continue to bring billions of dollars to their country; the increasing American reward only emboldens their conviction. The bulk of Al-Qaeda and Taliban leadership is now in Pakistan. That's where the United States should really be focused. The country, with a population six times larger than that of Afghanistan's, is both the heart of the problem and the key to its solution. The crux of Afghan instability is clearly embedded with the strategic rethink by Pakistan's military as to how it looks at national security. Thomas Friedman writes: "People do not change when we (the US) tell them they should; they change when their context tells them they must."[49] The United States needs to work on the direction of that "context." Most significantly, the manner in which the Obama administration decides to engage the Pakistani military to bring about a change in latter's perceptions on national security will be a determining factor in overcoming the current crisis in Afghanistan.

It is certain that Pakistan will not hang down its support to the extremist elements in Afghanistan. Like the Soviet's war in the 1980s where the largest beneficiary was the Pakistani intelligence agency which siphoned off more than 30 per cent of the billions of dollars aid the so called mujahedeen fighting against the Soviet backed regime in Afghanistan received from the United States,[50] Islamabad's policy is not much different today. The charade which has been going on in the United States' policy towards Pakistan is that the US cannot use its aid leverage to force Pakistan to stop supporting terrorist groups who kill US/NATO troops in Afghanistan day in and day out because US needs Pakistan's help in ferrying supplies to those very US/NATO troops.

Historically, it had often been difficult if not impossible to defeat an insurgency when it enjoyed a cross-border haven. In South Vietnam, allied forces were never able to seal off borders with Cambodia, Laos or North Vietnam. The self-imposed prohibitions against going outside South Vietnam with ground forces allowed the insurgents to use border areas for training, supply routes and sanctuary. Another example is that of the Algerians, who had havens in Tunisia when they were fighting to gain independence from France. Taliban uses the Pakistan border as its own barrier. Either Washington must find a way to get the Pakistanis to step up the fight against the terrorists, or consider operations across the border.[51]

The ANSF

The centrepiece of the American strategy in Afghanistan should be towards a greater effort to increase the size and quality of the Afghan National Security Forces (ANSF). From a long term point of view, developing ANSF is the most important strategic goal. If this cannot be accomplished, everything else is of little use since the ANSF must be adequately strengthened in order for the ISAF to be able to leave. The development of ANSF has to make enough progress so that, by July 2011, the ISAF can begin the process of turning over security responsibility to the ANSF.

Compared to 700,000 soldiers and police (plus 100,000 "volunteers") in Iraq which is slightly smaller and less populous nation, Afghanistan's 134,000 troop level is quite small. Standard counterinsurgency guidelines recommend 20 police and/or soldiers for every 1,000 civilians, implying that Afghanistan should have roughly, some 600,000 total security forces. Hence, it is quite necessary and entirely appropriate to increase the Afghan National Army (ANA) and Afghan National Police (ANP). At present, the Army is due to grow to 171,000 and the ANP will be increased to

134,000 by October 2011.[52] The cost will certainly run into billions of dollars. But this is probably cheaper than continuing to fight Taliban with western troops.

Like any other country, Afghanistan's national security depends most fundamentally on its economic strength. The present state of Afghan economy with GNP of 14 billion dollars is clearly unsustainable in terms of its security requirements vis-à-vis maintaining large armed forces. The US and the international community must work to build an Afghan nation that is self sufficient in its security requirements.

In the process, the US and the international community would have to make Afghanistan a frontline state for a possible war against Pakistan, i.e. to stop the Pakistani intervention in Afghanistan. It could no longer be the other way around. The Taliban/Al-Qaeda in Afghanistan-Pakistan region cannot be eliminated by traditional military strategies. Such attempts have failed in the past. What is required is a strong army and police force in Afghanistan, strong enough to provide internal security and to check cross-border insurgency across the Durand Line emanating from the Pakistani soil.

The Afghan army, however, is far from ready to take over operational command and to tackle security threats on its own. Till date (by first quarter of 2011), it remains a fragmented force with ethnic frictions and political factionalism undercutting institutional loyalty.

Resemblance of Soviet Occupation

Despite the 'surge', it is clear that the Taliban on both sides of the Afghanistan-Pakistan border as well as in many parts of Afghanistan continue to defy the American power. High profile military operations such as that of Helmand and Kandahar illustrate both abilities and limitations of a superpower. But this is not new in Afghanistan's turbulent history. The US-led war now resembles the failed Soviet occupation of Afghanistan in the 1980s, which lasted almost 10 years and cost the mighty Soviet military about 15,000 lives.

Both the Soviet Union and the United States entered Afghanistan for their perceived defensive reasons, with expectations of a time-bound engagement. But both the superpowers got fraught with a protracted conflict with Islamist resistance forces with main bases in the mountainous regions on the Afghanistan-Pakistan border.

Ironically, in both the circumstances, Pakistani intelligence agency (ISI) clandestinely channelized money and weapons to the insurgents, because of which both the superpowers suffered from a consequential inability to militarily crush the resistance and bogged down in a prolonged war. Pakistan's strategic calculations in Afghanistan, which were shaped and vigorously pursued during General Zia-ul-Haq presidency in the 1980s is also not different today. Zia's dream of establishing an Islamic fundamentalist regime in Kabul is yet to be fulfilled by his successors in Pakistani Army and ISI.

Throughout its war, the Red Army held little more than the main towns. The countryside remained largely in the hands of the mujahedeen. Similarly, today, 70 per cent of the country is ranked as "insecure" by the United Nations and the US, just as the Soviet Union, controls all the urban areas and especially provincial capitals and Kabul. The present war is primarily a rural insurgency just like mujahedeen's war against the Soviets in the 1980s. Soviet forces were able to take virtually any piece of territory, but could not hold that territory like the American position today. Like the Soviets, the Americans are finding that it is possible to wrest control of specific areas, but only as long as their troops are in occupation of those areas. As they move on for other operations, the insurgents make a comeback. Significantly, in their respective circumstances, both the United States and Soviet Union looked for various ways and means aiming to reinforce and build the Afghan Government's capacity (including that of the Army) to govern beyond Kabul and a few other urban strongholds.

Obama's current 'surge' policy also resembles the increase in the Soviet occupation forces in Afghanistan after the advent of Mikhail Gorbachev in 1985. At the height of the occupation, the Soviets commanded 120,000 troops in Afghanistan compared to the 140,000 (US + NATO) coalition troops in 2011. Gorbachev had ordered reinforcements similar in size to the American surge now ostensibly to give the Soviet armed forces one last chance to win the Afghan war. After the Soviet escalation of war, Gorbachev looked for a withdrawal plan which ultimately materialized as a "face saving escape" of a superpower from the Afghan war theatre. President Obama has already announced that American troops will begin to leave Afghanistan by June 2011. It is also interesting to note that after several years of the initial intervention and change of leadership both in Washington and Moscow, and high domestic cost of the war and its uncertain future, both the United States and the Soviet Union were compelled to re-evaluate their strategies. Both the superpowers saw their escalation to negotiate with the rebels from a position of military strength, but at the same time considered it as a prelude to a more significant troop reduction and eventual disengagement.

In 1986, when Gorbachev reinforced troops in Afghanistan, it was seen as last minute desperation of the Soviet leader. It was also seen as the Soviet's last attempt to alienate and suppress the mujahedeen. Now the American surge is viewed in that angle. When President Obama decided to increase the troop level to almost 100,000, critics saw it as a last desperate attempt by the United States before actually going for a draw down. Similarly, just as the present US/NATO versus Taliban war is in a stalemated situation, in the mid 1980s, Soviet war with the mujahedeen was also in the same condition.

Most significantly, like the mid-1980s war against the Soviets, rival militant organizations on both sides of the Afghanistan-Pakistan border have increasingly been teaming up in deadly raids to regain the initiative after months of American offensives. Different factions are setting aside their historic rivalries and coordinating attacks, combining their foot soldiers, granting one another safe passage through their areas of control, sharing new recruits and coordinating their propaganda responses to the American and allied actions on the ground.[53] In the process, like the former Soviet Union, America is creating enemies faster than friends in the ongoing war. To claim success in Afghanistan shows a poor understanding of the country.

During the Soviet war, many government, military, and police officials, including senior military commanders, secretly collaborated with the resistance; just as the Taliban, pro-Taliban, and their collaborators have infiltrated most ministries of the Karzai administration.

Conclusion

Apart from the above similarities between the unsuccessful bid of the Soviets to defeat the mujahedeen and the present US/NATO war against the Taliban/Al-Qaeda, few striking differences are also visible in the Afghanistan war. Compared to the Soviet war, the American and NATO forces operating in Afghanistan have far superior technology on the battlefield, such as communications, surveillance, precision-guided munitions, unmanned aerial vehicles, mine-resistant ground vehicles and air assets with advanced avionics, among others. On the other hand, the Red Army was untrained for the mountainous terrain and found themselves bogged down in an unwinnable guerrilla war against mujahedeen Islamist fighters backed financially and militarily by Washington. And yet, the US and NATO troops face a fiercer enemy today than did Soviet troops. Today, the situation appears more complicated, because the mujahedeen were more moderate than the Taliban, who are radical. Again, in those days, there were no suicide bombers which play a crucial role in the present war.

The Taliban is also well aware that the US cannot win this war. The strategy of Taliban will be to prolong this conflict and make the US and NATO forces desperate and tired. It is now nearly ten years since the US-led coalition invaded Afghanistan and despite their military and economic dominance, nothing has gone well with the western forces. For many observers of this war, the United States is repeating the mistakes that the Soviet Union made twenty years ago. The preceding resemblances as well as differences highlight one significant lesson for the big powers that they often overestimate their capacity to influence the political and military outcomes of weaker states. Afghanistan has been a victim of superpower rivalry for centuries. But its people have never been decimated and the country ruled by outsiders. No outside military doctrine, strategy or philosophy works in Afghanistan. It only brings death and destructions for the Afghan people. Therefore, before the situation in the Afghan battlefields look more dreadful, the United States and NATO forces should look for a face-saving escape from this war-torn country. The ultimate resolution of the conflicts in Afghanistan must come from the Afghans themselves.

Notes and References

1. Rajiv Chandrasekaram, "Nawa turns into a proving ground for US strategy in Afghan war," *The Washington Post*, 12 December 2010.
2. Chandrasekaram, "Nawa turns into a proving ground for US strategy in Afghan war."
3. See the text "Obama on New Strategy for Afghanistan and Pakistan," The White House, Office of the Press Secretary, Washington DC, Distributed by the Bureau of International Information Programs, US Department of State. http://www.america.gov, 27 March 2009.

4. Paul D. Miller has quoted Rep. Lynn Woolsey (D-Calif.) in "Congressional Oversight," *Foreign Policy* (15 February 2011).
5. For a background to the United States' surge policy, see Jagmohan Meher, "America's Coming War in Afghanistan: The 'Bloody' Iraq Model," in *Reconstructing Afghanistan: Prospects and Limitations*, Arpita Basu Roy and Binoda Kumar Mishra (eds.) (New Delhi: Shipra Publications, 2011), 93–111.
6. As quoted in Charlie Savage, "Obama's war on terror may resemble Bush's," *The Indian Express*, 19 February 2009, 13.
7. Bob Woodward, "Biden warned Obama during Afghan war review not to get 'locked into Vietnam'," *The Washington Post*, 28 September 2010.
8. As quoted in Mark Thompson and Aryan Baker, "A New General, and a New War in Afghanistan," *TIME,* 10 July 2009.
9. Thompson and Baker, "A New General, and a New War in Afghanistan."
10. See Dexter Filkins, "Stanley McChrystal's Long War," *The New York Times*, 18 October 2009.
11. See the tensed conversation of Military Generals and Defence Secretary with President Obama on troop surge in Bob Woodward, "Military thwarted president seeking choice in Afghanistan," *The Washington Post*, 27 September 2010.
12. Scott Wilson, "Obama: US security is still a stake," *The Washington Post*, 2 December 2009.
13. Wilson, "Obama: US security is still a stake."
14. See editorial, "The Afghanistan Speech," *The New York Times*, 2 December 2009.
15. David S. Cloud and Julian E. Barnes, "US strategy in Afghanistan may involve greater use of special operations forces," *Los Angeles Times*, 29 June 2010.
16. Peter Baker and Rod Nordland, "US Plan Offers Path to Ending Combat in Afghanistan," *The New York Times*, 14 November 2010.
17. Mark Mazzetti and Dexter Filkins, "US Military Seeks to Expand Raids in Pakistan," *The New York Times*, 20 December 2010.
18. Mazzetti and Filkins, "US Military Seeks to Expand Raids in Pakistan."
19. Mazzetti and Filkins, "US Military Seeks to Expand Raids in Pakistan."
20. Helene Cooper and Sheryl Gay Stolberg, "Obama Ponders Outreach to Elements of the Taliban," *The New York Times*, 8 March 2009.
21. For a comprehensive discussion on the subject, see Meher, "America's Coming War in Afghanistan," in Basu Roy and Mishra (eds.), *Reconstructing Afghanistan*, 93-111.
22. Rajiv Chandrasekaran, "US deploying heavily armoured battle tanks for first time in Afghan war," *The Washington Post*, 19 November 2010.

23. As quoted in Chandrasekaran, "US deploying heavily armoured battle tanks for first time in Afghan war."
24. The XM25, designed by Minnesota's Alliant Tech-systems, has been in development for about seven years. This 5kg, 29inch system costs up to $35,000 per unit. See "This gun can even target hidden foes," *The Times of India*, 1 December 2010, 12.
25. Ellen Nakashima and Craig Whitlock, "With Air Force's new drone, 'we can see everything'," *The Washington Post*, 2 January 2011.
26. Alissa J. Rubin, "Afghans to Form Local Forces to Fight Taliban," *The New York Times*, 14 July 2010.
27. Steven Simon, "The Price of Surge," *Foreign Affairs* (May/June 2008).
28. General Petraeus insists, "The local police has real potential to create problems for the Taliban. These are local community members who want to keep the Taliban out and are willing to defend their homes and their communities and to fight for it." "Petraeus: 'We're doing everything we can to achieve progress'," *The Washington Post*, 15 August 2010.
29. In a July 2010 Senate hearing, the incoming commander of the US military's Central Command, Gen. James N. Mattis was asked by Senator Jack Reed, (D-Rhode Island) whether the administration's July 2011 date for starting to withdraw American troops implied a shift in emphasis from counterinsurgency to a strategy concentrating on killing terrorists. "I think that is the approach, Senator," the four star General replied. See Helene Cooper and Mark Landler, "Targeted Killing is New US Focus in Afghanistan," *The New York Times*, 31 July 2010.
30. Cooper and Landler, "Targeted Killing is New US Focus in Afghanistan."
31. Petraeus also believes in the role of governance, development and other forms of soft power in stabilization missions.
32. Chandrasekaran, "US deploying heavily armoured battle tanks for first time in Afghan war."
33. Elisabeth Bumiller, "Intelligence Reports Offer Dim View of Afghan War," *The New York Times*, 14 December 2010.
34. Chandrasekaran, "US deploying heavily armoured battle tanks for first time in Afghan war."
35. Edward Cody and Karen DeYoung, "NATO adopts transition plan for Afghan war," *The Washington Post*, 20 November 2010.
36. Karen DeYoung, "NATO adopts transition plan for Afghan war," *The Washington Post*, 21 November 2010.
37. DeYoung, "NATO adopts transition plan for Afghan war."
38. Afghan President Hamid Karzai has confirmed this. See "Kabul Confirms US bases in Afghanistan," *Afghanistan News Centre*, 8 February 2011.

39. Joshua Partlow and Pamela Constable, "In Kabul, Biden promises US support beyond 2014," *The Washington Post*, 12 January 2011.
40. As quoted in Partlow and Constable, "In Kabul, Biden promises US support beyond 2014."
41. Peter Baker and Rod Nordland, "US Plan Offers Path to Ending Combat In Afghanistan," *The New York Times*, 14 November 2010.
42. Scott Atran, "Turning the Taliban against Al-Qaeda," *The New York Times*, 26 October 2010.
43. "Obama claims progress in bid to contain Al-Qaeda in Afghan, Pak," *The Indian Express*, 17 December 2010, 11.
44. As quoted in Rajiv Chandrasekaran and Scott Wilson, "Administration's next big Afghan battle: How many troops to withdraw," *The Washington Post*, 16 December 2010.
45. As quoted in Bob Woodward, "Biden warned Obama during Afghan war review not to get 'locked into Vietnam'," *The Washington Post*, 28 September 2010.
46. Greg Miller "US military campaign to topple resilient Taliban hasn't succeeded," *The Washington Post*, 27 October 2010.
47. See Jagmohan Meher, "Understanding the Dynamics of Afghan Instability," *Contemporary Central Asia* 10/3 (2006), 1-31, especially 10-12.
48. Bumiller, "Intelligence Reports Offer Dim View of Afghan War."
49. Thomas L. Friedman, "This I Believe" *The New York Times*, 2 December 2010.
50. Tim Warner, *Blank Check: The Pentagon's Black Budget* (New York: Warner Books, 1990), 152–53. Also see Jagmohan Meher, *America's Afghanistan War: The Success That Failed* (New Delhi: Kalpaz Publications, 2004), 145–46.
51. For the geo-political significance of this 2400 kilometers (1500 miles) porous border between Afghanistan and Pakistan, see Jagmohan Meher, "Afghanistan: Elusive Peace and its Geo-political Implications," in *Emerging Asia in Focus: Issues and Problems*, P.L. Dash (ed.) (Delhi: Academic Excellence, 2008), 118–20.
52. See Rod Nordland, "US approves training to expand Afghan army," *The New York Times*, 15 January 2010.
53. Thom Shanker, "Insurgents Set Aside Rivalries on Afghan Border," *The New York Times*, 28 December 2010.

Dimensions of State and Nation-building

8

Nation-building in post-2001 Afghanistan: Role of the International Community

Jamal Rahman

The term 'nation-building' had given rise to a lot of debate among western academicians and in developmental and political/military circles during the late 1950s and 1960s. The term nation-building conveys different meanings to different people.[1] For some, nation-building provides an analytical tool, focusing on the conditions and developments that lead to the establishment of nation-states. For others, it also provides a policy to create nation-states. As a policy tool we can distinguish two variants: nation-building as a strategy for development; and as instrument for competition in the cold war ("development" and "nation-building" as alternatives to "socialism" and "revolution").[2] The term nation-building became unfashionable after the Vietnam War. However, it has been revitalized since the end of cold war.[3] A distinction can be drawn between the following three basic elements for successful nation building which are closely interlinked in most cases:

1. An integrative ideology, that might be nationalist, but could also be religious, racist, developmentalist, or shaped along other lines, as long as it provides for integrating the subgroups of the inhabitants of a country into national society;
2. An integrated society, with its several elements communicating more often with each other than with outsiders. This implies a "nation-wide" integration of geographic regions, economic sectors, and politics. It also presupposes a functioning infrastructure and intellectual discourse of "national" scale;

3. An existing state apparatus, which actually fulfils its functions on all of the national territory.[4]

In nation-building, the more the establishing or development of a nation-state is advanced, the more are the three criteria fulfilled. This definition does not judge the legitimacy or usefulness of nation-building, nor the tools used for its purpose. Ethnic cleansing, massacres, and ethnic or cultural repression have been (used) utilized quite often. And sometimes ethnic, religious or geographical entities have been integrated that never wanted to be. The nation-state may have been and still may be the solution to a set of human and political problems, but it also has been the source of conflicts and suffering. Therefore, I use the term nation-building without implying any judgment about its usefulness in any specific case.

Nation-building in Pre-war Afghanistan

Culturally, Afghanistan is multi-ethnic country. These groups include Pashtun, Tajik, Hazara, Uzbek, Turkmen, Pashai, Pamiri and others. These ethnic groups participated in the country's political history and economic development. From time to time they have made great sacrifices for the freedom and protection of Afghanistan from outside invaders. For instance, the Hazara community in the early eighteenth century fought shoulder to shoulder with Shah Mahmood Hotaky against the Asfahan (centre of Safawi dynasty of Persian). They also took part in the Sher Sorkh Jirga that led to the selection of Ahmad Khan as a national leader and the establishment of modern Afghanistan in 1747. Successive Afghan governments have always had the support of all tribes in running the governments' affairs and maintaining peace and tranquillity. These groups have always taken active part in observing national ceremonies under the uniformed flag of being Afghan.

Normally, religion has played a pivotal role in Afghan society that has intertwined all ethnic groups. This in turn has brought all Afghans under the banner and direction of Islam and Afghan nationalism and thus has secured political stability and national unity. Practically, in Afghanistan nation building was a domestic process up to the year 1978. The central government was robust and it could implement its decisions not only at every province, but also in remote districts without any hinderances. There were no problems in joining

Afghan army since everybody was trying to complete the duty with full responsibility.

Traditionally, in Afghanistan schools were working well and state education system developed slowly until the 1960s but with numerous ups and downs. From the 1960s, state education started reaching out to the villages on an unprecedented scale. A look at the textbooks shows how successive governments have tried to use them to promote their own visions and interpretations of the history of the country, although sometime not very effectively.[5]

Historically, after liberal ideas made their way to the textbooks in the 1920s, following the 1928–9 civil war, the approach became more cautious: religion was reintroduced as a prime focus of public education and nation building principles were still emphasized. Throughout the 1930s and 1940s, the main political concern of the textbooks was developing reverence for the royal family and a number of 'national heroes'. During the 1950s, the idea of coordinated curriculum planning and specific educational objectives established itself for the first time in Afghanistan, even if the monarchy never developed a coherent national ideology.[6] Respect for the royal family and love for the Afghan nation became explicit objectives of education and the textbooks complied with the aspects of Afghan history and other patriotic themes.[7]

Additionally, in that era economic development was satisfactory. There was no religious, ethnic, or tribal conflict, and government was trying to ensure participation to all tribes. Every Afghan was proud of national flag, national anthem, and being an Afghan. People of different ethnic groups were living together and there were no discrimination based on ethnic line such as being Tajik, Hazara, Pashtun, etc.

Surprisingly, after the communist takeover in 1978[8] and the Soviet invasion in 1979[9] both communists and Islamist groups began to fight each other. The Islamist groups were accused of being reactionary while the communist were accused of being non-Muslims. Ironically, both ideologies had their root in internationalism and did not have a national basis in Afghanistan. However, during the conflict times, the support provided by the foreigners caused the spread of these ideologies in Afghanistan which consequently had a negative impact on the patriotism and Afghan nationalism.

Significantly, unlike neighbouring countries there has never been any religious sectarian violence between Shi'a and Sunni

Muslims in Afghanistan, and the proxy wars that have taken place in Afghan history have never been of a religious or ethnic origin. Even before Islam we had movements and religions (Buddhism, Zardoshtism) which had regional fronts, but there was no sectarian violence among them. They lived in harmony side by side with each other. On the one hand, Islam is the basic motive behind the defence of Islamic and national identification of the Afghan people; on the other hand, it granted unity and homogeneity to the multiethnic Afghan society.

Politically, Afghanistan has been ruled by one or another Pashtun tribe since its establishment. The Afghan rulers have tried to pursue the idea of national unity (integration) because their primary aim has always been the extension of the central power but not domination of other ethnic groups. Unlike neighbouring countries, the Afghan rulers had paid attention to the non-*Pashtun* minorities. Most Afghans see themselves as Afghans first, though this is not universal. They identify with their own tribes in their own valleys. This may not be a sign of backwardness either, but a sign of lack of mobility between main cities and rural areas. Due to lack of resources the central government could not provide social services and economic development to all remote areas of the country.

Moreover, despite its ethnical heterogeneous structure in the history of Afghanistan no ethnic group tried to establish their own state, but some of the main ethnic groups tried to seize the whole country. King Ahmad Shah Baba has wide vision and he did not try to have a Pashtun government. Taimor Shah shifted Afghan capital from Kandahar to Kabul. He wanted to abolish the tribal rivalries in Afghanistan and he gave more attention to the Qazal Bash. After that all other Afghan rulers followed the policy of national unity. When Amir Abdul Rahman Khan faced challenges he left for Bokhara[10] and not to the Pashtun areas. It means that all the wars that took place in Afghanistan were for sizing and extending the power.

As far as nation-building is concerned in the modern sense it is a European phenomenon and a product of a particular political, economic and social development in Europe, which took hundreds of years. The French Revolution provided the preconditions for its realization.[11] The nation-building process in European context worked in the United States, but Afghanistan has a different social and geographical structure. Therefore the nation-building process and the nature of Afghan nation are different than the nation-building process in Europe. For all the hurdles facing Afghanistan's nation builders, the country has significant advantages over countries like Iraq. Despite ethnic and regional rivalries, virtually no sentiment exists for separation or autonomy on ethnic ground. Afghans overwhelmingly favour the country's territorial integrity over joining ethnic cousins across the Iranian, Pakistani, Turkman, Uzbek, or Tajik borders.

Nation-building in Post-Taliban Era

Nearly a quarter century of armed conflict left the Afghan state broken, its national institutions virtually non-existent, and its economy ruined. Traditional authorities were undermined while many of the society's norms seemed transformed. After this prolonged conflict a political process launched in 2001 gave Afghanistan an opportunity to restore its lost political stability, build a functioning state, start nation building which was affected during the civil war, and launch an economic recovery. Much has been achieved since then, but challenges lie ahead. The progress Afghanistan has made since the 2001 Bonn Agreement offers grounds for hopes.

These positive developments led to the return of millions of refugees to the homeland in Afghanistan. State executive, legislative and judiciary pillars have been built, although the progress is uneven. A new constitution has been adapted. Presidential, parliamentary, and provincial council elections have been held. Seven million children have gone back to school. The Afghan National Army and National Police have been re-established and they should be transformed into credible and trusted national institutions.

In addition, in social sector basic health care coverage has expanded from just 8 per cent of the population to an estimated 80 per cent. A well-organized public-private partnership has delivered communications services to 75 per cent of the country, connecting people from the most isolated areas to each other, and to the rest of the country and to the world. The National Solidarity Programme is bringing small-scale development to over 32,000 villages, while also building or upgrading road networks access to services, trade and transit and these roads connected people in the provinces, districts even in the villages. Afghanistan has the necessaries and most important values of nation building, national flag and national anthem and national heroes.

Impacts of Regional Powers on Nation-building in Afghanistan

Interferences by neighbouring countries in support of clientele groups in Afghanistan have been a disruptive force. It has often helped feed resentments among ethnic elements. While competition among external powers can sometimes accelerate development assistance, as it did during the cold war, more often it has served to divide Afghans. However, since the Taliban's fall, Pakistan and Iran together with the former Soviet Republics and Russia have recognized their stakes in Afghanistan's economic recovery. Although none have thus actively worked to stabilize Afghanistan, all continue to hedge their bets and remain patrons to those groups and individuals in the country with whom they have held long association. Should Afghanistan, for whatever reason, begin to fragment, the regional powers stand ready to claim their spheres of influence.

The Idea of Partition

During the past three decades, Afghanistan has had no functioning government, but it remained united against foreign invasions. In a final attempt, before leaving Afghanistan, the former Soviet Union nurtured the idea of Afghanistan's partition to win the war. However, the Soviet leaders abandoned this strategy and accepted an unconditional withdrawal, even though by then they were in a stronger position for only Amu Darya divided the Soviet territory from Afghanistan.

Afghanistan is indeed an ethnic mosaic. Except for two or three out of 34-provinces of the country, you can hardly find a place identified with one ethnic identity. Separatism has never been an issue of concern in Afghanistan. During, the Soviet occupation and in the civil war period in the early 1990s a fierce internal competition for control of Kabul was raging. Despite of all these bitter experiences, no ethnic group and no warlord ever called for partition. The anti-Soviet resistance in the north remained always as strong as in the south. And let us not forget that there are millions of Pashtuns in the north as well and non Pashtun ethnics in the east, south and west of the country. Thus, Afghanistan's partition would lead to greater disintegration in the region. The effects of partition will spill over to Pakistan, where the separatist movements have long traditions. It will harm India, Iran and also the central Asian countries, because none of these countries is homogeneous in ethnic sense.

Moreover, it will strengthen the Taliban and other extremist movement beyond imagination and hearten Al-Qaeda for exploiting the crisis. It will lead to uncontrollable arms competition in south Asia and Middle East. Pakistan and India have nuclear weapons, and Iranian Government has been trying to achieve nuclear strength. The ripple effects will reach China and Russia, who are already keen on play their parts in the great game.

State Failure

A number of indicators for state weakness potentially leading to state failure have been identified: disharmony between communities, inability to control borders and the entirety of the territory, a growth of criminal violence, corrupt institutions, and a decaying infrastructure which are happening in the post-war societies. In Europe, a number of post-communist countries exhibited some of these symptoms. While the scope of public services reduced in almost all Eastern European countries and open criminal violence has been on the rise after the fall of communism, the new Caucasian states in particular have had grave difficulties in establishing their territorial integrity as well.

Furthermore, state weakness does not necessarily mean under-performance in all those categories. A number of states appear to be strong in terms of government institutions and control of territory while failing to deliver political goods, especially public services, to their citizens, such as North Korea, Belarus, pre-war Iraq, or Cambodia under Pol Pot. In such countries, however, the state structure consists largely of the coercive structure, so that the state is likely to collapse together with its coercive structure.

Post-war reconstruction efforts sometimes, though not always, focus on what is commonly called state-building, i.e. establishing an effective, central state that operates under the rule of positive law and in accordance with contemporary standards of transparency and accountability. Post-war reconstruction in Afghanistan is such a case. With previous state structures destroyed or neglected as a result of 25 years of war, general upheavals, and intermittent international sanctions, the internationally assisted reconstruction programme launched after the American-led intervention in November 2001 placed state-building at its core. By design and intent, however, this programme entailed much more than just reconstruction. Wrapped in a vision of modernity, it seemed to belong to a distinct genre of planned social change, typified by the ambitious modernization programs undertaken in earlier periods by Afghan and other Asian rulers.

Pre-requisites for Nation-building

- The first and prime requisite in nation building in Afghanistan as elsewhere is the provision of functioning state institutions. A rebuilt administration in Afghanistan calls for a functioning bureaucracy with a reasonable capacity to plan, budget, and recruit personnel, as well as enforce policy. The recovery of judicial institutions and a workable legal framework are necessary to restore an orderly society, protect individual rights, and also attract private economic investment. A national bank and stable currency are indispensable to a regulated economy. To realize a democratic polity, Afghanistan requires credible elections, a broadly representative parliament, multiple political parties, and institutional means to check the executive. A credible national army and police, expected to reinforce central authority, is usually cited along with an expanded and more effective police force as necessary to deliver greater security to the society.
- The second requirement is the reviving and strengthening of constructive national myths. These myths and the beliefs are necessary for social cohesion and raising national consciousness. Some consensus on values is essential for the adherence to laws and exercise of political and societal tolerance. Myths derived from recent and distant historical memories can contribute to resolving identity issues that involve the definition of who is an Afghan.
- The third is the need to resolve or at least manage outstanding, divisive political and constitutional issues. Foremost in Afghanistan is the centre-periphery struggle between the central government and regional commanders or warlords over local autonomy and access to coveted resources. Their conflict barely masks ethnic divisions that have intensified in recent years.
- Finally, state building is likely to falter without a reasonably capable and legitimate leader (leaders). Leadership is

> essential to providing purpose and direction for an Afghanistan emerging from its national trauma. To the extent that the leader transcends parochial differences and major societal cleavages, he can play a key role in helping to energize the national recovery and unify the country.[12]

Conclusion

In order to preserve peace and security in Afghanistan, it is necessary to give priority to the state-building instead of nation building in Afghanistan, because the weak state can give an upper hand to the neighbours and some local Afghans warlords that fuel ethnicity; a strong state will lead to national integration. Thus, state or nation-building process requires huge efforts in order to be successful. It is often assumed that strong leadership helps a country to mobilize the necessary resources.

Nation-building becomes more successful if the state has had experience in effective self governance and if it has had a viable economy. Nation-building in Germany and Japan was successful principally because both nations had existing functional governmental and economic structures. Though both were defeated in World War II, these nations was ripe for the seeds of democracy to take hold. The lack of democratic experience or economic institutions will remain formidable challenge to nation-building process in Bosnia, Kosovo, and Afghanistan.

Notes and References

1. For the emergence and different usage of the terms 'nation' and 'nation-building' in Europe, see Gerhard Guhler and Ansgar Klein, "Nationalismus," in *Politische Theorien von der Antike bis zur Gegenwart*, Hans-Joachim Lieber (ed.) (Bonn: Bundeszentrale fьr politische Bildgung, 1993), 611–56.
2. Hippler Jochen, "Violent Conflicts, Conflict Prevention and Nation-building—Terminology and Political Concepts," in *Nation-building—A Key Concept for Peaceful Conflict Transformation?* Hippler Jochen (ed.) (London: Pluto Press 2005), 3–14.
3. Jochen, "Violent Conflicts," 4ff.
4. Jochen, "Violent Conflicts," 6ff.

5. Antonio Giustozzi, *Nation-Building is not for all. The Politics of Education in Afghanistan*, Afghanistan Analysts Network, Thematic Report, 2010.
6. Ahady Anwar ul Haq, *Mili Massalae* (National Affairs) (Peshawar 2001), 29ff (in Pashtu).
7. The review of Afghan history school textbooks was conducted by Niamatullah Ibrahimi of the Crisis States Research Centre in Kabul. The 1972, 1977, 1992, 1993 textbooks for ninth, tenth and twelfth class were covered.
8. For the consequences of the Soviet invasion and emergence of Islamic fundamentalist resistance organizations, see Kakar M. Hassan, *Afghanistan, The Soviet Invasion and the Afghan Response, 1979-1982* (Berkeley, Los Angeles, London: University of California Press 1995).
9. Kakar M. Hassan, *The April Coup of 1978 and its Grave Consequences* (Kabul, 2010).
10. Kakar M. Hassan, *A Political and Diplomatic History of Afghanistan 1865-1901* (Leiden, Boston: Brill 2006), 11.
11. Tibi Bassam, *Vom Gottesreich zum Nationalstaat* (Frankfurt: Suhrkamp Verlag 1987), 15-26.
12. Weinbaum G. Marvin, "Nation Building in Afghanistan: Impediments, Lessons, and Prospects," paper presented in conference on *Nation Building: beyond Afghanistan and Iraq*, the School of Advanced International Studies, 13 April 2004.

9

State-building and the Continuation of Warlordism in Afghanistan

Zubair Popalzai

After the ostensible decline of the state in the post-cold war neo-liberal order of a uni-polar world, which viewed the state as a problem and not a solution, the widespread globalization meme in the early 1990s was that the state would wither away. However, the emphasis in the development literature that state incapacity is an impediment to development[1]—and in the discourses on international security that state weakness, failure or collapse generates terrorism, HIV/AIDS, instability and refugees among other problems[2] has brought the state back into academic and policy debates. The problem of state weakness and failure is thus seen to be at the heart of a worldwide systemic crisis that constitutes the most serious challenge to global stability in the new millennium.[3] Whereas prior to the 11 September attacks on the United States, the focus was largely on humanitarian intervention in weak or failed states, following the attacks the focus shifted from humanitarianism to security threats. The 2002 US National Security Strategy formulated after the 11 September attacks clearly states that, "America is now threatened less by conquering states than we are by failing ones."[4] Because security is now described as a "global public good" for its arguably inextricable link with development in poorer and less stable countries,[5] security and development discourses in international relations are focused on how to rescue the technically advanced states in the West from the pathologies of state failure elsewhere. This perspective ensures that state-building, "constructing or reconstructing institutions of governance capable of providing citizens with physical and economic security"[6] will remain a preoccupation of the international community for some time to come.

If the problem emanates from state weakness, failure or collapse,[7] then the solution naturally seems to be state-building. However, viewing state failure and state-building in pure security terms, as has been the case since the beginning of the global war on terror, is too narrow and fails to tackle the problem it aims to address. When combined with local factors it may, instead, perpetuate state weakness and failure which, in certain situations, might lead, to state collapse.

In this article I want to argue that the state-building agenda in Afghanistan, which should have gradually built the infrastructural power of the state to overcome its weakness, was overshadowed by the short-term stability and international security imperatives. These imperatives placed a number of limitations on the ability of the technocratic core of the weak central government in Kabul and forced them to co-opt warlords. The co-optation strategy, however, was often used as a tacit pact for often-short-term alliances of convenience for personal gain at the expense of institution-building. The concept of state-building as a process whereby operations of the state and its institutions and actors are depersonalized and formalized was thus replaced by building and extending the power and influence of individuals, often but not always with military backgrounds. Although developments in Afghanistan are closely tied to regional and international politics and today it is the Taliban that present the greatest threat to the nascent Afghan state, it remained a valid point that the Afghan and foreign actors failed to align themselves around a common set of objectives culminating in the formation of a strong state. Instead, each actor pursued their own military, political and economic interests, subsequent developments perpetuating weakness of the Afghan state.

I will begin with a quick look at the history of the most recent state formation exercise to show how it began with the handover of Afghanistan to militia groups with a history of rivalry and violence among themselves. Next, I will discuss the subsequent seizure of state administration for the centralization and distribution of patronage, the incentives to remain armed and powerful despite undergoing a disarmament process and an apparent break with military practices. I will also show that co-optation was used to build and maintain power networks. I will then reflect on the process of building the coercive apparatuses of the state namely the army and police.

The Post-Taliban[8] State-building in Afghanistan

The United States intervention in Afghanistan in October 2001 was triggered by the new Pearl Harbour[9], the attacks on 11 September 2001 on the Twin Towers, temples of American commerce, as their Arab attackers identified them, and the Pentagon, the closest the United States has to a temple honouring war. Prior to that, US embassies in Kenya and Tanzania were bombed in 1998. The larger context of the invasion of Afghanistan, however, was that the weakness or failure of the Afghan state had enabled rogue elements and international terrorists to use the Afghan soil against the West. Despite the opposition of the Afghans to the Taliban rule, the US military invasion of Afghanistan with the help of fighters of the Northern Alliance as "boots on the ground" did not necessarily come under domestic pressure but rather under external pressure as a top-down imposition of a normative vision of good state which would fight terrorism and fundamentalism. The invasion marked the beginning of the so-called "Global War on Terror." Once the Taliban were rounded up in the northern and other major cities, to further its counter-terrorism campaign in the south and east of the country, the United States adopted an approach that relied on warlords for the provision of intelligence, logistics security and physical help in the search for the remnants of Taliban and Al-Qaeda fighters.

At the time of the US attack, the Northern Alliance and the warlords comprising it were largely defeated by the Taliban and controlled less than 10 per cent of Afghanistan. The Alliance's politico-military leader, Ahmad Shah Masud, had been assassinated allegedly by two Al-Qaeda suicide attackers posing as journalists on 9 September 2001, two days before the September 11 attacks. With the exception of Jami'at-e Islami Afghanistan (Islamic Society of Afghanistan) and Shora-ye Nezar (Supervisory Council), a military-political semi-autonomous sub-group within Jami'at-e Islami led, until his assassination, by Ahmad Shah Masud, other military commanders of the alliance only had a few hundred men each. By early 2002, however, the number of militias funded and armed by the United States had grown to hundreds of thousands.

The Taliban Islamic Emirate of Afghanistan was toppled within two months, but the Taliban were not defeated on the ground. They had left major cities to retreat into districts and villages and across the border into Pakistan. Many of them who had returned to their homes were later harassed by warlords and their men as well as by the US forces and thus forced to re-join the Taliban. President Hamed Karzai, who was then chairman of the Interim Administration, later admitted that he had made a mistake to return a Taliban surrender note to them asking them to announce their surrender on the radio, which they took as an insult and chose to fight instead.[10] Questions about where the Taliban went, their numbers, their thinking seemed to be on nobody's mind and certainly not on the mind of US officials. It was later discovered that the Taliban alone had more than 100,000 fighters and could recruit between 70,000 to 100,000 fighters for major fighting. The number of foreign fighters was also hugely underestimated. It was initially thought that foreigners were may be all in all 5,000 consisting of 3,000 Pakistanis, 2,000 Arabs and some Central Asians from Chechnya, Uzbekistan and so on. It was later discovered that the Pakistanis alone were more than 10,000. The Arabs were more than 5,000.[11]

While the war was still continuing in Afghanistan, the roadmap for a new political set up for Afghanistan was discussed and determined at the UN-sponsored Bonn Conference in Germany. The UN Secretary General's Special Representative, Lakhdar Brahimi, organized the conference and along with the US Ambassador to the Northern Alliance, James Dobbins, made decisions about which groups should attend. Participants at the Bonn Conference were either exiles or leaders of armed factions in Afghanistan. They represented four groups: 1) The Northern Alliance, which had a strong military presence in Afghanistan; 2) The Rome Group, a group of politically desirable Afghan exiles with ties to the former king, Zaher Shah, living in Rome, Italy since 17 July 1973 when he was deposed by his cousin, Sardar Mohammad Daud Khan; 3) The Cypress Group, a group of Afghan exiles who held their meetings in Cypress hence the Cypress Group and also said to have had ties to Iran; and, 4) the Peshawar Group, a group of mostly ethnic Pashtun exiles based in Peshawar, Pakistan.

Among the four groups, the Northern Alliance, whose representatives were flown into Bonn in a Royal Air Force jet,[12] dominated the conference. The second most important group in terms of its political influence emanating from the role of the former Afghan king was the Rome Group. The Northern Alliance delegation leader, Yonus Qanuni, had previously expressed his concern to James Dobbins about giving the émigré groups the same status as the

Northern Alliance,[13] which he thought should be afforded special treatment in view of its armed resistance to the Taliban in Afghanistan. At the conference, the Northern Alliance delegation secured key ministries and Hamed Karzai was elected as chairman of the Interim Administration as a compromise leader. Karzai, who had entered southern Afghanistan from Pakistan with a team of American Green Berets from the US Army's 5th Special Forces Group to rally tribes against the Taliban, was not at the conference. However, he was in contact with James Dobbins via satellite phone and also spoke to all delegates on his election.

It merits a mention that in a rare display of unity, a gathering of about 1000 Afghan tribal, political and military leaders was held in Peshawar, Pakistan, about three weeks after the bombing campaign against the Taliban began. These leaders wanted the Taliban government replaced, but they were critical of the US bombing campaign. Among the participants was Sayyed Ahmad Gailani, the spiritual leader of the moderate Mahaz-e Melli Islami Afghanistan (The National Islamic Front of Afghanistan). Since the participants were critical of US methods, the United States largely ignored their meeting and regarded them more as an obstacle. A former anti-Taliban Pashtun mujahedeen commander, Abdol Haq opposed the US bombing campaign, ventured into Afghanistan by himself to rally forces against the Taliban. However, unlike Hamed Karzai who was besieged by the Taliban and immediately rescued by the US forces, Abdol Haq was captured by the Taliban and killed.

The Bonn Conference adopted the Bonn Agreement,[14] which laid the roadmap for the post-Taliban Afghanistan and served as its interim constitution. The Bonn Agreement also made reference to reconciliation, but it was not a peace deal as it excluded the main warring party, the Taliban. The Taliban, who came mostly from the largest ethnic group, the Pashtuns and who, until then, had controlled 95 per cent of the country, were not represented at the conference. This not only left a warring party out of the agreement but was also interpreted as its marginalization.

The Bonn Agreement set out a process of four events: an Interim Administration until June 2002, followed by an Emergency Loyah Jergah (a grand assembly of delegates from different parts of Afghanistan) to elected a transitional administration, a constitutional Loyah Jergah to draft the new constitution of Afghanistan, and finally presidential and parliamentary elections in 2004. Hamed Karzai, who was elected chairman of the Interim Administration, was elected as chairman of the Transitional Administration at the Emergency Loyah Jergah. The constitution was ratified in January 2004 and after having chaired the Interim and Transitional administrations of Afghanistan, Hamed Karzai was elected President of the Islamic Republic of Afghanistan in October of that year. Parliamentary elections were delayed and held in September 2005.

The theoretical design of the post-2001 Afghan state envisioned in the Bonn Agreement called for a state that would perform an extensive set of functions as the principal governing agent in the lives of its citizens, but international assistance to enable the state to perform its functions remained less than modest especially during the critical early years. At the Tokyo donor conference for Afghanistan in 2002, the United States, for example, pledged 290 million dollars, less than 5 per cent of the total 5 billion pledged and the same amount of money Afghans would have received under the Taliban.[15] The paucity of aid was reflected in comparative per capita figures. In the two years following US invasion, Afghanistan received $57 per capita whereas Bosnia and East Timor received $679 and $233 respectively. Development aid remained a fraction of military spending which was around $30 billion dollars a year and $100 million a day whilst the average volume of international aid by all donors was $7 million a day until at least 2008.[16]

Discussions about the formal structures of the new state took place prior to and at the time of the Constitutional Loyah Jergah. Among Afghans there were widely differing answers to the question of how the government should be structured to enable different interests to be incorporated and aggregated. A number of minority ethnic leaders pushed for either power-sharing within the central state or recognition of their identities through mechanisms of local self-government.[17] In the end, the 1382 (2004) Constitution affirmed the nature of Afghanistan as a unitary state, although some still continue to argue that provisions for more autonomous regions need to be made.[18] The idea of a federal solution has recently emerged in a number of northern Afghan political circles. However, that option is currently not formally a topic for discussion, either among the international actors or within the Afghan Government.

The Northern Alliance leaders remained in control of all four phases of the Bonn process until the end of 2004 when Afghanistan completed the Bonn roadmap. Although all the benchmarks of the

Bonn Agreement were achieved, the nature of the agreement as handover of Afghanistan to militia groups with a history of rivalry and enmity among themselves and absence of a citizen-centric approach, exclusion of the Taliban as a major warring party and the short-term US security imperatives did little to address the long-term state-building challenges and alleviate the possibility of another war cycle, the civil war that Afghanistan is experiencing today. In Saikal's words, "The Bonn Conference was an exercise in elite power-sharing and not popular legitimation."[19] The Pashtun-Northern Alliance divide, a legacy of the recent Afghan history percolated down to the Karzai-led transitional administration and was well-reflected during the Constitutional Loyah Jergah as well as in the run-up to the presidential elections held on 9 October 2004. The controversial 2009 presidential elections witnessed the repetition of divisions along ethnic lines. This time, however, at least one warlord governor appointed by President Karzai himself openly opposed Karzai's candidacy and supported the former Northern Alliance foreign minister Dr. Abdollah.

Seizure of State Administration

Once the Taliban withdrew from Kabul on 13 November 2001, the military forces of the Northern Alliance swept into the capital triumphantly despite the agreement that the city will remain demilitarized. The Northern Alliance justified the military takeover of the city by citing absence of any security forces to prevent possible chaos, looting and plunder in the city as a reason. The Northern Alliance delegation at the Bonn Conference led by the "Panjsheri trio," Yonus Qanuni, Dr. Abdollah and General Qaseem Fahim, claimed key government positions for their role in the overthrow of the Taliban government. Mohammad Qaseem Fahim was appointed as the first deputy chairman and defence minister of the Interim Administration, Yonus Qanuni as interior minister and Dr. Abdollah as foreign minister. This was one of the other reasons the Taliban, who rose to prominence initially because of their success against the corruption of local commanders, held back from the new setup in Kabul. Not only did the Northern Alliance entrench themselves at the national level but also at the provincial, district and village levels. In just five or six weeks between his arrival in Kabul in mid-November and the installation of the Karzai administration on 22 December, the formerly exiled Northern Alliance President of Afghanistan and leader of Jami'at-e Islami Afghanistan, Borhanoddin Rabbani, and his aides appointed 1200 civil administration officers in the president's office alone and every one of his ministers had done the same in their ministries.[20]

ISAF and NATO Deployment

Participants as the Bonn Conference also agreed that an UN-mandated security force, which came to be known as the International Security Assistance Force (ISAF) should be deployed in Afghanistan. The United States initially blocked ISAF expansion beyond Kabul because where multi-national forces might have filled the breach; the concern among US military planners was that such a force would get in the way of American military operations. Commander of the US forces General Tommy Franks feared that international peacekeeping forces especially nation-wide might clash with local commanders useful to US forces. This was coupled with the perception of Afghans as world-renowned xenophobes and peace-keeping as a failed concept.[21] Washington insisted that International Security Assistance Force (ISAF) troop levels be held to 5000 and its presence limited to peace-keeping and service activities in Kabul and vicinity. When conflicts occurred between General Dostum and Atta Mohammad Nur in Balkh between 2002 and 2004, the then US defence secretary Donald Rumsfeld was still unwilling to allow or encourage the expansion of ISAF to other provinces arguing that no government had volunteered to man the force and citing the lack of volunteer states as a reason, but it was also true that a nation-wide security force had until then not been requested internationally. Moreover, since Rumsfeld had made his opposition to any such force known, other countries were less likely to have pushed or volunteered. The then US foreign secretary Colin Powel national security advisor Condoleezza Rice and Donald Rumsfeld later came to an agreement that the American liaison teams already working with most of the major Afghan warlords would use their influence to keep the peace among their charges. Governance, however, was not a priority and warlords were given a free hand to treat the Afghan citizenry as they pleased. [22]

The first contingent of foreign peace-keepers called the International Security Assistance Force (ISAF), with *Assistance* added on US insistence to eliminate any suggestion that international forces themselves will provide security, was put in place in 2002.[23] The presence of a small international security assistance force initially served the US and its interests, but when it later asked for a greater European and NATO involvement, the international community chose not to field a major enforcement presence to fill the security vacuum. The Pentagon's refusal to entertain a deeper overall US commitment was no doubt influenced by its already evolving plans for military action in Iraq. The US refused to take a leadership role in the civilian sphere where it would have had to organize police training, judicial reform, prison reform, and build capacity within the nascent Afghan state institutions and coordinate international aid.[24] The course was gradually corrected in the subsequent years, but the momentum had already been lost. Consequently, the period between Taliban ouster in 2001 and their comeback in 2005 was missed in terms of service delivery including security. Warlords strengthened their grip on provinces, districts and villages as well as on the capital Kabul.

Incentives to Remain Armed

At the Bonn Conference of 2001 senior government positions were distributed among the anti-Taliban Northern Alliance forces for an initial period of six months only until the Emergency *Loyah Jergah* could be held. Therefore, military power was a weapon to use in the subsequent phases of state formation to maintain, win or extract more political power. Although the Japan-funded and UN-implemented Disarmament, Demo-bilization, and Reintegra-tion (DDR) programme sought to demobilize Afghanistan's militias (or, in UN par-lance, the Afghan Military Forces, or AMF), warlords retained their core militias and better military hardware. For example, in the 2005 parliamentary elections, Jami'at-e Islami's different factions elected about 20 per cent of the MPs while General Dostum's Junbesh Melli appointed 9 per cent of the MPs. For both parties arms proved useful in campaigning which included intimidation and assassinations as militias were mobilized to bolster their political allies' campaigns, as well as their own.[25] Of a total of 200 "former military leaders, the Joint Electoral Management Body, removed the names of only 32 candidates for failing to hand in their weapons during the parliamentary elections.[26] Peer competition, the US unwillingness to intervene in local governance issues and the inability of the United Nations to provide any kind of security guarantee or keep peace provided more reasons to remain armed.

Public calls for transitional justice provided warlords with another reason to resist being undermined and to maintain and build their power-bases and networks. The disarmament programme destroyed major armies and the patronage network in defence ministry, but it failed to significantly reduce armed groups in rural areas. The challenges to the DDR process included resistance from the Afghan defence ministry, the limiting of targets to those under the defence ministry only, fear of destabilization and finally, the entrenchment of armed groups within the country's new economic and political structures.[27] This left large amounts of weaponry in the hands of individuals and groups that were seen to have the potential to reconstitute themselves at any time. The United States was complicit in sustaining militias even during the disarmament process.[28] It created major obstacles refusing to fund or support the DDR process or allow US troops to help the United Nations carry out the job and the CIA refused to divulge which of the militias were still on its payroll.[29] The disarmament that did occur was a "façade process of disarmament" that left military commanders in control of their local areas and allowed short-term stability and legitimisation at the cost of long-term negative effects due to dashed expectations.[30] The disarmament process was declared "completed" in July 2005, but the reintegration of the former combatants had not taken place. In fact, much of their reintegration was centred on reorganizing them into the new structures of the Afghan National Army and police and private security companies. By 2005 a paltry 35,000 light and 9,000 heavy weapons had been collected from more than 60,000 militiamen and large amounts of weapons were hidden by various commanders who went through the DDR process. Although by June 2006 large armies under Marshal Qaseem Fahim, General Dostum and Ismail Khan among others were disbanded, small militias continued to exist. Irregular armed groups had not been tackled at all until the Disbanding Illegal Armed Groups (DIAG) process was launched in 2005 with only partial success. The marked lack of progress by the government in the disarmament of the virtually moribund state of the DIAG process by the end of 2005 also called into question the efficacy of the results officially claimed for the DDR process before DIAG.[31] At least 2753 "illegal armed groups" numbering some 180,000 armed men were reported to exist in 2006.[32]

The need to maintain a degree of militia power grew after 2005 when the Taliban began to exert themselves with greater vigour.

Whereas in Kandahar the Taliban re-emerged in late 2003, the Taliban insurgency became more visible in the north from 2009 onwards using scattered Pashtun villages as its bases. Warlord militia groups also reappeared around the same time in Balkh with their numbers surging ahead of parliamentary elections in September 2010 and growing significantly. Atta Mohammad Nur is reported to be running at least two such militia units citing lack of security personnel as reason.[33] According to a Wall Street Journal report, the 452 militiamen affiliated with Atta Mohammad out-number the 280 policemen in Chimtal and Charbolak districts in Balkh.[34] In the south of Afghanistan, some warlords enjoy mutually beneficial relations with the US and coalition forces based on their provision to these forces of military, intelligence, security and logistics support. In Kandahar, for example, coalition forces have been working with Ahmad Wali Karzai's Kandahar Strike Force or militias of the Achekzai militia leader, Abdol Razeq. In 2010, there were reports about US forces employing Gol Agha Sherzai's militias to fight the Taliban in Kandahar. Interestingly, one report quoted a senior US military officer as saying, "There is no distinction between them and any other policemen from any other tribe or any other family."[35]

The Co-optation Strategy

Whereas the international security imperative put one kind of strain on the state-building agenda, the other problem emanated from the Afghan Government's policy of co-optation of the warlords. The political leadership in Kabul remained content as long as it was able to build and strengthen its own power networks. The Afghan leadership equated personal power with state power and used the centralization of patronage as a tool to buy often short-term allegiances at the expense of state-building. Although the technocratic core of the Kabul administration did press for a degree of successful centralization against the powerful presence of the warlords, national, regional and provincial actors focused on building their personal power networks and propped up individuals to strengthen their own positions in the capital Kabul and provinces. For example, whereas Hamed Karzai focused on building his network in the south, Marshal Fahim worked to consolidate his position in the north. Co-optation for alliances of convenience served as a tacit pact between the central government in Kabul and warlords and allowed both parties to flourish often through marriage of military interests with economic and mafia type interests. The doling out of official government positions legitimized warlord control over polities and enabled them to shield their militias and questionable activities earning the state a bad name and crippling it from within. The concept of state-building as a process whereby operations of the state and its institutions and actors are depersonalized and formalized was thus replaced by building and extending the power and influence individuals who treated the state as a set of institutions that should be captured and manipulated for personal ends. Giustozzi notes that there are documented cases in Afghanistan in which warlords entered office in an attempt to increase their power. "In June 2003, Fahim stood out as the most successful warlord vis-à-vis the state, controlling the ministry of defence with almost complete autonomy," while Ismail Khan and General Dostum "made concessions, but maintained substantial power bases."[36] Larry Goodson paints an even darker picture: "Virtually all of these warlords have used their power to enrich themselves and their followers, coming to control well over half the cash economy, with access not only to heroin trade but also to customs revenues, illegal real-estate deals, mineral wealth, timber, and road tolls."[37]

In order to entrench themselves, Afghan leaders have dispersed power to weaken resistance to their power. This has given warlords or in Rubinp's words, "competing armed groups" an incentive to maintain the status quo,[38] but the status quo is not contributing to the state-building agenda. Power-holders are using public office as a sort of pension plan due to their uncertainty as to how long they might remain in power. Rule of law does not develop and power is not depersonalized under such circumstances.[39]

Building the Afghan National Security Forces (ANSF)

Monopoly over the legitimate use of violence is a hallmark of statehood. To be able to gradually overcome centrifugal tendencies, provide the Afghan citizenry with physical security against predatory warlords and military commanders and to extend the legitimate authority of the state, coercive apparatuses are needed. Whereas warlords and individuals have grown more powerful in their own ways, progress on building Afghanistan's security forces has been dismal despite the acceleration of efforts in the past two years. In what follows, I will look at the progress on building Afghanistan's security forces.

The Afghan National Army (ANA)

The Afghan National Army (ANA) falls under the authority of defence ministry. As of March 2011, the ANA comprised 159,363 personnel. The target for the ANA is to grow to 171,000 by October 2011.[40] The ANA is structured within five. As of September 2010, of the 26 ANA corps and brigades assessed by the ISAF training teams, only 17 were assessed as effective with assistance or advisors, and nine were assessed as "dependent on coalition forces for success." None were assessed as "independent."[41]

Serious measures aimed at building the Afghan army began only in 2009 when the full force of the insurgency and the weakness of the Afghan security forces became more visible. However, The ANA continues to suffer from a number of problems. These include shortfalls in training personnel, faulty equipment, poor infrastructure and logistics, and high attrition rates. The US ambassador to Afghanistan, who previously served as the top commander of the US forces in Afghanistan, Karl Eikenberry, himself had serious doubts about the ability of the Afghan police and military forces to take over security duties in the country by 2014. "The Army's high attrition and low recruitment rates for Pashtuns in the south are crippling," he wrote. "Simply keeping the force at current levels requires tens of thousands of new recruits every year to replace attrition losses and battlefield casualties."[42] The development of the ANA has been characterized more by a focus on quantity rather than quality, and a focus on infantry training at the expense of attention to non-combat training and the development of logistics capabilities.[43] A US Department of Defence report to Congress in November 2010 acknowledged that "logistics planning remains more of a discussion topic than a tool for execution," that partnered units were heavily reliant on ISAF to control operations, and that staff members' low literacy levels hindered their ability to effectively manage staff functions and exercise command and control.[44]

The gradual handover of security responsibilities to Afghan forces—the so-called "Afghanization" of security, which seems to be both the gradual withdrawal of foreign forces and handover of the burden of fighting the insurgents from international forces to Afghan forces—began in July 2011 and is scheduled to be completed by 2014, but there is a widely-held belief that the army is not ready. The nature of training is often described as too conventional and not very effective in tackling guerrilla attacks by the Taliban and other insurgent groups.

Though much better equipped than the police, the ANA is poorly equipped and uses the former Warsaw Pact rifles. Each brigade is also equipped with eight Warsaw Pact D-30 howitzers, but about 40 per cent of them are not functional.[45] The army lacks a fully functional air force and is highly dependent on the NATO-led ISAF and coalition air support administered through the embedded training teams. Even in the capital Kabul, coalition helicopters had to intervene to bring the attack on the Intercontinental Hotel to an end.[46]

A key element in terms of the sustainability of the ANA is its composition. Information about the ethnic composition of the ANA is securely guarded, but there is a general perception that ethnic Tajiks are overrepresented. A 2009 RAND report states that while other ethnic groups such as the Hazaras and Uzbeks are underrepresented, the Tajiks are overrepresented especially in the officer and non-commissioned officer categories.[47] This is partly due to the influence on the defence ministry of the Shora-ye Nezar group of the Northern Alliance especially during the early years of the US invasion and partly due to the shortage of recruits from the eastern and southern parts of Afghanistan especially Kandahar and Zabol provinces. The feeling of exclusion from the government and the intimidation of the families of soldiers by the Taliban and other insurgent groups are some of the factors for fewer Pashtun recruits. This gives rise to the possibility of inter-ethnic conflict and disintegration of the army once foreign forces withdraw from Afghanistan especially because many in the officer rank are believed to be affiliated with different Afghan factions pursuing different political and military interests.

The Afghan National Police (ANP)

After many problems with the German effort to build the Afghan police, which falls under the authority of the interior ministry, the United States began playing a greater role in support of the police forces in 2003. Germany continued to train Afghan police forces, but in 2005 the US assistance surpassed that of Germany despite the latter being the lead donor. Germany was replaced in 2007 by EUPOL which provided some support to the police, but EUPOL has a small presence in the country and thus a limited impact. As of March 2011, the ANP counted 125,589 police in its ranks with the expectation that this number would grow to 134,000 by October 2011.[48]

The model used to build the ANP until 2009 rested on "recruit-assign-intend to train" strategy. This meant that a new policeman was recruited and assigned to a police district with the intention to train him at some future point. As a result, there are now "several tens of thousands" of police who have still not received even the most basic training.[49] Those who were trained were put through a programme that was heavily focused on military skills, with just one week out of eight devoted to the basic civilian policing functions of investigating crimes and upholding the rule of law. Despite some improvements, the focus has remained on training policemen as fighters against the insurgents and not civil officers conducting community police work. In fact, it is the police which is often attacked by the Taliban and other insurgent groups or which takes on these groups militarily. It is for this reason that the casualties among the police are far higher than among the army. As noted in the chapters on Kandahar and Balkh, sections of the police also remain loyal to former and current warlords and armed commanders and often work to serve their group or factional interests. As such, the police are often regarded by the people as predatory armed men rather than trusted law enforcement officials.

US and Government-funded Militias

A number of "self-defence" initiatives, which are basically the creation of new local militia units, have also, at places, complicated law enforcement and the counterinsurgency campaign. These militias, which do not directly fall under either defence or interior ministry, are armed by the government and the United States to present the first layer of resistance against the insurgents, but the units are often former militias which reportedly engage in predatory actions against villagers, settling scores with former rivals and enemies and harassing members of the public. They are often commanded by the same former militia commanders who were arguably disarmed. Due to their own vested interests and affiliations, they often provide wrong information against their rivals to the army and the US or ISAF forces. The subsequent raids, especially night raids, then result in civilian casualties and resentment among the populations especially in the south and east of the country which bear the brunt of the war. In June 2011, there were reports that the United States wanted to triple the size of these local armed groups.[50]

Despite recent steps to develop the numbers and capabilities of the Afghan security forces, these forces have remained weak, unprofessional, largely unaccountable and, more importantly, unmotivated. When Hamed Karzai describes the Taliban as "disenchanted brothers," Afghan security forces naturally ask themselves who they are fighting and why if their president does not regard the insurgents as enemies. The Afghan army and police ranks are also sometimes infiltrated by Taliban and other insurgent groups who then often kill foreign trainers or fellow soldiers or policemen. In view of the growing insecurity and targeted assassinations of key politico-military personalities, there are serious concerns regarding the capability, professionalism and accountability of the Afghan security forces. A clear reporting mechanism against the excesses and violations by the security forces is missing and despite the emphasis on the casualties caused by the insurgent groups, the government does not even count casualties caused by the Afghan security forces.

The size of the army and police may also present a major problem if US military aid is withdrawn. Internal revenues barely cover the nondefense expenses such as the civil service salaries. It is unclear how Afghanistan will sustain even the current levels of forces if foreign aid is withdrawn or reduced. The Afghan state is now well advanced along an unsustainable trajectory. The Afghan army and police depend for their salaries and equipment on supplemental appropriations of the US Congress, which cannot be projected from year to year. Internal licit GDP revenues, about 7 per cent in 2009,[51] do not cover even the recurrent nondefense costs and the parallel government created by international donors and aid agencies with expenditures outside government controlled mechanisms generates a "tsunami of corruption" according to Rubin.[52]

Inadequate Results

Afghanistan was initially conceived by the United States as essentially a military operation. Little thought was given in this Pentagon directed mission to a political vision or imagination for the post-Taliban Afghanistan beyond conceding to others the responsibility for pressing Afghan political figures to agree on an interim government and raising international aid donor interest. As the Afghan and foreign actors failed to align themselves around a common set of objectives culminating in the formation of a strong state and each actor pursued their own interests, subsequent developments perpetuated the same state weakness that the international intervention aimed or should have addressed. While the United States and its allies pursued a narrow security agenda, the Afghan leadership failed to act in ways that would have enabled it to underwrite their social contract with the Afghan citizenry.

Because they were in a position of power, the initial phase of post-Taliban state-building placed a heavy and unmet burden on international actors to work with the Afghan players on a unified strategy and secure the division of labour and mechanisms of accountability. It was necessary to take stock of and map the interest groups to identify the forces that would resist the creation of a sustainable state.[53] Although the political change in Afghanistan after the Taliban delegitimized association with militias and armed groups and, to some extent, forced commanders of medium to large militias to publicly distance themselves from their military past, they maintained their influence and connections over their core militias and continue to play dominant roles. The initial compromise with the warlords for stability not only blocked a rapid consolidation of the state but also resulted in public disenchantment and gradual loss of momentum and legitimacy. The subsequent electoral processes and international support for the Government of Afghanistan failed to strengthen this fast eroding legitimacy because legitimacy comes from the people. Crisis deepened further when both presidential and parliamentary elections of 2009 and 2010 were marred by allegations of fraud. At any rate, legitimacy is not a one-time event conferred through elections or the establishment of a charismatic authority. It is rather an ongoing process of deepening and broadening the rights and obligations of citizenship.[54] Through the "contract industry" especially in the south of Afghanistan, US and coalition forces poured millions of dollars into the pockets of the very same elements (militias and even the Taliban indirectly) that the state-building agenda should have undermined. Governance and institution-building including the rebuilding of the Afghan security forces and strengthening an independent bureaucracy with its own motivations and professional cadre came a paltry second however.

Conclusion

The discussion on post-Taliban state-building in Afghanistan must revert to the pre-Taliban state weakness or state failure which triggered an international military response. From the beginning of its invasion of Afghanistan in 2001, the United States has been involved in attempts to further the aims of two overarching and contradictory agendas: the Global War on Terror and state-building in Afghanistan. Reconciling these two agendas has been problematic at best. The state-building agenda, which should have gradually built the infrastructural power and resources of state institutions, however, was undermined by the short-term stability in Afghanistan and international security imperatives. These imperatives placed a number of limitations on the ability of the central government in Kabul and forced it to co-opt warlords due to its own weakness and absence of a robust international force to control centrifugal tendencies and consolidate fragmented authority. This coupled with patronage politics resulted in the continuation of warlordism, emergence of personality-dependent governance and perpetuation of state weakness.

Today, Afghanistan is a double failure of both the Afghan leadership and of the international community. The official policy of the international community is to strengthen official governance institutions, but is has simultaneously strengthened and enabled those forces which undermine and manipulate formal government. The Afghan Government is defined by the role of individual power-holders and not of the enduring state institutions that inspire public confidence. Afghanistan remains dependent on international financial and military aid and continues to suffer from weak state institutions incapable of providing economic and physical security to the population. Addressing these issues requires a strategy that takes account of the entirety of these issues and integrates scattered and contradictory efforts at state-building. The dominant security strategy must now be enveloped in a wider political strategy. There is a need for political imagination which goes beyond reconciliation with the Taliban and other insurgent groups. The political imagination should produce solid state institutions with which ordinary Afghans identify themselves. Identification can be made if stake-holders are produced and if stakes are significantly high for the future of the people to rise and defend. Although the majority of Afghans do not want the Taliban to rule them again, the US security imperative and the narrative of war on terror will not give Afghans a stake nor will a political order legitimizing the power of personalities that Afghans believe are part of the problem.

Notes and References

1. The World Bank, *The State in a Changing World*, vol. 1. (New York: Oxford University Press, 1997), 278.
2. See for example, Stephen D. Krasner and Carlos Pascual, "Addressing State Failure," *Foreign Affairs*, 84 (July/August 2005); Francis Fukuyama, *State-Building: Governance and World Order in the 21st Century* (New York: Cornell University Press, 2004); Ashraf Ghani and Clare Lockhart, *Fixing Failed States: A Framework for Rebuilding a Fractured World* (New York: Oxford University Press, 2008).
3. Ghani and Lockhart, *Fixing Failed States*, 4.
4. *The National Security Strategy*. September 2002. http://georgewbushwhitehouse.archives.gov/nsc/nss/2002/.
5. Ghani and Lockhart, *Fixing Failed States*, 159.
6. David Chandler, *Empire in Denial: The Politics of State-building* (London: Pluto, 2006), 1.
7. State weakness, failure and collapse have been defined in a number of ways which are often overlapping and controversial. A state can be defined as weak when it lacks the "capacities to penetrate society, regulate social relationships, extract resources, and appropriate or use resources in determined ways." See Joel S. Migdal, Strong *Societies and Weak States: State-society Relations and State Capabilities in the Third World* (Princeton, NJ: Princeton University Press, 1988), 4. Where these capacities are high states are, in Mann's terms, possessed of "infrastructural power." See Michael Mann, *The Sources of Social Power. A History of Power from Beginning to AD 1760*, vol. 1 (Cambridge: Cambridge University Press, 1986), chapter 14. Weak states, which lack this infrastructural power, are rather based on despotic power as state officials centralize, or try to centralize, decision-making rather than embed it in society. See Aidan Hehir and Neil Robinson (eds.), *State-Building: Theory and Practice* (London and NY: Routledge, 2007), 4. State failure, on the other hand, is difficult to define authoritatively and the distinctions drawn by scholars between state weakness and failure are controversial at best because the difference between a weak state and a failed state can be eroded by time and practice. The Crisis State Research Centre defines state failure as: "a condition of "state collapse"—e.g., a state that can no longer perform its basic security, and development functions and that has no effective control over its territory and borders. In a failed state "the structure, authority (legitimate power), law and political order have fallen apart and must be reconstituted in some form, old or new." See William I. Zartman, "Introduction: Posing the Problem of State

Collapse," in *Collapsed States. The Disintegration and Restoration of Legitimate Authority*, I.W. Zartman, (ed.) (Boulder, CO: Lynne Reiner, 1995), 1. Robert Rotberg notes that in failed states "ruling cadres increasingly oppress, extort, and harass the majority of their own compatriots while privileging a more narrowly based party, clan, or sect." See Robert I. Rotberg (ed.), *State Failure and State Weakness in a Time of Terror* (Brookings Institution Press, 2003), 6.
Armstrong and Rubin conceptualizes state failure as "the transformation of public power into privately held and often fragmented power" although "sometimes individuals within a regime fragment and disperse power to weaken resistance to their regime and entrench themselves." See Andrea Armstrong and Barnett R. Rubin, "The Great Lakes and South Central Asia," in *Making States Work: State Failure and the Crisis of Governance*, Simon Chesterman, Michael Ignatieff and Ramesh Chandra Thakur (eds.) (Tokyo: United Nations University Press, 2005), 83. At the other spectrum, commentators like John Warnock are of the view that the concepts of "rogue" and "failed" states in the British and American foreign policy have served as instrumental tools to intervene in the internal affairs of weaker countries unilaterally for self-serving purposes through regional organizations such as NATO and international organizations such as the United Nations. See John W. Warnock, *Creating a Failed State: The US and Canada in Afghanistan* (Winnipeg: Fernwood Publishing, 2008), 22-23. From Warnock's point of view, a "successful" state in the eyes of western powers would be one with a "liberal democratic government, a high standard of living and a free market economy, and is more or less aligned with the United States" (4). A collapsed state is a "rare and extreme version of a failed state" where "the structure, authority (legitimate power), law and political order have fallen apart and must be reconstituted in some form, old or new." See Zartman, "Posing the Problem of State Collapse," 1.

8. By post-Taliban, I do not imply that the Taliban are no longer relevant. I use the expression to refer to the political process initiated after the collapse of the Taliban regime.
9. The only difference is that the Japanese attack on 7 December 1941 was not on the mainland USA whereas the 9/11 attacks targeted the heart of New York City.
10. "Karzai should answer the nation," *Arman-e Melli*, Kabul, 7 June 2010.
11. The Brookings Institution, *Memo to the President: expand the agenda in Pakistan*, Washington D. C., 18 December 2008. http://www.brookings.edu/~/media/Files/events/2008/1218_transition/20081218_afghanistan_pakistan.pdf (accessed on 30 January 2010).

12. *RAF flies Northern Alliance representatives to Bonn*, November 26, 2001. http://webarchive.nationalarchives.gov.uk/+/http://www.operations.mod.uk/veritas/bonn_flight.htm (accessed on August 22, 2011).
13. James Dobbins, *After the Taliban: Nation-building in Afghanistan* (Washington D.C.: Potomac Books, 2008), 8.
14. Agreement on Provisional Arrangements in Afghanistan Pending the Re-Establishment of Permanent Government Institutions, 2001, available on the website of the United Nations Assistance Mission in Afghanistan (UNAMA), http://unama.unmissions.org/Portals/UNAMA/Documents/Bonn-agreement.pdf.
15. Dobbins, *After the Taliban*, 120.
16. Matt Waldman, *Falling Short: Aid Effectiveness in Afghanistan*, Oxfam International Afghanistan, March 2008.
17. Rubin Barnett, "Crafting a Constitution for Afghanistan," *Journal of Democracy*, 15/3 (2004), 5-19.
18. Amin Saikal, "Afghanistan's Weak State and Strong Society," in Chesterman, Ignatieff and Thakur (eds.), *Making States Work*.
19. Saikal, "Afghanistan's Weak State and Strong Society," in Chesterman, Ignatieff and Thakur (eds.), *Making States Work*, 201.
20. The Brookings Institution, *Memo to the President*.
21. Dobbins, *After the Taliban*, 125.
22. Dobbins, *After the Taliban*, 131.
23. Dobbins, *After the Taliban*, 102.
24. Dobbins, *After the Taliban*, 126.
25. Antonio Giustozzi, *Empires of Mud: Wars and Warlords of Afghanistan* (London: Hurst, 2009), 93.
26. Giustozzi, *Empires of Mud*, 92.
27. Sarah Lister, *Understanding State-Building and Local Government in Afghanistan* (London: Crisis States Research Centre, 2007).
28. International Crisis Group, "Afghanistan: Getting Disarmament Back on Track," *Asia Briefing* 35, Kabul/Brussels (23 February 2005).
29. Ahmed Rashid, *Decent into Chaos: The United States and the Failure of Nation Building in Pakistan, Afghanistan, and Central Asia* (New York: Viking, 2008), 84-86, 209.
30. David H. Ucko and Mats Berdal, *Reintegrating Armed Groups After Conflict: Politics, Violence and Transition* (Abingdon: Routledge, 2009).
31. International Crisis Group, "Afghanistan: Getting Disarmament Back on Track", 23 February 2005.
32. Giustozzi, *Empires of Mud*, 91.
33. Maria Abi-Habib, *Ethnic Militias Fuel Tensions in Northern Afghanistan, The Wall Street Journal*, 21 April 2011. http://

online.wsj.com/article/SB10001424052748704530204 57623205337 5098340.html (accessed on 30 August 2011).

34. Abi-Habib, *Wall Street Journal.*
35. Claire Truscott, "US enlists ex-warlord's men for Afghan police force," AFP, 14 June 2010. http://www.google.com/hostednews/afp/article/ALeqM5hWycXw_iOQqgsY8g3djRtNcLfWtw (accessed on 18 May 2011).
36. Antonio Giustozzi, *Respectable warlords? The politics of state-building in post-Taliban Afghanistan,* Working Paper 33 (London: Crisis States Research Centre, 2003), 4.
37. Larry Goodson, "Building Democracy After Conflict: Bullets, Ballots, and Poppies in Afghanistan," *Journal of Democracy,* 16/1 (January 2005), 24-38.
38. Armstrong and Rubin, "The Great Lakes and South Central Asia," Chesterman, Ignatieff and Thakur (eds.), *Making States Work*, 83.
39. Neil Robinson, "State-building and International Politics: the emergence of a 'new' problem and agenda," in Hehir and Robinson (eds.), *State-Building*, 4.
40. US Department of Defense, *Report on Progress Towards Security and Stability in Afghanistan and United States Plan for Sustaining the Afghanistan National Security Forces* (April 2011), 13.
41. US Department of Defense, *Report on Progress Towards Security and Stability*, 31.
42. Eric Schmitt, "U.S. Envoy's Cables Show Worries on Afghan Plans," The New York Times, available at: http://www.nytimes.com/2010/01/26/world/asia/26strategy.html?hp, (accessed on 26 May 2011).
43. US Department of Defense, *Report on Progress Towards Security and Stability*, 30.
44. US Department of Defense, *Report on Progress Towards Security and Stability*, 30.
45. Obaid Younossi, Peter Thruelsen Dahl, Jonathan Vaccaro, Jerry M. Sollinger, and Brian Grady, *The Long March: Building an Afghan National Army,* National Defense Research Institute (RAND) (Santa Monica: CA, 2009), 23.
46. BBC News, "Kabul's Intercontinental Hotel attacked by gunmen," 29 June 2011, http://www.bbc.co.uk/news/world-south-asia-13947169, (accessed on 3 October 2011).
47. Younossi et al, *The Long March*, 21, 57.
48. US Department of Defense, *Report on Progress Towards Security and Stability*, 13.
49. Inspector General, US Department of Defense, *Assessment of US Government Efforts to Train, Equip, and Mentor the Expanded Afghan National Police*, Report No. SPO-2011-003 (2011), 1.

50. Jim Michaels, "Measure lets size of Afghan militias triple," *Army Times*, 29 June 2011. http://www.armytimes.com/news/2011/06/gannett-afghanistan-militias-may-triple-in-size-062911 (accessed on 7 August 2011).
51. Barnett R. Rubin, "The Transformation of the Afghan State," in *The Future of Afghanistan*, J. Alexander Their (ed.) (Washington: United States Institute of Peace 2009), 17.
52. Rubin, "The Transformation of the Afghan State," Their (ed.), *The Future of Afghanistan*, 18.
53. Ghani and Lockhart, *Fixing Failed States*, 177.
54. Ghani and Lockhart, *Fixing Failed States*, 8.

10

International and Regional Contributions to Afghan Reconstruction

Gulshan Sachdeva

Ahmad Shah Durrani founded Afghanistan in 1747. The country served as a buffer in "The Great Game" between the British and the Russian empires in the late nineteenth century. Following the third Ango-Afghan war, the country regained independence from the notional British control. Beginning from 1933, King Zahir Shah ruled the country till 1973 when he was overthrown in a bloodless coup. The Soviet Union invaded in 1979 to support Afghan communist regime. As part of the cold war strategy, the United States started funding various factions of anti-communist mujahedeens, who all shared conservative Islamic ideology. Pakistan and Saudi Arabia provided further logistic and financial support to these groups.

After the Soviet withdrawal in early 1989, the Nazibullah regime was able to last a few more years till 1992. In 1992, different mujahedeen groups established the Islamic Republic of Afghanistan with the introduction of rotating presidency. Between 1992 and 1996 Afghanistan saw one of the worst periods in its history. Different parts of the country were controlled by different warlords. During this period, much of the infrastructure in Afghanistan was destroyed. In this chaotic situation, a new Taliban movement emerged in the south, seizing control first of Kandahar and surrounding areas and later Kabul in 1996. The Taliban had strong backing from the Inter Services Intelligence (ISI), Pakistan's intelligence agency, which assisted in recruitment, provided weapons, training and technical assistance. In the beginning Taliban were well received and quickly they established new political and social order in the country. The world was horrified when it learned the way Taliban were treating the women and minorities. In 2001, they also destroyed sixth century monumental statues of standing Buddha at Bamyan because they declared that statues were against the tenets of Islam. However, Afghanistan was still a forgotten place for most western countries as their larger strategic objective of defeating Soviets was achieved. Still, some of the regional countries (India, Iran, Russia and Tajikistan) were helping the Northern Alliance which was fighting the Taliban regime in Afghanistan. These regional countries had better understanding of the dangers of Taliban than many western capitals. The US became active only when Taliban's links to Osama Bin Laden became clear. Finally, when 11 September 2001 happened President Bush delivered an ultimatum to Taliban to extradite Osama. Later, at a press conference in Pakistan, Taliban ambassador to Pakistan asked proof and refused to extradite Osama to the US. Consequently, on 7 October 2001, Operation Enduring Freedom was launched with the initial objectives of (a) destruction of terrorist training camps and infrastructure within Afghanistan; (b) capturing of Al-Qaeda leaders; and (c) cessation of terrorist activities in Afghanistan. Initially, the US and the UK led the aerial bombing campaign, with ground forces supplied primarily by the Northern Alliance. In 2002, US, British and Canadian infantry along with some special forces from other allied nations also joined the Afghan war effort.

After the fall of the Taliban, all Afghan factions who were opposed to Taliban met in Bonn in December 2001. The meeting was sponsored by the United Nations. Decades of war, followed by the Taliban regime, had already destroyed the core institutions of Afghan state. The heavily war torn economy faced high levels of absolute poverty, ill health, large scale illiteracy and complete marginalization of the female population. In addition, millions of Afghans had left the country and became refugees mainly in the neighbouring countries. The Bonn Agreement charted the roadmap for the political transformation of the county into a democratic state. The UN Security Council endorsed the agreement through its resolution 1383. Under the leadership of Hamid Karzai, a Transitional Administration was established to guide the process of transformation. The interim administration derived its authority through the Loya Jirgha (Grand Council) convened by former Afghan king Zahir Shah. In early 2002, international donors gathered in Tokyo and pledged about \$4.5 billion for the reconstruction efforts in Afghanistan. In March 2002, the UN also established the UN Assistance Mission in Afghanistan (UNAMA). The constitutional Loya Jirgha adopted a new constitution in January 2004, with the presidential form of government. In April 2004 in Berlin, 23 donor nations pledged a total of $8.2 bn. aid to Afghanistan over three years. Under the new constitution, presidential elections were held in October 2004 and parliamentary elections in September 2005. More than 75 per cent voters participated in the presidential election and a significant number of women to the National Assembly were elected. The constitution also established legal protection for private property and it was presumed that economic development in the country will be based mainly on the market economy. These were remarkable achievements for a country destroyed by decades of war. Once these landmarks were achieved, international community and the Afghanistan Government agreed on the Afghanistan Compact at the London Conference in 2005. The compact set ambitious targets for security, governance, development, regional cooperation and counter narcotics. While reviewing the Afghanistan Compact, at another international conference on Afghanistan in Paris in June 2008, international community made further commitments for the next five years. Despite serious difficulties, the process of second presidential and parliamentary elections was completed in 2009 and 2010 respectively.

International Community and Reconstruction

In the last three decades, Afghanistan has witnessed diverse projects of nation building and socio-political transformation. The current international project of building democracy and market economy is mandated by the United Nations and being implemented mainly by the western alliance led by the United States. More than 70 nations have committed over US$ 70 billion for Afghan reconstruction. As of December 2009, the United States had pledged US$ 51 billion, out of which $ 22 billion had already been disbursed by February 2009. More than 50 per cent of this aid had gone into building Afghan National Army and Afghan National Police. Other commitments are in the areas of economic and social development, governance, counter narcotics and support to many civil society activities. Apart from this, the number of US troops serving in Afghanistan touched 100,000 in November 2010.

Next major commitment to Afghanistan is from Europe. Individual member states of the European Union (EU) and the European Commission are making significant contribution to security and justice reforms, development and reconstruction, counter narcotics and regional cooperation activities in Afghanistan. EU has also deployed a police mission. Together they have committed around EUR 8 billion (around $11.5 bn) for reconstruction activities. Besides, 25 out of 27 EU nations are participating in NATO-led ISAF mission with around 30,000 troops. Their military involvement in Afghanistan has been controversial at times because of limits of their deployment and "national caveats" on many of their troops. Many EU nations committed themselves thinking that it would mainly be a peacekeeping and reconstruction effort rather than a project of "War on Terror" in which they have to engage with the resurgent Taliban. There have also been problems of coordination with other international partners as well as within the EU nations themselves. On reconstruction, the UK has spent over 740 million pounds (around $1175 million) in the last eight years and have committed to more than 510 million ($810 mn) over the next four years. Germany has also increased its funding in 2008-09 and by 2010, it is likely to have made available resources worth some EUR 1.2 billion ($1.72 bn).

From Asia, Japan has pledged around $1.8 bn. to Afghanistan including reconstruction ($ 919 mn.), security involvement ($212 mn.) and governance ($ 247 mn.). Together with the UN, Japan is a lead nation in Disarmament, Demoblisation and Reintegartion (DDR) and also involved in construction of Kabul-Kandahar highway and Kabul international airport terminal. After the collapse of the Taliban, Chinese authorities showed relatively little interest in Afghanistan's reconstruction. According to the Chinese Government sources, China has provided more than 900 million yuan ($US 132 million) grants to Afghanistan. It remained disengaged in the country until Afghan administration opened its energy, mineral and raw material to foreign investors. With large investment commitment of about $ 3 billion in copper mines, it is becoming clear that China will be more involved in Afghanistan than hitherto.

India's Role in Afghan Reconstruction

With broad understanding that peaceful and stable Afghanistan is crucial for regional stability, India has been playing an active role in the reconstruction since 2002. So far it has pledged assistance worth about $1.3 billion, with projects covering the whole of country mainly in the areas of road construction, power transmission lines, hydro electricity, agriculture, telecommunication, education, health and capacity building. Details of these projects can be classified under three major heads:

Infrastructure Projects

One of the major infrastructural projects completed by India is construction of 218 km Zaranj-Delaram road project in the southwestern Afghanistan. This road has a strategic significance for India as it is going to facilitate movement of goods and services from Afghanistan to the Iranian border and, onward, to the Chahbahar Port. This road, together with 60 km of inner-city roads in Zaranj and Gurguri, was completed in January 2009 at a cost of US $150 million. During construction 6 Indians and 179 Afghans lost their lives due to insurgent attacks. Another major project, which was completed in 2009 was construction of 220kV DC transmission line from Pul-e-Khumri to Kabul and a 220/110/20 kV sub-station at Chimtala. Built at the cost of $120 million, this line has facilitated almost 24 hour power supply from the northern grid to Kabul city. Further, Indian engineers will also be setting up of additional 220/20 kV sub stations at Charikar and Doshi along the Pule-e-khumri Kabul transmission line. With the Indian help, construction and commissioning of $ 184 million, 42 MW Salma Dam power project on Hari Rud River in Herat province is also going to be completed in by the end of 2010. At the cost of $180 million, Indian Government is also going to construct Afghan parliament building by 2011. It has also restored telecommunication infrastructure in 11 provinces and expanded national TV network by providing an uplink from Kabul and downlinks in all 34 provincial capitals. Earlier, it also supplied vehicles (400 buses and 200 mini-buses for mass urban transportation, 105 utility vehicles for municipalities) and 3 airbus aircrafts and spares to Ariana Afghan Airlines. The Indian Government also supplied equipment for three sub stations in Faryab province and for 125 km transmission line from Andhkhoi to Maimana plus rehabilitated Amir Ghazi and Quargah reservoir dam. It further helped in restoration/ revamping of information set up, including setting up of Azadi (Freedom) printing press. Other infrastructure projects include solar electrification of 100 villages; construction of 5000MT cold storage in Kandahar; establishment of modern TV studio and 1000W TV transmitter in Jalalabad; setting up of a mobile TV satellite uplink and five TV relay centers in Nangarhar; digging 26 tube wells in 6 north-west provinces; drilling of 24 deep wells in Herat; planned construction of Radio television Afghanistan (RTA) building in Jalalabad and leasing of slot on Indian satellite INSAT3A for RTA telecast since 2004.

Humanitarian Assistance

The Indian Government is providing a daily supply of 100 grams of fortified, high-protein biscuits to nearly 1.2 million children under a School Feeding Program. This programme is administered through the World Food Programme and will cost $ 460 million when completed in 2012. It has also reconstructed Indira Gandhi Institute of Child Health in Kabul and is providing free medical consultation and medicines through 5 Indian medical missions in Kabul, Kandahar, Jalalabad, Heart and Mazar-e-Shrif to over 300,000 patients annually. Apart from supplying blankets, tents, medicines, vegetable seeds, etc. during 2002-2004, the Indian Government also announced gift of 250,000 metric tonnes of wheat in 2009.

Education and Capacity Development

India is playing an important role in this field through provision of 675 long-term university scholarships annually. These fellowships are sponsored by the Indian Council for Cultural Relations for undergraduate and postgraduate studies in India. In addition, 675 annual slots for short term technical training courses are provided every year since 2006. At the January 2010 London Conference, Indian External Affairs Minister announced further 200 graduate and 100 post graduate/PhD fellowships for 5 years in the field of agriculture and related fields. In 2005, the Habibia School in Kabul was reconstructed by India and about 9000 educational kits to students of this school were provided. Further, it provided 20,000 school desks to the Ministry of Education and laboratory equipments and sports goods to schools in Nimroz as well as teacher training and books to Kandahar and Khost Universities. In cooperation with the UNDP, the Indian Government is also deputing 30 Indian civil servants as coaches and mentors annually under the Capacity for Afghan Public Administration programme since 2007. It has also provided services of Indian banking experts to Da Afghan Bank and Millie Bank; Indian English teachers in 5 cities; vocational training to 1000 Afghans (through the Confederation of Indian Industries); Women's Vocational Training Centre in Baghe-Zanana for training of 1000 Afghan women;

computer training centres, and established Hindi and English departments at Nangarhar university. Special training courses have also been provided to more than Afghan diplomats, dozens of civilian officials, police officers, teachers, and doctors and paramedics. In addition, Indian institutions are also providing training to Afghans in various fields through training programmes organized by many international agencies independently.

With the help of the Indian Government, nearly 100 small development projects in the areas of agriculture, public health, rural development, education are also under different stages of implementation in 19 provinces of Afghanistan since 2007. In 2002, India also contributed $10 million to Afghan Government budget and has also been contributing to the Afghan Reconstruction Trust Fund regularly since 2002. In 2005-06, it also provided 150 trucks, 15 ambulances, 120 jeeps, bullet proof jackets, bullet proof helmets, laser aim points, mine detectors, winter clothing, medicines, etc., to Afghan National Army. It also helped setting up of Common Facilities Service Centre and Tool Room at Pule-e-Charkhi Industrial Park and trained 5000 self help groups in Balakh.

Positive Impact

It seems that the population of Afghanistan has very positive perception of Indian activities in the country. This fact has been brought out by many opinion polls. In the latest nationwide survey conducted by the BBC, ABC News and German news agency ARD in December 2009, 71 per cent of Afghan population had favourable opinion about India. Corresponding figure for the US, UK and Iran and Germany was 51 per cent, 39 per cent, 40 per cent and 59 per cent respectively. Similarly, 44 per cent Afghans think that India is playing a neutral role and 36 per cent think it is playing a positive role. India is also very popular among ordinary Afghans because of Indian films and serials, which are shown on different TV channels every day.

Involvement of China, Iran and Russia in Afghan Reconstruction

China condemned Soviet intervention in Afghanistan and later cooperated with the US in arming Afghan mujahedeen groups against Soviet occupation. After the collapse of the Taliban, Chinese authorities showed relatively little interest in Afghanistan's reconstruction. According to Chinese Government sources, China has provided more than 900 million yuan ($US 132 million) grants to Afghanistan. Main projects include Jomhuri hospital, and Parwan irrigation project and training for about 500 Afghan officials in diplomacy, trade, finance, agriculture, counter-narcotics, etc. It remained disengaged in the country until Afghan administration opened its energy, mineral and raw material to foreign investors. In November 2007, the Metallurgical Construction Corporation of China (MCC) and Jiangxi Copper Limited (JCC) consortium was selected as a preferred bidder for the Aynak copper mine project by the Afgahnistan Ministry of Mines. In 2008, Afghan cabinet approved the project. Aynak copper deposit, a 28 sq. km field is in Logar province, some 60 km southeast of Kabul. This is the second largest copper mine in the world. According to the Afghanistan Investment Support Agency, MCC plans to invest 2.9 billion in the project with investment reaching to five billion in the future. MCC will pay $400 million annually to the Afghan Government to operate the mine. MCC will also pay $ 800 million Afghanistan Government as assurance to start extracting of the copper mine. MCC has also agreed to build a 400 MW Power station that will be used both for the mine and for the residents of Kabul. MCC will excavate the coal mine deposits in the area for its energy resource and is committed to build a railway line from Logar Province to one of Afghanistan's borders to facilitate the export of copper abroad. It is expected that this large investment including subprojects will create direct and indirect employment opportunities for 15000 people. Based on the facts from Ministry of Mines, Aynak copper mine is believed to contain almost 20 million tones of copper. The construction period of this project is 5 years with the production period of 30 years. There has been allegations that $30 million bribe was paid to award this contract. However, Minister of Mines rejected all bribery allegations and said that MCC bid was the strongest bid for the project. In March 2009, at the special conference on Afghanistan, organized under the auspices of the Shanghai Cooperation Organization, members "stressed the importance of concerted and combined efforts in the region to counter terrorism, illicit narcotics and organized crime, in particular coordination and cooperation of Afghanistan and its neighbours."

In recent years, the Chinese have begun to understand that as a major power, China has to take some major responsibilities in Afghanistan. Broadly three views of Chinese involvement have emerged. The first view is that China should stop seeing it as an exclusive American problem as it has long term security implications for China. Second, a more cautious view indicates many negative consequences for its involvement in Afghan problem. A third view suggests instead of regular army China may send police and paramilitary forces into Afghanistan. Whatever position Chinese Government takes in future it is becoming clear that there will be greater involvement in Afghanistan than hitherto.

Similarly, Iran has spent about $300 in Afghan reconstruction mainly in infrastructure and capacity building. Pakistan has also committed about $300 million to reconstruction efforts in Afghanistan. Russia has also made settlement of Afghanistan's debt to former USSR which according to some Russian expert estimates totals to $10 billion.

Signs of Economic Revival

According to the Afghanistan National Development Strategy (ANDS) more than 5 million Afghan refugees have returned home since 2002. The number of school going children has grown from under one million in 2001 to about 6 million in 2008 (one third of them are girls). The number of teachers has increased seven fold to 142,500, which include 40,000 female teachers. In the health and nutrition sector, more than US$1 billion has been invested in the last five years. As a result, the percentage of people living in areas where basic health care facilities are made available has increased from 9 per cent in 2002 to 85 per cent in 2008. The infant mortality rate has been reduced by 26 per cent in five years. 76 per cent of children under the age of five have been immunized against childhood diseases. Between 2002 and 2008, there has been 38 per cent reduction in child mortality and 40 per cent in maternal mortality. As a result, the lives of approximately 500,000 children have been saved since 2003.

It is remarkable that despite a difficult legacy, the macroeconomic stability in Afghanistan has been maintained with high growth rates. Till 2007, inflation remained reasonably low and exchange rate has been stable. More than a dozen private commercial banks, four private airlines and 13 microfinance institutions are operating successfully. About 150 cities across Afghanistan now have access to mobile phone networks and internet provider services. Many multinationals which include Coca Cola, Siemens, Nestle and Etisalat are already in Afghanistan. Today over 12 million Afghans have access to telecommunication services, compared to 20,000 in 2001. The process of constructing a 3,200-kilometer optical-fiber network connecting major provincial capitals with one another and also with neighbouring countries is almost complete. Broadly free and privately owned media sector has developed. Presently Afghanistan has seven national TV stations (out of which six are private), numerous radio networks, plus a diverse and increasingly professional print media. According to government sources about 12,000 kilometres of roads have been rehabilitated, improved, or built. This includes the 2200 km long ring road which connects all major town of Afghanistan, national highways, provincial roads and rural roads. A sum of more than US$ 2 billion has been spent on roads. All these projects are implemented in difficult security situations.

Control of Opium Cultivation

The opium production continues to be a serious problem in Afghanistan although 2008 and 2009 opium surveys by the United Nations Office of Drugs and Crime (UNODC) have shown that there has been some moderate decline. In 2008 it was shown that 98 per cent of the total cultivation was confined to seven provinces with serious security problems. Five out of these provinces were in the south and two in the west of Afghanistan. The seven provinces that contributed to 98 per cent of Afghan opium cultivation and production in 2008 were Hilmand, Kandahar, Uruzgan, Daykundi, Zabul, Farah and Nimroz, clearly showing strong linkages between opium production and security situation. Opium cultivation in Afghanistan has decreased by 22 per cent, from 157,000 hectares (ha) in 2008 to 123,000 ha in 2009. In 2008, Hilmand remained the single largest opium cultivating province where 66 per cent of total Afghan cultivation was done. In 2009 cultivation declined by a third, to less than 70,000 ha. in Hilmand. The 2009 survey also shows that compared to 13 in 2007 and 18 in 2008, 20 provinces (out of 34) were poppy cultivation free. All the seven provinces in the northern region are poppy free in almost a decade. The UNODC survey rightly asserts that "controlling drugs in Afghanistan will not solve all of the country's problems, but the country's problems cannot be solved without controlling drugs." It has been clearly shown by many studies that drug money has significantly contributed to corruption and poppy money is used by the Taliban to fund insurgency.

Importance of Afghanistan for India and the Region

Strategic location of Afghanistan will always be important for India, particularly in the context of difficult India-Pakistan relations. However, importance of Afghanistan for India is much bigger than normally perceived in this narrow context. Once Afghanistan becomes stable, trade through Pakistan and Afghanistan could also alter India's continental trade. By 2015, India's trade with Europe, CIS plus Iran, Afghanistan and Pakistan would be in the range of US$ 500 to 600 billion annually. Even if 20 per cent of this trade is conducted through road, US$ 100-120 billion of Indian trade would be passing through Afghanistan and Central Asia. With improvement in India-Pakistan relations, an important portion of Indian trade (particularly from the landlocked northern states including Jammu & Kashmir) will be moving through Pakistan and Afghanistan. With the possibility of this trade passing through Afghanistan and Central Asia, most of the infrastructural projects in the region will become economically viable. These linkages will also transform small and medium industries and agriculture in Central Asia and Afghanistan. For this to happen, first of all a massive effort is needed to rebuild Afghanistan's transport network and economy. From the commitments of international community and multilateral institutions, it seems that this would happen immediately once Afghanistan becomes relatively stable. The second major impediment in realizing this potential is existing difficult relations between India and Pakistan. While looking at the regional economic dynamics, it is clear that both India and Pakistan would be paying huge economic costs for not cooperating in the Afghanistan. If trade stops in Pakistan, many road and other infrastructural projects will never become viable because of low volumes. Direct linkages between Central Asia and India will also give huge boost to all economies in the region, particularly to Afghanistan.

Despite difficult security situation and limited capacities, Afghanistan could emerge as an important player in regional economic cooperation. All international and regional players have appreciated its approach towards regional cooperation. This has major implications for regional peace and stability as well as India's linkages with the Eurasian region. High economic growth in both Central and South Asian regions is also pushing policy makers to work for integration strategies. Policymakers in Afghanistan believe that after decades of war now the country has a unique opportunity to realize its potential as a 'land bridge' between Central Asia, South Asia and the West Asian region. Increasingly it is pointed out that with enhanced cooperation, land-locked energy-rich Central Asia could be connected to energy deficient South Asia. Similarly, Afghanistan could also realize significant revenue as transit fee and improve its economic activities in the process. So far Afghanistan has been able to market itself as an important player in regional cooperation. The country is already playing an important role in various regional organizations like Economic Cooperation Organization (ECO), South Asia Association for Regional cooperation (SAARC), Central Asia Regional Economic Cooperation (CAREC), etc. It has also initiated an institutional mechanism called Regional Economic Cooperation Conference (RECC) on Afghanistan. The first RECC was held in Kabul in 2005, second in New Delhi in 2006, third in Islamabad in 2009 and fourth in Istanbul in 2010. Through various declarations, countries in the region have also accepted the centrality of Afghanistan for economic cooperation.

Conclusion

Afghanistan has witnessed diverse projects of nation building and socio-political transformation. The current international project of building democracy and market economy is mandated by the United Nations and being implemented mainly by the western alliance led by the United States. More than 70 nations have committed resources for Afghan reconstruction with US being the biggest donor. In addition, many European and Asian countries have also committed significant resources. A major portion of these resources have gone into building Afghan National Army, Afghan Police as well as education, health, community development projects and institutions of governance. As a result of these efforts, large gains have been made in education, health, infrastructure, economic development as well as in women empowerment, which needs to be consolidated. These gains have been made despite difficult and deteriorating security situation in many parts of the country. Many regional countries including India, China and Iran are also actively involved in reconstruction and development. The current security situation in the country is serious but not hopeless. The only possible way is to increase the numbers and capabilities of Afghan security forces, put pressure on anti-government forces and also continuously work for political solutions. It is also realized that despite major challenges, Afghanistan has the potential to play an important role in facilitating regional integration for different economies of South and Central Asia. If proposals concerning regional economic cooperation originating from Afghanistan are implemented by other countries in the region, this could ultimately improve chances of peace not only between India and Pakistan but also in the entire Eurasian region.

11

Processes of Policymaking Leading to Strategies for State Building: The Case of Afghanistan

Sayed Mohammad Shah

State building encompasses wide gamut of areas that include political, social and economic interventions. The paper would deal with the strategies of social and economic development that came out of different rounds of policymaking processes in Afghanistan after 2001. It will also deal with the subsequent failure to implement these same strategies in a successful way due to political influences on policy in an aid-dependent environment, lack of capacity and lack of political commitment to achieving the policy goals.

The current state building discourse in Afghanistan is dominated by a general belief that the priority agenda of the United States and its allies is the War on Terror and fighting the Taliban insurgency. State building was only a byproduct of the War on Terror and success in that has necessitated the formation of a functioning state able to provide its citizens with certain benefits on an inclusive basis. The foundation for formation of such a state was laid through the UN-sponsored Bonn Agreement in December 2001, in which the representatives of Afghanistan's political and social arena decided to end the conflict in the country and promote national reconciliation, lasting peace, stability and respect for human rights. They reaffirmed the independence, national sovereignty and territorial integrity of Afghanistan, acknowledging the right of the people of Afghanistan to freely determine their own political future in accordance with the principles of Islam, democracy, pluralism and social justice. This agreement contained all the key elements of modernity including social justice and women's rights. Thus a dream was set to modernize a country, which had never been truly modern and which even functioned in anti-modern ways.

This was the difficult journey on which the international community along with its Afghan partners decided to embark up on. Afghanistan is unlike other post conflict countries such as Iraq and Bosnia, where the states had functioned before the war or conflict. The governments of these countries had been able to extend services to their populations through state institutions and systems which were in place. Afghanistan was not a functioning state for at least the last three decades before 2001 due to political turmoil, foreign invasion, *Jihad*, civil war and the interference of neighbouring countries who wanted to define the state and its legitimacy. Thus a necessary precondition for state building in a post conflict environment was missing in Afghanistan and that made the task more difficult for its newly established interim government and its international partners.

However, to operationalize the dream of a modern state in post-Taliban Afghanistan, there was a need for strategic documents that would explain how to reach this goal and hence the first national development strategy was developed in 2002 for the Interim Government of Afghanistan and some national priority programmes were identified for the emergency period. This first ever post-Taliban development strategy was called the National Development Framework.

The NDF was followed by a series of strategic planning exercises and after two years, another document was produced by some 100 international experts from the United Nations (UN) and multilateral development institutions in collaboration with their Afghan colleagues. This was called "Securing Afghanistan's Future" (SAF) and was aimed at putting forward a programme of investments designed to lay the foundations for the sustained economic growth needed for a financially sustainable state capable of undertaking social development and poverty reduction.[1]

The Afghanistan Compact (AC) and the Interim Afghanistan National Development Strategy (I-ANDS) process began in early 2005 with a discussion of Afghanistan's Millennium Development Goals (MDGs), which the Government of Afghanistan envisioned to improve the well-being of its people. An Oversight Committee headed by the Presidential Advisor on economic and social development and seven key ministers of the Afghan cabinet worked throughout 2005 and 2006 to develop and refine the contents of the I-ANDS and to oversee the process. Based on the MDGs, the I-ANDS was elaborated.

It was followed by the London Conference, held from 31 January to 1 February 2006, which brought together 60 delegates from the Government of Afghanistan, the UN and the international community. The delegates met to agree on the AC and I-ANDS with the Government of Afghanistan and subsequently pledged US$10.5 billion in funds to support Afghanistan's reconstruction. The event was a precursor to the development of a full ANDS which would lay out the strategic priorities and mechanisms for achieving the government's overall development vision and would serve as the country's Poverty Reduction Strategy Paper (PRSP).

Following the London Conference, the Afghan Government and the international community agreed to establish the Joint Coordination and Monitoring Board for overall strategic coordination of the implementation of the AC. UNDP subsequently devised a two-year, USD$8.2 million project[2] with funding from different donors. The practical development of the ANDS began in March 2007 and was completed in April 2008 and then presented to donors at the International Conference in Support of Afghanistan in Paris on 12 June 2008. Under the ANDS process, 24 sector strategies, including 6 cross-cutting issues were developed for which different government ministries and agencies had ownership.

In January 2010, again in a conference on Afghanistan in London, there was re-emphasis on Afghan Government's accountability and the transfer of security matters to the Afghan Government as well as the announcement of the planned reconciliation and reintegration initiative to end conflict.[3] It was followed by another conference in July 2010 in Kabul with the attempt to recommit to the priorities of the ANDS and embark on a process of refining and improving the ANDS document through the clustering of its sectors and developing National Priority Programmes (NPPs) under each cluster. This process of developing the National Priority Programmes is on-going and it has been named the Kabul process.

From the National Development Framework in 2002 up to the Kabul Process in 2010, many strategic documents were produced that defined state building plans and activities but ironically, none of them have been implemented in a way that could be counted on to achieve results. The failure to implement one strategy led to the starting of another process to develop yet another strategy and this cycle is currently moving on. This failure has reinforced a common pessimism about the time and resources spent on policies and programmes which do not get implemented.

The implementation failures have been due fundamentally to politically-driven strategies, their ambitiousness and their unrealistic nature in terms of understanding the contextual facts in Afghanistan and the lack of political will on the sides' of the government and donors'. This is further exacerbated by an enormous capacity gap both within the government and donor institutions and the hasty processes aimed at meeting the deadlines that leads to ignoring any focus on the quality of work.

Political Influences on Strategies

Policies are both political and technical in nature. The political aspects of policies are mainly linked with the commitment of a country to achieve international targets such as the MDGs, the donors' agenda for the aid-dependent country and their conditional funding commitment for the specific development programmes in their specific regions of interest. For example, if the British forces are being stationed in Hilmand province of Afghanistan then the maximum focus for British development aid will be on this province. The technical aspects refer to the understanding of contextual facts and realities and the alignment of policies with them to make them more realistic, practical and achievable.

Like many other aid dependent countries, Afghanistan needs donor financial assistance for development programmes. The majority of the donors have priority programmes for the sectors and areas of their interest and these condition their funding for the national strategies to ensure the accommodation of their agenda items with the national strategies. The aid-dependent status of the government weakens its position to challenge the donors' options with contextual facts and realities and eventually it compromises with them. The donors also have conflicting agendas and programmes amongst themselves while some of them have the mandate to achieve international targets through their policies and programmes.

Here, I will review only two cases as examples: first the development of the Afghanistan National Development Strategy

(ANDS) which was fundamentally aimed at developing a Poverty Reduction Strategy Paper (PRSP) for Afghanistan that would enable Afghanistan to become part of (HIPC) Heavily Indebted Poor Countries initiative. It is worth mentioning that the IMF and World Bank require a PRSP from those countries which are seeking debt relief within the HIPC initiative. The IMF and World Bank provide debt relief and low interest loans to reduce external debt repayments to sustainable levels. To qualify for assistance, the national governments of HIPC countries must meet a range of economic, management and performance targets.

In April 2007, Afghanistan became the 41st HIPC through unique circumstances. The Government of Afghanistan had come under pressure from Russia and the IMF to accept a debt of USD$10.6 billion from Russia based on the amount of funds transferred to Afghanistan during the communist regime from 1978 to 1989. However, Afghanistan's status as a HIPC country meant that it would be able to write off the debt. Although the Afghan Parliament reacted strongly against the move, the decision was made to go ahead, on the basis that the country would be more likely to receive support and future funding from donors.[4]

The second example of political influence is at a sectoral level about policymaking in the primary and secondary education sub-sectors. In mid-2008, the Ministry of Education decided to revise its National Education Strategic Plan (NESP), this started in early 2009 with the aim to enable the country to become part of a Fast-Track Initiative (FTI) for increased funding to the education sector to achieve the Education for All (EFA) targets linked to the MDGs.[5]

The EFA FTI is a global partnership to assist poor countries in meeting the primary and secondary education MDGs. The World Bank launched the partnership in 2002 in collaboration with other donors and hosts the FTI Secretariat. The World Bank has set up collaborations with developing countries and country level donor partners as well as global level donors as a high priority for realizing the promise of FTI. To receive FTI endorsement, a country must have a PRSP and an education sector plan that is endorsed by in-country donors. These donors lead the endorsement process through a coordination forum, with one donor acting as the lead coordinating agency with responsibility for organizing the assessment of the country's programmes, using FTI appraisal guidelines and an indicative framework. In Afghanistan, the coordination forum of in-country donors is called the Human Resource Development Board (HRDB).

The Ministry of Education in Afghanistan shared at least five drafts of a revised National Education Strategic Plan with the HRD Board but the donors did not approve it, even though they were part of the process of the development of Education Strategic Plan but they waited for an FTI assessment of the education sector and the NESP to take place. The assessment happened during the months of March, April and May in 2010 and the FTI assessment team gave their recommendations, which again did not lead to the finalization of the NESP. The team instead recommended developing an interim one year plan before the approval NESP that would elaborate how to achieve EFA targets in Afghanistan.[6]

These examples not only explain the great political influences of in-country donors on the process of national decision making but also bring the marginalization of national ownership on the processes under limelight.

Lack of Capacity

Another issue that has a deep correlation with the political influence on policies is the lack of capacity at different levels. Capacity needs to be seen broadly, it does not imply only the capabilities of human resources to perform their specific tasks, but it also refers to efficiency of systems, administrative structures, realistic policies and programmes as well as rules and procedures.

On part of the Afghan Government, it had inherited poor capacity both in terms of dysfunctional institutions and an inefficient workforce as the legacies of the civil war and protracted period of turmoil. At the same time, there was an unprecedented demand from Afghan society for service delivery as millions of Afghans started return migration to their homeland from different parts of the world, particularly the neighbouring countries, with the dream of living on their own land with a better future. Thus state institutions needed tremendous technical support from the international community to meet the demands of Afghan society and come up to their expectations, at least to some extent. The state institutions were injected with numbers of technical advisors, which according to a recent study by the Ministry of Finance was as follows:

Estimated numbers of TA in key ministries

Ministry	*National TA*	*International TA*
Education	1,248	11
Finance	300	71
Commerce	25	16
President's Office	90	10
MRRD	1,134	49

Source: *Scaling up Technical Assistance and Capacity Development in Afghanistan*, September 2009

These technical advisors took the key functions in the government ministries, from programme implementation to design and development of policies and programmes. The already weak position of government in determining the content of policies and programmes due to its aid dependent status was made worse by a lack of professional capacity with its own staff to draft strategies. The control of processes thus drifted into the hands of mainly those TAs who are on donor contract and the majority of them ensured the agenda of their contracting organizations were represented in the strategic documents.

Other than the lack of professional staff, another disability of the government ministries was inability to spend their development funds. According to Ministry of Finance sources, the government ministries spent only 39 per cent of their development budget during the last fiscal year (1388), although over 60 per cent of the development funds are spent outside the government budget directly by donors through their implementation partners. This disability is due to the highly complicated and bureaucratic system of financing and budgeting in the government institutions, which despite many attempts at reform is still inefficient.

When it comes to the donors' capacity, although they have efficient systems in place in their institutions, the majority of their technical staffs are largely ignorant to the context of Afghanistan but they led processes and wrote the strategies. Many of these people replicated their experiences from other parts of the world in Afghanistan, without tailoring them according to the specific needs and realities of the country. Their capability to write the documents in English language put them on the driving seat, which by itself is enough to put into question the local ownership on the processes.

Undoubtedly, English has been a big factor to define capacity in the context of Afghanistan. Some even blame the professional bureaucracy in the UN and other international organizations for smelling money in the post conflict environments and then rushing in with their tailored development models to become engaged in policy development processes and find reasons for spending money.

Unrealistic Timeframe

Policymaking requires adequate time and proper time management. In Afghanistan, national level policymaking has mainly been hasty, driven by unrealistic deadlines. Pushing processes within an unrealistic timeframe, the quality of work is often sacrificed over the process. This undermines confidence in and satisfaction with, the soundness of policies and planning, which then leads to their hasty revision, as happened in the agriculture sub-sector. Within a year of the development of ANDS sector strategies, the Ministry of Agriculture, Irrigation and Livestock (MAIL) developed another policy document called the National Agriculture Development Framework (NDAF).

Dearth of Political Commitment

The processes of development of national development strategies have been extremely zealous: government, donors, parliamentarians, NGOs, think-tanks and academics got engaged in tremendous activities to ensure their contributions. There were uncountable coordination meetings, consultations, working group activities, workshops, conferences, traveling into and out of the country, along with conflicts of interest among the actors and compromises. Millions of dollars have been spent on organizing these events. Then finally the strategies get approved at formalized and impressive events such as the Paris and London Conferences where dignitaries from key contributors of Afghan rebuilding announce their funding commitments. Once the funding commitments are obtained, suddenly everybody gives up their enthusiasm for the strategies as if they have achieved all of their objectives.

At least this was the case with the ANDS, all the actors rather disgracefully forgot about it after the Paris Conference in June 2008. The Secretariat, which was established to manage the development of the document, suddenly lost their office, top leadership quit and the website died for sometime due to lack of funding. The Secretariat was then divided into two sections, one responsible for budgeting of sector strategies was merged into the Ministry of Finance while the other section, which was responsible for monitoring and evaluation of the ANDS sector strategies, was handed over to the Ministry of Economy. Both of these sections ran into severe management problems with their managing institutions since these institutions had their own priority programmes and ANDS implementation was allocated only secondary importance compared to their institutional mandates.

During the development phase, President Karzai spoke several times about the importance of the formulation of ANDS, but after its formulation, he never spoke about the importance of implementing it, which shows a decrease in political commitment in implementation phase.

Conclusion

The failure to implement strategies that formed the state building agenda does not mean that there has not been progress at all. Development has taken place in major sectors such as agriculture, the private sector, education, health and others but the last nine years of reconstruction could have meant a lot more than they did, if the development actors had developed more consensus and common vision, if military activities had not been associated with development practices, political choices had not dominated technical choices in policies and strategies and there was more practice than words and papers.

Many believe that the attention of the United States shifted towards Iraq after 2003 and Afghanistan did not get the required financial assistance compared to Bosnia and Iraq, and this slowed down progress on state building. However, there is another view, to which I subscribe, that there was a lot of money for and in Afghanistan, which was spent in an irresponsible and unaccountable way that not only darkened the chances of the development planned but also brought further destabilization by increasing corruption and strengthening existing and nascent mafias. A recent study by Andrew Wilder for Tufts University which was partially funded through AREU and conducted in Khost, Uruzgan and Paktiya provinces of

Afghanistan, argued that unaccountable aid money corrupted the system and brought further destabilization in these areas. Andrew found that some people on key government and social positions deliberately created insecurity for their personal benefit to make reasons for the inflow of further aid to the area since the development landscape is dominated by a false belief that more aid brings stability.

Today a fear prevails about the future of Afghanistan as a state and people keep questioning each other that what happens if United States and its allies leave Afghanistan? Would the country be able to sustain itself and provide essential services to the people through its institutions? Unfortunately, after over nine years of international interventions to build the state of Afghanistan and many rounds of policymaking and strategy development, the answers to these questions are not positive.

Notes and References

1. Sayed Mohammad Shah, *ANDS Formulation Process: Influencing factors and challenges*, Afghanistan Research and Evaluation Unit, February 2009, 9.
2. Shah, ANDS Formulation Process.
3. Sarah Parkinson, *Means to What End? Policymaking and State building in Afghanistan*, Afghanistan Research and Evaluation Unit, Synthesis Paper Series, November 2010.
4. Shah, ANDS Formulation Process, 10.
5. Sayed Mohammad Shah, "Is Capacity Being Built? A Study of Policymaking Process in the Primary and Secondary Education Subsector," Afghanistan Research and Evaluation Unit, Case Study Series, July 2010.
6. Shah, *Is Capacity Being Built?*

The Government and the Taliban

12

Improvement of Governance and Rule of Law in Afghanistan

Abdul Rahman Ulfat Mahmoodi

The United States' prime strategic objective in Afghanistan over the last nine years has been defeating the Al-Qaeda network. The second tier priority was strengthening and sustaining the Afghan Government which was ranked far behind military operations. Clearly, any effort by the United States to strengthen government was only as a means of "dismantling, disrupting, and defeating" the Al-Qaeda terror network.

Practically, it is necessary to build legitimate, responsive, and self-sustaining Afghan Government institutions if the United States and its NATO International Security Assistance Force allies are to withdraw their military forces from Afghanistan. It is also necessary to prevent Afghanistan from descending into civil war and regional proxy fight. To accomplish this objective, the Congress, the Obama administration and the American public need to have a clearer understanding of the full dimensions of Afghan governance along with the many international actors and programs whose activities affect the issue. This paper's purpose is to aid that understanding.

Building even a minimally functioning state in Afghanistan will be incredibly difficult. The task is not helped by 30 years of war, and an Afghan Government plagued by a lack of capacity and political will. It is understandable that the Obama administration wants to show quick results to the American people. The American people are growing increasingly frustrated over the human and financial costs of almost nine years of war. However, the administration officials are paying too little attention to the sustainability of the programs and state building process in Afghanistan. They need greater clarity of purpose in defining the goals of American policy toward Afghanistan.

Strategically, the Obama administration began to focus on the state-building effort in Afghanistan in 2009 to a much greater extent than the Bush administration. Further, Obama placed a stronger rhetoric on strengthening governance at all levels in Afghanistan as part of its overall strategy. The strategy asserted that state institutions are essential to weaken the insurgency and extremism at a broader level. One can observe it by the action of Under General Stanley McChrystal who commanded NATO's International Security Assistance Force; it identified the need to "separate insurgent influence from the populace and support Afghan Government's sub-national structures to establish rule of law and deliver basic services" as one of the three principal efforts in its current campaign plan.

The main purpose of this paper is to discuss the relationship between rule of law, good governance and sustainable development along with the elements of the good governance and challenges for the rule of law in Afghanistan.

Governance in Afghanistan

Governance is affected seriously, in almost entire Afghanistan, both nationally and sub-nationally. Since 2001, many stakeholders including international community and aid organizations have contributed a lot to maintain good governance at national and sub national levels. Several obstacles, such as presence of illegal armed groups, political interferences, ethnic discriminations and nepotism did not allow steady improvement in governance. Consequently, it requires efforts to facilitate application of good governance in order to win the trust of public across the country.

What Role can Good Governance play to stabilize Afghanistan?

Good governance lays the foundation for stabilization and rebuilding processes in war-torn societies. International standards of good governance are only emerging, but at least the following indicators are widely shared: public accountability, transparency and institutional quality. Good governance is measured on these dimensions and it is assessed against qualitative and quantitative components. Enhancing good governance requires not only institutional capacity, but also knowledge and understanding of the role of different factors and actors within a country.

In addition, establishment of good and capable government is vital for winning the hearts and minds of Afghans which has been lost. Such government should ensure equitable representation of all social, ethnic and geographical realities of the country. Further it needs to ensure a functional judicial system; provide good social services to public; ensure balanced development and bring peace and security to the people. By fulfilling these tasks, the government could win the trust of people and bring stability to the country and prosperity to the nation. In fact, the volatile security situation in Afghanistan is an impediment to recovery (socio-economic, governance, etc.), stability and development. One of the key contributions that can be made at this stage is to help reinforce the human capacity in governmental institutions at all levels along with the civil society organizations with the aim of improving access to key services for the entire people.

Ironically, the capacity of the national government is weak and its presence is limited outside of Kabul. The country is currently facing serious threats from opium production and its illegal trade and insurgency, increasing the concerns about corruption and intensifying popular discontent. In order to prevent these threats short-term action is urgently required. However, it is clear from the recent experience of Afghanistan and other fragile states that long-term solutions will only come from comprehensive improvements in governance and service delivery system. These steps can result into the emergence of a stronger state that can be accountable to its citizens.

Effective state building through democratization requires careful consideration of the general and specific policy lessons outlined above. It may be that the big changes of early post-conflict efforts require closer attention to the micro-formal/informal sources of legitimization, rather than radically trying to alter them at the macro-level. In the current Afghan milieu, this means addressing the questions such as what services is most urgent, how to deliver it, and what type of representation and modes of interaction between people and state are required to do so. Fortunately, Afghanistan can derive many constructive lessons from its own experience since 2001 and from the democratic peace building initiatives spearheaded by the United Nations since the end of the cold war. It would be patronizing and misguiding to say that the Afghans are not ready for the political transformation that democracy entails.

Elements of Good Governance

A number of multilateral organizations, e.g., the United Nations Development Programme (UNDP) and the Organization for Economic Cooperation and Development (OECD) have reflected on the elements of good governance and on their relation to development. As the ethos and experience of these organizations vary, so, too their perceptions of what constitute good governance. The World Bank's interest in governance stems from its concern with the effectiveness of the development efforts it supports. From this perspective, sound development management, in the broader aspect, is critical for ensuring adequate returns and efficacy of the programs and projects financed, and for the World Bank's underlying objectives of helping countries reduce poverty and promoting sustainable growth. Hence, the World Bank's emphasis in recent years has shifted from its own interventions to the overall country context (i.e., the governance climate) within which those interventions take place. In doing so, it has been guided by the nature of its operations and the opportunities for action that these offer. Accordingly, the key dimensions of governance identified by the World Bank are (i) public sector management, (ii) accountability, (iii) legal framework for development, and, (iv) transparency and information.

Rule of Law in Afghanistan

Historically, Afghans have distrusted state judicial institutions for valid reasons and have turned to their customary systems of mediation and arbitration to resolve large number of their disputes. They view their informal systems as less corrupt, more efficient, and less time consuming than the state system that is vying to displace them. Nevertheless, they are compatible with state system of justice and in rural areas government officials use them as tools for maintaining social stability. To date, attempts to reform the Afghan legal system have been stymied by a broad range of interests that agree on little other than blocking reform. One particular problem is that many international and western trained legal experts espouse a formal, codified system of justice and are disdainful of other forms of conflict resolution.

Additionally, the culture of impunity that undermines the legitimacy of the Kabul government magnifies the systemic problems in the judiciary. Corrupt officials and criminals enthusiastically display their ill-gotten gains. Even the best efforts to reform the judiciary and staff it with competent officials will have little effect if the government fails to muster the will and resolve to bring powerful lawbreakers to justice. Moreover, failure to tackle these problems also raises the question whether the Afghan state has the power to do so or not, subsequently, the implication of this undermines respect for state authority.

Apart from these developments, a number of ideological laws have been duplicated and translated from other laws without taking into account the local circumstances in Afghanistan. It must be recognized that Afghanistan has traditionally relied on traditional councils and assemblies in solving problems. Moreover, under good governance, there are clear decision making procedures at the level of public authorities, civil society participation in decision-making processes, and the ability to enforce rights and obligations through legal mechanisms.

Implementation of the Rule of law

The Afghan Government is failing to deliver rule of law to its people. The lack of an effective judicial system is a common complaint against the Kabul government. Indeed, the claims by the Taliban insurgents that they deliver justice are a key selling point in their strategy for gaining legitimacy as a "counter-state" competitor to the Kabul government. But this is hardly a new problem.

Beside this, the rule of law has never been strong, but after 23 years of warfare and civil war it has been displaced almost completely by the "rule of the gun." In the large part of the country, regional power-holders, whether they hold official positions or not, effectively exercise political, police and judicial authority through their control of militia. In some places in Afghanistan they are still in power ruling through their own constitutions and not obeying central government.

The definition of rule of law is transparency and accountability of state to the public. The judicial system in Afghanistan is an independent body and makes the decision and the trial take place in public. The prosecutor as part of the government has responsibility to protect the society from the crime, so has been tasked to improve the immunity of society. The defense lawyers as another part of fair trial defend the rights of their clients, but it is not meant to affect fair decision of the court. Most of the laws have been enacted to fill the gaps; however, in the field of criminal procedure in Afghanistan the gap exists. Since there are three applicable laws of Criminal Procedure

Code (CPC), amendment of CPC and Interim Criminal Procedure Code has to be enacted after falling of Taliban.

Although, the new constitution in Afghanistan has been enacted in 2004, it has root in the earlier laws. For instance, the criminal code which is called penal code in Afghanistan was enacted 30 years ago and amended in 1983, and is still being applied. The major challenges to rule of law in Afghanistan are insecurity, corruption, low salary, lack of infrastructure for judiciary, lack of space for prosecution, lack of proper correction facilities, like juvenile center, male and female prison, interference of high ranking officials in the cases, lack of ability of prosecuting the high corruptors and crimes perpetrators.

Afghan System of Law

The system of law in Afghanistan is very complex. There are various sources of law in Afghan's law system. Some parts of the system are based on Islam. Other parts are based on the *Qanoone Tamoli* and rest is based on modern laws. For example, the civil code of Afghanistan says that since everyone enjoys the rule of law, all civil cases should be decided by the law. According to the Afghan statutory law, the first source of law is the law, the second source of law is *Sharia*, and the third source of law is customary. But then in the Afghan Constitution, it says that Islam is the basis of the law. Accordingly, one can see that the statutory law and the constitution contradict each other on several places.

Most sections of the Afghan Constitution are based on Islamic *Sharia* (*Hanafi* Doctrine). For a long time, the formation of particular madrasas (religious schools) was considered to belong to the traditional rights of the people. Hence there were no bans or prohibitions placed upon them by the government. The teaching of religious knowledge was a part of the programme of primary, secondary, and higher education in the educational institutes of the government. As a result, we can say that as an Islamic country, religion, nationalism, and politics form a cornerstone in Afghanistan.

Where no punishment is imposed according to *Hodood*, the criminal law of Afghanistan could still be applied. For example, if someone commits a murder he is not jailed if he gives adequate compensation and this is accepted by the victim's family. The laws of Afghanistan's courts are made according to *Hanafi* jurisprudence. The reliable thing in this regard is *Mujalatul Ahkam* (commandments' magazine), which was written in *Usmani* Caliphate in Turkey, but on occasions where *Hanafi* jurisprudence is complicated and difficult to implement, then other jurisprudences are utilized. For example, *Hanafi* jurisprudence stipulates that in the case of "missing" or losing her husband, the wife has to wait for her husband for a period of 90 years; but in *Hanbaly* jurisprudence a period of four years is stipulated. Accordingly, four years is mentioned in Afghanistan's law.

There are two major challenges to law in Afghanistan. First there is the pressure of modernization. The pressure is to have a system of law which conforms to international law. Second is to have a system of law that conforms to *Sharia*. In Afghanistan, *Sharia* has been considered the primary source of law from the past two decades. Can these two systems of law be reconciled? If not, how does Afghanistan deal with the demands of the two opposing systems? There is a conundrum in that aligning *Hanafi* jurisprudence with international charters which is likely to incur the objection of religious scholars (Article 3 of the Afghan Constitution states that no law shall contravene the tenets and provisions of the holy religion of Islam in Afghanistan). On the other hand, interpreting international charters close to that of *Hanafi* jurisprudence is likely to meet with opposition from the international community.

These aspects of good governance neither in themselves ensure that society is run well nor do they guarantee sustainable development. However, their absence severely limits that possibility and can, at worst, impede it. Without proper functioning of the governing institutions based on the rule of law that promote social stability and legal certainty, there cannot be investment and assumption of risk that form the basis of market economy development, let alone sustainable development.

Indeed, the strength of the rule of law is the best predictor of a country's economic success. Furthermore, deficiency in the rule of law encourages high rates of corruption, with further devastating consequences on the confidence of economic actors. This lack of investment, in turn, slows economic growth and consequently deprives the governments of resources to invest in education, social safety nets, and sound environmental management, all of which are critical for sustainable development.

Challenges for Law in Afghanistan

Introduction of good governance and rule of law, however, cannot be done overnight. The process is often a gradual one, involving changes to long-standing practices, entrenched interests, cultural habits, and social and even religious norms. A significant step was taken in this endeavor in 1998 when countries adopted the Convention on Access to Information, Public Participation in Decision-making and Access to Justice in Environmental Matters ("The Aarhus Convention"). The Convention recognizes that sustainable development with elders, khans, and those who presides councils as key figures in this. The following are the challenges for the rule of law in Afghanistan:

1. Government authorities are themselves not observing laws, because they are arrogant and conceited by power.
2. We have failed to explain to people the significance and values of laws and their implementation.
3. Disparate and divergent laws have been ushered in by various outfits including royalists, republicans, Communists, the mujahedeens, the Taliban, and democrats. None of these have been national laws in the true sense of the word.
4. A number of ideological laws have been duplicated from other laws without taking into account the local circumstances in Afghanistan. It must be recognized that Afghanistan has traditionally relied on traditional councils and assemblies in solving problems, with elders, khans, and those who presides councils as key figures in this.

Key Recommendations for the Improvement of the Governance in Afghanistan

Stability in Afghanistan requires that its people accept state authority as legitimate and trust its institutions. This will happen only if the central government addresses the people's "hierarchy of needs"—security, justice, and economic development—through good governance.

If improvements in governance do not happen quickly, then the international community may scale back its commitment to Afghanistan and cut support—risking a return to the anarchy and tumult that drew international forces into the country in 2001.

In light of the 20 August presidential elections and the sharp increase in violence, the issues most important for bringing better governance demand immediate attention. The window is closing on the chance to bring change. After the election, the international community, led by the United States, should press for and support the following reforms:

1. *Improve the appointments process for senior officials*, especially provincial governors, so that the corrupt and unqualified do not get important offices and undeserving incumbents can be removed for cause.
2. Alongside the U.S military and civilian surge, *commit to a comprehensive "Afghan civilian surge"* that parallels the effort to build a capable, competent Afghan national security force.

Conclusion

It is widely recognized that good governance is essential for sustainable development. Well-functioning legal institutions and governments bound by the rule of law are, in turn, vital to good governance. Weak legal and judicial systems—where laws are not enforced and non-compliance and corruption are the norm—undermine respect for the rule of law, engender environmental degradation, and undermine progress towards sustainable development. Practitioners in the development field have increasingly turned their attention to reforms to improve legal and judicial institutions and promote the rule of law and good governance.

References

"What is Good Governance?" (Bangkok: UN Economic and Social Commission for Asia and the Pacific, 6 September 2003) <http://www.unescap.org/huset/gg/governance.htm>.

http://www.bu.edu/aias/reports/governance_short.pdf)

13

Complicated Aspects of War in Afghanistan

Sanaullah Tasal

Having declared during the election campaign that Afghanistan was the central front in the fight against terrorism—the war on which America should have been focusing all along—American President Obama took some quick steps to show how serious he was about winning it; he sent thousands of troops to Afghanistan.

Within days of taking office he asked Gen. Stanley McChrystal to review the US and NATO war strategy in Afghanistan. Gen. McChrystal delivered the results of his 60-day strategic assessment to US and NATO commanders. He described the situation in Afghanistan as serious, but added that success was achievable subject to revised implementation strategy, commitment and resolve, and increased unity of effort. He wanted the American troops to be reinforced by 40,000 if the war was to be won, and his announcement of a new strategy aimed at protecting Afghans instead of hunting down insurgents was supposed to be aimed at reducing civilian casualties and winning people's hearts and minds.

On the request of Gen. McChrystal, President Obama unveiled a comprehensive strategy for Afghanistan in March 2009 and decided to surge 30,000 more troops to this country. Although the number of US and other foreign forces in Afghanistan has increased, there has been a steady resurgence of the Taliban and other insurgent groups. They have increased their attacks by more than 40 per cent in each of the last two years, causing an escalation in military and civilian casualties, and systematically attacking and intimidating civilians associated with the Afghan Government.[1] Taliban now have control or influence over more than half the country, having expanded from the south and southeast to parts of the north, centre and west.

At ten years and counting, the US war in Afghanistan is the longest in its history, surpassing even the Vietnam War, and it will shortly surpass the Soviet Union's own extended military campaign there. It has become complicated to the extent that neither the international community nor the Afghan state could bring significant change in the situation in the country despite utilizing all tactics and weapons. The more international community increases their soldiers and military equipments the more they lose their troops and lower their outcomes. The international forces are as anxious towards the insufficient military gains over the Taliban as they have so far conducted several failed military expeditions by the names of Joint, Desert Scorpion, Dagger, Lion, etc., without having any positive impact. The result of these military expeditions has been destruction of houses, harvests and killing of civilians.

The international community not only failed in bringing security and stabilization, but also failed in political and economical grounds as well because they could not achieve what have been anticipated. The government is weak and the democracy that the international community wants to put forward in Afghanistan has had a setback in the worsening political situation after the elections with breakdown of rule of law.

There is also feared among the Afghans that NATO and US, in looking for the political alternative to stabilize Afghanistan, will depend more on regional countries, especially Iran and Pakistan, to end the war and find a settlement with the Taliban. Afghanistan has a long history of its neighbour's intervention; both Iran and Pakistan used Afghanistan as a battlefield against their rivals and used the Afghans and their lands for their strategic need. These countries do not want their neighbour Afghanistan to be independent and having elected government and not being used any more for the proxies.

This paper attempts to talk about the complicated aspects of the war in Afghanistan and would like to analyse failure of the international community in term of winning the hearts and minds of Afghans and providing security. It would also like to talk about the capacity and necessity of Talib fighters and the international forces. Furthermore, the analysis will elucidate factors of failure of the international community and talk about their military tactics, possibilities and their modalities. It will also mention how it has become possible for the Taliban and Al-Qaeda to recruit volunteer fighters in their lines and how they could defeat forces of 40 countries with very little fighters.

Complicated Aspects of the War

War for the implementation of two different ideologies: Democracy or Islamic Amara

In opinion of some analysts Afghanistan is graveyard for the super powers, however Afghanistan can be said to be not only graveyard for the super powers, but also graveyard for any ideology whether it is Islamic or non-Islamic. The West deems that implementation of democracy to be the solution to the Afghan problem. However, the aim of the USA and NATO to implement democracy in a land of different ideologies like Islam, communism, Talibanism, etc., has already proved to be a failure as no ideology has yet been decisively implemented here.

The western powers have promised people's government, reconstruction, development works, etc., that means that they want to implement democracy in lieu of money and material assistance. Thus they have spent millions of dollars in Afghanistan.

The Taliban, on the other hand, tell the Afghans that democracy is a thoroughly western phenomenon that totally contradicts Islam. They tell people that democracy means allowing women to freely do what they want such as going out without permission of husband, which is considered much more serious than suicide in Afghan society. According to the Taliban the only way of peace and improvement is implementation of Islamic laws.

Moreover, the rivals of Americans and their allies (Taliban and Al-Qaeda) invite people to be strict Muslims because they believe that their tranquility and prosperity are only in implementation of Islam and if they want to be good Muslims, they shall only think about the doomsday and forget about this world. They tell people that all human beings are created and inhabited in this world only for a limited time and there perennial life is afterlife. They also illustrate that the livelihood of the Prophet (PBUP) and his companions was very simple as they have been surviving in very poor circumstances only to worship Almighty Allah. By extensive spread of such preaching, Al-Qaeda and Taliban could influence views of Muslims and cause obstacle against Americans and their allies.

Winning the hearts and minds of Afghans

The USA wants to win the minds and hearts of the people who were always against foreigners and were proud of defeating several super powers. Taliban are members of the Afghan community and in comparison with the international community can much more easily attract the people in light of religious and cultural beliefs. In areas of southern and northern Waziristan, where Pashtun tribes reside, there are blood relations between those tribes and Al-Qaeda members. Thus they often shelter them.

Their first motivation is retaliation for perceived military aggression by foreign forces, especially with civilian casualties and abusive raids or detentions. As one southern insurgent put it, "The foreigners here do not observe the rules of their own countries; they are far wilder than the animals of the jungle. They bomb weddings, for example in Shindand, killing over two hundred innocent civilians. They shout about human rights more than most but then they kill people and call it a mistake. How can they call it a mistake after eight or nine years? If this continues, the resistance will continue." The USA and its allies with all sorts of possibilities and large amounts of money could not attract Afghans' hearts, and thus compelled the Afghans to go to the Taliban for help.

The issue of *Ansar* and *Muhajirin* (Islamic brotherhood) and fraternity was so important in Islam.[2] Referring to this the Al-Qaeda found that there was cultural and economic disparity among the *Ansar* and the *Muhajirin*. So with the guidance of the Islamic history, they established the bond of brotherhood between the *Ansar* (FATA) and the *Muhajirin* (Al-Qaeda) and declared them to be brothers of each other. Referring to this bond of brotherhood, they convinced the FATA people that Allah says: "Those who believed, migrated and fought in the way of Allah [i.e. Al-Qaeda], and those who gave shelter and helped [i.e. FATA] were the true believers, and for them forgiveness is a noble sustenance.

Some of the FATA (*Ansar*) went beyond the call of duty in fulfilling the rights of *Ansar*: they divided their entire wealth into two and gave one-half to their immigrant brother-in-faith. And they also married their daughters. This shows that one of the first steps towards building relationship with FATA and gaining their hearts and minds were the model of *Ansar* and *Muhajirin*.

Al-Qaeda saw Afghanistan as the first state in the multiregional caliphate. It used Afghan territory to train 10-20,000 terrorists, according to the 9/11 Commission. It has high stakes in the victory of the Taliban in both countries.[3]

Afghans and their strong feelings of Jihad/Islam

Afghans have a long history of being extremely conscious of the tenets of Islam. From Amanullah Khan to the present day, many authorities have been ousted and exiled for being "infidels."

And yet our problem is more complicated than this. The Taliban are using the propaganda that the present government in Afghanistan are infidels, and that they are deliberately aggravating the situation; convincing the people to support them. Thus they have been propagating the idea that our so-called "infidel" governments are cursed by Allah: they neither utilize their intellect nor do they learn their lessons from bad experiences; thus, they fail to open the door for mutual understanding and negotiation with the nation to prove themselves as true Muslims. Our so-called infidel governments are deliberately aggravating the situation by imposing the culture of the West on the Afghan people. This is enough to be spread in the villages that the government has became infidel. Even if the government increased mosques and delivered Azans no one would accept it.

Kabul and the rest of the provinces are full of graveyards. Some of those buried have been killed in the name of being infidels, and others were killed while killing infidels. This notwithstanding, no one has looked at where, in a 99.9 per cent Muslim country, such a number infidels have come from? Even worse is that we still feel proud of killing each other.

Fighting and expecting an early win in this type of complicated society is itself a big challenge for the international community, because it is difficult to fight with those who pride the killing of his brother and pride to destroy their country for the so called *Jihad*.

Division and strife among the foreign troops/and unity among the Taliban

There is more division and strife between US political leaders, the State Department, Secretary Hillary Clinton, Secretary Richard Holbrooke, Ambassador Karl Eikenberry, and the DOD (Dept Defense) than any time in the course of Operation Enduring Freedom.

Basically some 40 countries have used their efforts for suppression of terrorism which was a unified goal. However, things have changed in recent times. We are also witnesses of the differences between the US and UK, as well as between the US and the NATO allies. There have also been differences between the western allies and the Afghan Government.

Some of NATO member countries like Germany and Australia have come to Afghanistan only to please the USA. They sit in their bases, do not fight against Taliban and signed the contracts with someone to safeguard them.

There are three major Taliban groups posing primary threat to Afghan security: the Quetta Shura Taliban, the Haqqani Network, and the Hezb-i-Islami Gulbuddin. According to the US military, these groups often operate together, coordinating activities loosely, but they do not share a single formal command and control structure. Nor do they have a single overarching strategy or campaign plan. Each group has its own methods of developing and executing plans each has adapted over time.[4] They have different spokesmen, different ideologies (some are the followers of Wahabisam, some are Deobandi and Ekhwanism) but their goal is to defeat the US and NATO in Afghanistan. The US and NATO along with the government of Afghanistan has not been able to divide the Taliban by deploying them money and promises of sharing the power.

President Karzai vs NATO and US

Mutual suspicions have marked the relationship between Karzai and Obama at least since the Afghan leader's trouble-packed reelection last year. Obama has fumed over an unaccountable leader who has done little to stem rampant corruption, while Karzai has blasted an arrogant foreign presence in his country, going so far as to recently charge the US with seeking a "servant government" from the Afghans.

President Karzai's government could not attract hearts of the Afghans. High ranking officials are isolated from the nation and the significant achievement of this government is to increase discrimination. The best example of this is allotment of ministries, departments and governors' position based on regional, tribal and other discriminative measures that paves the way for dividing of people. If we do away with the national foundation while the government is already weak, the country will face with big disaster and continuation of the President Karzai's government will very soon lead to civil war.[5] Thus the international community noted that Karzai was not a good ally, and he lost the credibility in the eyes of the US and NATO in Afghanistan.

From the point of view of the majority of the Afghans this is the drama of both invaders and their puppet to deceive the Afghans. They argue that condemnation of civil casualties by President Karzai as a result of foreign military operations does not mean that Karzai has sympathy with the nation because he gathered (as his supporters) around him lots of those who have been perpetuating crimes against people and have been killing people. Existence of such individuals will never allow real representatives of people to be in high ranking positions and serve their people and country.

Both sides strive to undermine each other. Karzai tries to manifest existence of foreigners illegal in the country and thus plans to attract the people, while the USA and its friends want to show the people that Karzai is source of problems. But people believe none of them and suppose that both of them deceive people by playing such games.

Talib Fighters are Stronger than US/NATO

Since 2006, the Taliban have made a dramatic comeback in Afghanistan after being driven from the country in 2002. As security has deteriorated, they have steadily taken control of more and more territory.

The Taliban groups have made significant inroads in Afghanistan, especially in the southern and eastern portions of the country. Violent attacks constitute the most visible part of this insurgency; targets are the ISAF forces, Afghan security forces, and the civilian population. In addition, the Taliban wage a silent war of intimidation and persuasion to gain control of the population. These efforts make possible the existence of Taliban shadow governments in virtually every province that actively seek to control the population and displace the national and local governments and traditional power structures.

They have developed tactics that the western soldiers find it harder and harder to defend against. Their roadside bombs have become more powerful and advanced. Inside Taliban fighters every third individual knows about bombs and explosive tools and every Talib is familiar with technology of bomb making. Using bombs that are made by Taliban themselves against Afghan National Army, Afghan National Police, American and NATO troops is a very successful and cost effective means that creates serious casualties between the foreign troops. Making such bombs may cost 500 Afghanis, but their explosion may kill several soldiers at once and damage vehicles and equipments of the troops that are very expensive.

They instill fear with their complex attacks on army bases and government buildings, in which they combine shooting and suicide actions.

Equipment and warriors' distinction

1. Al-Qaeda and Taliban train people who are volunteers and do not seek any privilege. They are the people who are not only thinking about Afghanistan, they think about the world and want Emarah Islamiah around the world. Therefore, they choose either to be victor (*ghazi*) or martyred (*shaheed*). Moreover, some of those who join Taliban or Al-Qaeda intend taking revenge.
   One southern commander explained how an attack by foreign forces incited him to fight for the revenge:
   I am a landowner and was working on the land. I was not a Talib. But some years ago American Special Forces came and entered my home without my permission at night and killed my two sons, my father, and two uncles without any reason. Another time they did the same thing in another village in my district. When I saw their acts and knew they came only to kill us, not to help, I started fighting against them. They forced me to fight them and now I will continue to fight them so long as they are in Afghanistan.[6]
   Another commander argued that "if international forces keep bombing and killing civilians not only the Taliban but also all the rest of the nation will fight them."
2. Taliban and Al-Qaeda could find volunteer soldiers, train them and whenever newly recruited soldiers are killed, they can find twofold of the soldiers they have lost. Every year thousands of youths graduating from Pakistani madrasas are joining the Taliban. Up to the year 2006, Al-Qaeda and Taliban conducted military, physical and Islamic training for around some 16,000 children and the number might have increased since then.
3. If a general of the international troops is killed, there might be vacancy in the frontline, but if a member of Taliban or Al-Qaeda is killed, there is no vacancy remaining (Azzarqawi in Iraq and Mullah Dadullah in Afghanistan, who were killed are good examples that after their murder no changes has come to being in the war).
4. Most of the troops of the neighbouring countries are trained ideologically, for example, Pakistan trained their soldiers to fight the enemy of the Islam and their enemy country India,

> fanning Islamic emotion and patriotism. Iran is another good example. Unfortunately our National Army does not have any ideology, they have been trained how to fight the enemy of Afghanistan, West and US (Taliban and Al-Qaeda). On the other hand it has been decided during Peace Jirga that no more Taliban shall be called terrorists, it directly had impact on the morality of the Afghan soldiers who fight with Taliban because they will no longer fight with them as fighting with the terrorists and instead they will think that they are their unhappy brothers. In most of his speeches, President Karzai refers to them as unhappy brothers.

Fighting against these classes of people is very difficult and their defeat will need more time and years, it needs sacrifices and losing more troops. We can exemplify oppression of Marja of Helmand Province that was carried out by 15000 solders, but the outcome became obvious to everybody.

Whether this intervention has actually changed anything for better for the Afghans?

Afghanistan was burning in the fire of mutual wars between a number of warlords after defeat of the former Soviet Union and before coming of Taliban. Neither family members nor wealth of the people was safe during these wars and the nation was thirsty of peace and good security.

In 2001, when western leaders ordered the invasion of Afghanistan, they set out their objectives for it as their war against terrorism. They talked of bringing peace to the region, establishing a government which is accountable, promoting economic and industrial development, ending opium trade and securing the rights of the Afghan people.

Afghanistan today is more corrupt than it was in 2001.[7] It produces more drugs than in did in 2001 and it has less security than it did in 2001.[8] At the end of the decade, the West has been unable to deliver in Afghanistan. Instead, the people of Afghanistan have been subjected to a brutal occupation, thousands of civilians have been killed and many Afghans have witnessed firsthand the West's empty promises of 'freedom' and 'human rights' when detained and tortured in Bagram and Kandahar. The Karzai regime, thoroughly discredited by ineptitude, corruption and dealings with brutal warlords, continues to be propped up by both London and Washington. The opium trade is booming and politicians with close ties to the West are alleged to be wrapped up in it. There is no economic or industrial development and despite pledges of billions of dollars in aid, there is little evidence of the rebuilding of Afghanistan that was promised.

Serious crimes of the twenty-first century are being committed in Afghanistan and killing of civilians has become news headlines. I have to say that nowadays the anti-humanity crimes that take place in Afghanistan is responsibility of those who are directly perpetrators, or of those who keep silent towards the killing of civilians or put the innocent Afghans in jails without trial or cut their heads because they teach the children in the villages' schools.

Difference between the Civil War and the Current War

From many Afghans points of views, that the present war has worsened the situation in Afghanistan and it destabilized the rural areas which were saved during the civil war. Thus they say that the main difference of the current war with civil wars is that the mentioned wars took place in urban cities while the current war is spread in the rustic areas of the country.

Solution for the Afghan war

I would like to give you and analogy which I heard from Mr. Shah Mahmood Miakhel (Country Director of USIP Afghanistan): if we compare Afghanistan with a patient, when a patient goes to doctor, the doctor would ask for the history of the symptoms, then the doctor recommends some lab examination or X ray, and after diagnosing the problem, the doctor gives prescription. The patient and doctor should make sure to use the full dose of the prescription otherwise the symptoms will return back. If symptoms return back next time the doctor will prescribe the stronger dose of medicine. If the prescription is not according to the symptoms, it will have side affect no matter it is high dose or low dose.

The patient by the name of Afghanistan, having more than 50 doctors, and no one has recommended him some lab work or x-rays, no one want to diagnose the problem, but they are giving him prescriptions. And some time they would like to test the expired dose, some time these doctors recommend the dose that already had bad affect on the health of Afghanistan (like withdrawal, blind bombardments, night riding) and some time they recommend the dose of Pakistan interferences is the better option for the treatment of Afghanistan. Unfortunately, these doctors pretend that they know the patient before sending him for lab tests or X-rays, but they do not know that the patient's disease is transferrable and fatal, it may will madness the doctors and compelled him to go themselves to the hospitals.

In case of Afghanistan, the different stakeholders have different solution for this country. Some want to be in Afghanistan till the end of the last Talib fighter, while the other is willing to leave Afghanistan as soon as they can, some others support the idea of reconciliation and reintegration with the Taliban, while others supports the idea of partition of Afghanistan (dividing Afghanistan to the north and south).

The Afghans are themselves divided, debating whether the presence of foreign troops is driving the conflict or the only thing keeping the Kabul government from total collapse. And their reactions to the war vary based on geography. In the south, intensified military operations have made people realize the very real costs of war. The threat of rolling violence has forced thousands from their homes, further disrupting social and economic rhythms and they expect that coalition forces should leave sooner rather than later.

Residents of the north and capital, a so called honey pot for foreign money by the southern residents, seem to think that 2014 is far too soon and they worry that a premature pullout would undo some of the socioeconomic advances made since the fall of the Taliban.

I do not like to challenge good ideas or programs but the problem is that this patient, Afghanistan, is in life support, need to be saved, and status of this patient should be changed from critical to stable condition, then we can implement good ideas or programs in the long run.

Is exile of the alien troops a path of solution?

If now the international troops withdraw from Afghanistan and Afghan troops take their place, in their opinion then there will be peace in Afghanistan and Taliban will halt the war. However, such thinking is not valid because the Taliban and those who fight in Afghanistan deem that they fight for the sake of Almighty Allah and their struggles are not limited to the existence of foreign troops in the country. They may prove by some verses (Ayahs) of the Holy Quran and prophets Hadith that they shall prolong the battle against bondsmen of the infidel since the Afghans who are backed and trained by the foreigners are the same as them. Thus it is prioritized to combat against those who serve the infidel and show themselves as Muslims.

Conclusion

The United States should by no means abandon Afghanistan, but it is time to abandon the current strategy that is not working. Trying to pacify Afghanistan by force of arms will not work. A costly military campaign there is more likely to jeopardize America's vital security interests than to protect them. America and its allies should try to win the hearts and minds of Afghans and should work closely with the Afghans to rebuild their country, politically and economical.

In light of the above, I make the following suggestions to the Government of Afghanistan:

1. The government should endeavor in accordance with new methodologies of political and social sciences not to appear non-Islamic to the people. Corrupt governments never could be reckoned Islamic ones. No official task should be in clash with religious principles.
2. The organs established for religious affairs should not be symbolic, but they might study the causes, on an academic basis, of why opponents utilize them in excommunicating governments.
3. The experiences from the Amanullah Khan era up to the present are in front of us. Analysing these experiences may bring solutions. Another solution is to increase mutual understanding and open opportunities for negotiation. This entails the government leaving its barricades and fortifications and communicating with the nation, thereby increasing public awareness of government programs.
4. It is also necessary that we should arrange all official and governmental affairs in accordance with Afghani traditions and national values, and not copy alien ideologies soiled with non-Islamic and non-Afghani guidelines and policies. This, however, does not mean that we may not learn from and utilize instruments, technology, and science from the West.

Notes and References

1. See the quarterly reports of the Afghan NGO Safety Office, 2006–10, http://www.afgnso.org/index_files/Page447.htm (accessed on September 2010).
2. Soon after migrating to Medina, the first important social decree of Prophet Muhammad was on the issue of brotherhood. The Muslim community of Medina was divided into two groups: the *Ansar* and the *Muhajirin*. "*Ansar*" (Helpers) was a title used for the natives of Medina, whereas "*Muhajirin*" (Immigrants) was a title used for those Muslims, mostly from Mecca, who had migrated to Medina. Among the *Ansar*, there were two tribes known as the Aws and the Khazraj who were bitter enemies and had fought each other for more than a century. The Prophet had resolved this conflict even before he migrated to Medina. With the advent of Islam, the Aws and the Khazraj put their past animosity behind and accepted the bond of Islamic brotherhood. See *Seera-tul_ Al Nabi (SUW)* (Jamia Islamia Al-Alamia, 1989), 321.
3. www.afghanistanstudygroup.com
4. http://www.longwarjournal.org/archives/2010/02/the_military_strateg.php#ixzz14aL6q1bR
5. http://www.allvoices.com/contributed-news/7330965-karzai-wants-reduction-in-us-military-operations-in-afghanistan
6. http://www.usip.org/files/resources/SR%20256%20%20Dangerous%20Liaisons%20with%2 0the%20Afghan%20Taliban.pdf
7. http://www.winnipegfreepress.com/world/afghanistan-among-most-corrupt-nations-report-finds-105846628.html
8. www.bbc.co.uk/news/world-south-asia-11442411

14

Pakistan's Strategic Interest in Afghanistan

Savita Pande

> The centre of the Pakistani solar system is not the sun, as innocents may tend to believe, but our elephant-like neighbour to the east, from whose bosom once-upon-a-time we were carved: India. We may be fighting a war on our western frontier and the greatest threat to the idea envisioned by our luckless founding fathers may come from the forces of religious extremism... whose creation in present form and shape is one of the singular achievements of our defence establishment... but all our war doctrines are based on the real or presumed threat from the east.
>
> Ayaz Amir, *The News*, 24 December 2010[1]

Pakistan's strategic interests in Afghanistan are rooted in geographical contiguity of the two nations and hence the shared social, cultural, religious and ethnic linkages, which in turn, underline the nature of relationship between the two. This also explains why the United States forged alliances with it, particularly in Afghan War and in Global War on Terror. In the background of cold war bipolar rivalry, Soviet intervention in Afghanistan made Pakistan the frontline state of the United States. In a bid to counter Soviet action, an arms "pipeline" was established through Pakistan to through which flew arms and money to rebels—the mujahedeen.[2] Pakistan recognized seven Islamist Afghan parties and permitted the leaders to regulate the distribution of relief supplies to the rebels who had fled and sought refuge in Pakistan. Thus from 1982 to 1990 the CIA, together with the ISI and Saudi Intelligence funded "training, arrival and arming of some 35,000 Islamic militants from 43 Muslim countries in Pakistani madrasas. This global *jihad* launched by Zia and Reagan sowed the seeds of

Al-Qaeda and turned Pakistan into world centre of Jihadism for the next two decades."[3] As the Soviets withdrew, anti-Communism *Jihad* became anti-America *Jihad*![4]

Post-Soviet withdrawal Pakistan became extremely interventionist in an Afghanistan fraught with inter-mujahedeen rivalry as well as instability. It started backing Hekmatyar whose party (Hizb–i-Islami) received the largest Pakistani aid.[5] When he failed to turn the situation in favour of Pakistan, the latter changed gear and brought to the fore the Deobandi, puritanical Islam followers from Taliban who were Pushtun and fundamentalists, nurtured in the Pakistani refugee camps, trained in Pakistani seminaries (madrasas).[6] The Taliban came to power as a brainchild of Benazir's Interior Minister, Naseerullah Babar.[7] In 1996, the Taliban assumed power in Afghanistan, (renaming it as "Amarate-Islami Afghanistan," Islamic state of Afghanistan) after defeating the Northern Alliance, a Pushtun conglomerate led by Ahmad Shah Masud.[8]

Post 9/11 Pakistan had to make a U-turn in Afghanistan policy. There were a number of factors which brought about this "volte face." According to Amer Rizwan, these ranged from "coercive diplomacy by the US to the realization on the part of Pakistani elite that had it not acted decisively and quickly on that count, the country might have been pushed into a blind alley. Pakistan was *also haunted by the traditional Indian nightmare in case of Pakistan's failure to take a somersault; that any foot-dragging on the part of Pakistan in this regard might imply playing India's game which was more than ready to pounce on the opportunity and let the US and international community decimate Pakistan,* as they later did in case of Taliban."[9] (Emphasis added.)

Strategic Interests

According to Oliver Roy, the permanent strategic goals of Pakistan are: (a) to have a friendly government in Kabul to prevent the reconstitution of a Kabul-New Delhi axis; (b) to establish strategic depth against India, by using Afghan territory and a corridor towards Central Asia, which could be used to import gas and oil; (c) to enact a 'Sunni Islamic policy', which is the very basis of Pakistan's legitimacy, both internally and regionally. The policy would serve to help the Pakistani Government procure the support of militant religious networks in the country and diverting their attention from internal politics to regional militancy.[10]

For Weinbaum and Harder, Pakistan's policy goals in Afghanistan are: (a) counter Afghan moves to carve out Pushtunistan; (b) minimize India's influence and presence in Afghanistan; (c) see Afghanistan as an asset in providing strategic depth in the event of a wide conflict with India; (d) foster friendly if not subservient regimes in Kabul; (e) use of Afghanistan to attract of regional and extra-regional powers, (especially US) for security leverage in its disputes, especially with India.[11]

However, at a macro level, the objectives and interests evolved as Afghan saga moved from situations to situations. Thus as the Soviets withdrew, Pakistani objectives were: to install a Pushtun-dominated government, which would (a) accept the Durand Line; (b) would allow Pakistan to expand its sphere of influence into Central Asia, thus becoming a bridge between latter and the Arabian Sea.[12]

Pakistan's objectives in creation of Taliban was no different, namely secure a strategic depth against India as well as have camps to train militants to infiltrate into Jammu and Kashmir; to get recognition of Durand Line; to assuage fear of Pushtun nationalism; create an outlet for Pakistan's Islamic radicals, thus preventing a radical Islamist movement at home, a move that clearly boomeranged; securing trade routes to Central Asia and get a reliable and alternative source of gas supply from that region; to have the pipelines laid to India and Arabian Sea through Pakistan so as to accrue economic dividends (the United States initially supported the anti-Iran, pro-West Taliban, also because of plans to build a gas pipeline from Turkmenistan across Afghanistan to Pakistan by US firm Unical, a move reversed in 1998).

Post 9/11 a definite turn came to these interests. The issue now was how to retain these objectives as well as continue to maintain a balance between keeping a pro-Pakistan future government option alive as well as seen to be complying with the US demand, failing which, it could be "bombed to Stone age"!

The United States, got, apart from logistical support, "access to bases and over flight rights." Pakistan deployed 80,000 to 120,000 troops from the paramilitary Frontier Corps and regular army units along the Pakistani-Afghan border.[13] Most of the money, channeled by US to Pakistan, "however, went to build up Pakistan's defenses with India, as al Qaeda and the Taliban regrouped in the wilds of Western Pakistan."[14]

A consequence of Pakistan's U-turn on Afghanistan policy was rise of FATA as an epicenter of terrorism. The emergence of a Pakistani

Taliban is a post-2001 development, a reaction to Pakistani military assaults in the tribal areas. Operating since2004 in different agencies, leaders like Baitullah Mehsud, Maulvi Nazir, Mullah Fazlullah, Maulvi Faqir, et al, in late 2007 they coalesced under the banner of the Tehrik-e-Taliban under the purported leadership of Baitullah Mehsud of South Waziristan, who was succeeded by Hakimullah Masud on his death. "Talibanization" of the Pashtun belt initiated n North and South Waziristan of Pakistan in 2004, soon engulfed Mohmand, Orakzai and Kurram agencies as well as frontier areas of Bannu, Tank, Kohat, Lakki Marwat, Dera Ismail Khan, Swat and Buner. Thus in the post 9/11 phase Pakistan has continued providing sanctuary and support to the Taliban.

Strategic Depth and India

Pakistan's strategic planners have long worried about absence of its strategic depth. This deficiency of Pakistan's geographic paradigm is reflected in the narrowness and the location of cities and communication networks within short striking range of its prime adversary India. A weak dependent as well as pro-Pakistan Afghanistan was believed to give Pakistan this much desired strategic depth.

The quest for strategic depth dominated Pakistani thinking beginning in the late 1980s. Afghanistan was chosen to provide safe harbor for Pakistani forces in the event of conflict with India. Articulated in 1989 by the then Chief of Army Staff, General Mirza Aslam Beg, the notion of 'strategic depth' in the context of Pak-Afghan relations essentially meant "...hiding Pakistan's military assets in Afghanistan beyond the current offensive capabilities of the Indian military... Its pursuit entailed five assumptions: a) in a crisis, Pakistan would have the leisure of time; b) Pakistan would transfer its equipment to a place of its choosing; c) logistical support for such an undertaking would always remain available; d) the places west of the Durand Line would remain safe from Indian attacks; e) Pakistan would dominate, maintain and sustain huge safe houses in areas hundreds of miles deep into Afghanistan."[15] Interestingly, Ahmed Rashid has talked about retired ISI officers' claims before 9/11 "for Pakistan's support to the Taliban regime was to gain access to vast former Soviet underground storage bunkers built at major airfields such as Bagram. Here Pakistan could stash away conventional and nuclear-tipped missiles in order to enhance its second-strike capability against India in case of war."[16]

Weinbaum says, a cooperative, if not altogether satellite Afghan state would be an insurance against threat from India or any forces aligned with in the northwest frontier; and "a pure Islamic state in Afghanistan not only promised to neutralize Pashtun irredentism but also helped to train and indoctrinate jihadis for the struggle against India in Kashmir."[17] Thus in Pakistan's perspective, the mujahedeen *jihadists* were "valuable paramilitary irregulars" who could supplement Pakistani security forces in the event of conflict. And, instead of controlling them it was better to keep them occupied, first on the eastern border fomenting trouble for India, and then on the other border with Afghanistan.[18]

According to Ahmad Rashid, "Kashmir dispute continued to be a key factor in the intense rivalries that erupted between India and Pakistan after 9/11. *Islamabad viewed its Afghan policy through the prism of denying India any advantage in Kabul*."[19] Interestingly, it has been argued that "Pakistan does not want an Afghanistan controlled by the Taliban" as that could "lead to an alliance between the Afghan and Pakistani Taliban," who could benefit from "reverse strategic depth" inside Afghanistan.[20]

It is therefore hardly surprising that Pakistan left no stone unturned to deny India an advantage. As it decided to reverse its policy on Taliban, Musharaf in his famous speech of 19 September 2001, put the onus on India, arguing it could be advantage Kashmir for the latter.[21] Terror attacks in India continued regardless of massive deployment of troops by Pakistan on the other border, notwithstanding Musharaf's claims to the contrary in his January 2002 speech.

There is no doubt that India's increased presence is seen as worrisome by Pakistan establishment. India has consulates in Jalalabad, Kandahar, Herat, and Mazar-e-Sharif, and is alleged by Pakistan to back rebels in Baluchistan. India built a 215-km long, 600 crore Delaram-Zaranj highway in January 2009.[22] India's other major infrastructure projects include, construction of Afghan Parliament, 220kV DC transmission line from Pul-e-Khumri to Kabul; 220/110/20 kV sub-station at Chimtala, Salma Dam project in Heart, besides humanitarian assistance projects like gift of 250,000 metric tonnes of wheat, feeding school children, medical and sanitation and community development projects.[23] Writes Kaplan, "When India talks of building dams in Kunar, the ISI thinks that India wants to help

Afghanistan steal Pakistan's water. *Karzai's open alliance with India is nearly a casus belli for the ISI.*"[24] (Emphasis added.)

However, India does not maintain troops in Afghanistan. The offer to effect was turned by the US in view of Pakistan's resistance. After Taliban killed an Indian engineer in 2006, India sent in a company of paramilitary troops to protect the engineers working on the road construction projects, a development discomforting to Pakistan.[25]

Analysing the impact of India Weinbaum and Harder conclude that "sponsorship of Afghan leaders and political groups has regularly calculated their expected or demonstrated partiality toward India. But attempts to intervene have only increased Afghan leaders' efforts to offset Pakistan's influence by turning toward India and strengthening the impression that Afghanistan would allow India to use its soil against Pakistan."[26]

Pushtunistan

After India, Pakistan's strategic concerns lie in preventing the rise of Pashtunistan, an independent state carved out of Pushtun dominated land across Pakistan and Afghanistan. The term, though coined by the Pushtuns on the Afghan side was never clearly defined and may not have got the targeted popularity but has been compelling enough to make Pakistani leaders insecure. Barnett Rubin says the Afghan war gave Pakistan "*a golden opportunity to act on its long-standing desire to weaken Pashtun nationalism.*"[27] (Emphasis added.) Others have also argued that the presence of large Pashtun populations on both sides of the border between Afghanistan and Pakistan has also been a source of tension between the two. Although these tensions were latent since the 1960s, Pakistan's interest in seeing a friendly government in Afghanistan is also rooted in apprehensions of a Pashtun secession movement in Pashtunistan, the North West Frontier region in Pakistan, which might be supported by Kabul.[28]

This was sought to be done through fomenting active support to pan-Islamism among the Afghan refugees as it sponsored Pakistani Islamist parties in the border region. This resulted in a newer brand of "Pashtun Islamism," spread exponentially as Taliban rose to power—pan-Islamist solidarity surpassed tribalism and ethnic cohesion.

The demand has been supported by various regimes of Afghanistan, albeit with varying intensity. Thus during the reign of

Zahir Shah's monarchy, Muhammad Daud's republic (1953 to 1963 and again after 1973 when he overthrew former in a coup), forcefully championed Afghan royal claims to a greater Pashtunistan; with the post-1978 communist governments in Kabul, the movement saw an upswing, either an independent Pushtunistan to be carved out of Pakistan or a "Greater Afghanistan" annexing lost Pushtun areas in Pakistan. Pakistan's response, like its general response to ethnic conflict has been repression. Thus during its role as a frontline state in the aftermath of Soviet intervention in Afghanistan, it prevented flow of aid, arms and money, to groups close to Zahir Shah, a strong proponent of Pashtunistan.[29]

There have been differences between Afghanistan and Pakistan Pushtunistan supporters on the issue. In 1969 the Afghan Government had published a Pashtunistan postage stamp on which Pashtunistan included only the areas of FATA, the NWFP (now Khyber Pukhtunkhwah) and Baluchistan. Pakistani Pushtun nationalists like Ajmal Khattak was not pleased with "this not-so-subtle gimmick of the Afghan state" excluding the Pashtun territories under their control from Pashtunistan.[30] Adeel Khan says in the post independence Pakistan KKM sought a new identity, Ghaffar Khan shifting focus from demanding an independent state to increased autonomy.[31] The NAP moved towards pragmatism, former forming coalition government in 1972 with the JUI in the then NWFP (now Khyber-Pukhtunkhwah) was banned by Bhutto in 1975 when it merged with other parties and formed ANP.[32] This notwithstanding, the Pakistani establishment has frequently cited the Bannu Declaration of 22 June1947, whereby Ghaffar Khan had sought the option of independent Pashtunistan versus joining Pakistan (rather than joining India and Pakistan) in the referendum to be held for partition. On being denied its demand the Red Shirt movement led by Ghaffar Khan boycotted the Referendum.[33]

Historically, secular Pashtun nationalism was much stronger in the first two decades of Pakistan's political history, when hostility between Islamabad and Kabul were quite high with each side backing low-level subversive activities against the other.[34] As Pashtun economic interests emerged in Afghanistan and as Awami National Party decided to join hands with Pakistan National Alliance to overthrow Zulfikar Ali Bhutto's government, nationalist fervor declined. The trend continued as Pashtun migration to other places like Karachi began, labour movement accompanied Pashtun entrepreneurs joining and then dominating certain sectors like transportation in most big cities of Pakistan. In the post Zia Pakistan, as the Pashtun nationalist political parties got elected to national and provincial assemblies, they moderated their demand, replacing "Pashtunistan" with "Pashtunkhwa," the latter was to be province for all Pashtuns "living east of the Durand Line" to include "NWFP, some districts of Baluchistan, and the tribal agencies."[35]

Nasreen Ghufran argues that Taliban is not an ethno-nationalist movement. At best the movement may have taken advantage of the Pushtuns' disgruntlement with the (poor) delivery of public goods, the inequitable distribution of resources, and the general lack of provincial autonomy under the garb of religious fanaticism in Pakistan. To quote her, "The majority of the TTP members are said to be Pushtuns, but no studies exist that provide statistics regarding the percentage of Pushtuns, Punjabis, or other ethnic groups in the TTP. The existence of Punjabi Taliban and Taliban of Central Asian descent brings into question the often-assumed strictly Pushtun identity of the movement." Notwithstanding this, the Taliban has attracted Pashtun attention as they have invoked religious card—*jihad* against the US and its forces who have spilled "Pushtun blood" across border.[36]

The worst case scenario is presented by Selig Harrison who argues that the radicalization of the Pashtun areas on both sides of the Pakistan-Afghanistan border "has intensified both Islamist zealotry and Pashtun nationalism. In the conventional wisdom, one or the other, either Islamist or Pashtun identity, will eventually triumph, but an equally plausible possibility is that the result could be what Hussain Haqqani has called an 'Islamic Pashtunistan'."[37] Seth Jones has also argued there were deep divisions among the Pashtun ethnic majority regarding the Taliban. While the Pashtun Ghilzai tribes, as well as such Durrani tribes as the Alekozai, Eshaqzais, and Norzais supported them, most Durrani Pashtuns and a number of other eastern and southern Pashtun groups did not support the Taliban.[38] Again, even though many Pushtuns belong to TTP, the latter has not used Pushtun nationalism card as that "would deprive the organization of other (e.g., Saudi, Uzbek, Turkmen, etc.) sources of financial, military, and political support."[39]

Pashtun resentment towards the Musharraf government's policy of cooperation with the US had manifested itself during the October 2002 general elections in Pakistan, as evident from the success achieved by the candidates of the religious parties' alliance, the MMA (Muttahida-Majlis-I-Amal).[40] Weibaum says Pakistan's support to Afghan Taliban has an eye for the future in the post withdrawal Afghanistan. Pashtuns "will serve Pakistan's interests as a proxy force in creating a Pashtun buffer zone in southern and eastern Afghanistan."[41]

Durand Line

In the process of making Afghanistan an isolated buffer state between their empire and Russia, on 12 November 1893, the British signed an agreement with the then Amir of Afghanistan which laid down Durand Line defining the southern and eastern limits of the Amir's dominion, beyond which he renounced any claim. Post independence, Afghanistan does not agree to the agreement, which it holds was signed under duress. Afghan parliament, in June 1949 proclaimed cancellation of all the treaties that former Afghan Governments has signed with the British-India government, including the Durand Treaty, thereby announcing that the Afghan government does not recognize the Durand Line as a legal boundary between Afghanistan and Pakistan, a stand it holds today.[42] Dispute also extends to time scope, with some claiming that the treaty expired after the lapse of hundred years.

There is no consensus on details among the Afghans.[43] Those who advocate of Pashtun ethnic unity claiming the Afghan nation beyond Afghanistan set their boundary at the Indus River to create a Pashtunistan, independent or otherwise; others would draw the boundary at the limits of the settled zones of the NWFP saying the Frontier Agencies were never directly administered by the British, the frontier residents freely crossing the Durand line do not consider it legal. Still others do not mind settling the issue with Pakistan, using it as bargaining chip for Afghan interests. Part of the reason for the difference is that the partially demarcated boundary is largely theoretical, existing more in theory or maps than otherwise and is rarely policed and is managed by Maliks. In fact till 2001in the adjoining tribal areas military was confined to small bases, practically nonexistent. Under an agreement with the tribals in 1947, Pakistan had promised not to place any troops in Khyber, Kurram, and South and North Waziristan; elsewhere also it had isolated cantonments.

By contrast, Pakistan holds Durand Line as a formal international boundary; as a successor state to the British Raj, it claims legal title to the lands up to the line. From Pakistan's point of view, the issue is not open to negotiation, even though Pakistan, like the British, failed to establish direct state administrative authority in the tribal areas. Pakistan's official claim is "there is no move to renegotiate the Durand Line; this question is closed, and there is a proper Pakistan-Afghanistan border and there is no agreement of free move across the border. It is recognized and it is verifiable through modern technical means."[44] Pakistan claims that the Durand Accord specified no time limits, and the boundary, as demarcated under this accord, should be formally recognized as the international border between Afghanistan and Pakistan. Lack of unitary version of Durand Line is further complicated by free movement of people across the border.

In the 1960s and 1970s diehard Pushtun nationalists claimed that Afghanistan's borders "extended up to Indus River, well south of Peshawar, a claim if acknowledged would have cut Pakistan into half."[45] However, argues Ahmed Rashid, "Pakistan Government did not push the Afghans to recognize the Durand Line as it suited Pakistani expansionist ambition to keep the border situation fluid."[46] Interestingly, as Oliver Roy pointed out, the Taliban, who did not want the establishment of 'Pashtunistan' on both sides of the Afghan Pakistan border but, nevertheless, were "still reluctant to define the Durand Line as an international border."[47]

The issue of Durand Line also dogs the fencing of Pakistan Afghanistan border as proposed by Pakistan. Afghan objections ostensibly are rooted in the fear that it might be seen as tacit support for the Durand Line, notwithstanding the fact "the measure could reduce the smuggling of contraband."[48] It would also lie to rest Pakistan's claims of support of its rebels through the border.

Economy, Trade

Landlocked Afghanistan has had trade linkages (dependence) with Pakistan by virtue of being its neighbour. Its economy suffered adversities due to periodic impeding transit of goods from the port of Karachi. A trade blockade in 1963 facilitated quick fall of Afghanistan's pro-Pashtunistan Prime Minister Mohammad Daud.

Between 2001 and 2006, trade between Pakistan and Afghanistan increased from $100 million to $1.6 billion.[49] The economy of the tribal areas saw a radical transformation, from subsistence pastoral agriculture to dependence on unregulated trade including drugs, exploiting the Afghan Transit Trade Agreement provision that permits duty-free goods into Pakistan for re-export to Afghanistan. India would like to expand its trade with Afghanistan, but Pakistan continues to block the overland transit of Indian goods through its territory.

One of the fallouts of Afghanistan's reconstruction and foreign aid has been "rampant inflation compounded by the replacement of food crops by poppy cultivation" which may have helped Pakistan sustain the elimination of its own narcotics production, but "has also raised wheat prices to twice the level prevailing in Pakistan, prompting large-scale smuggling of food and essential commodities into Afghanistan and contributing to nationwide shortages of wheat flour in Pakistan. Estimates (2008) of the annual volume of gray market trading run as high as $10 billion—five times the official volume of trade between the two countries. A strong parallel economy run by Afghan Pashtuns has also emerged in Baluchistan."[50]

More recently Pakistan and Afghanistan agreed that no Indian export to Afghanistan would be allowed through the Wagah border but Afghanistan would have the opportunity to export to India and reciprocally Pakistan would be able to export its goods to Central Asia through Afghanistan.[51]

In 2008, 60,000 Pakistanis were reportedly employed in Afghanistan. Private investment in Afghanistan shows signs of growing: annual exports account for US$1.2 billion, (as opposed to the US$25 million in exports during the Taliban era) imports more than US$700 million worth of goods.[52] Pakistan has reportedly helped to improve airports, civil aviation, roads, and highways are all meant to create a better infrastructure for trade. A promised US$200 million development aid package, containing some 20 projects, is also pledged for education, health care, housing, and other social sectors

Afghanistan is also a potential route for access to Central Asian energy. A pipeline from Turkmenistan across Afghanistan to Pakistan (and India)—the 1,700-km-long Turkmenistan-Afghanistan-Pakistan-India (TAPI) —was conceived in 1990s (the last, India, joined much later). However, owing to major differences with the Taliban regime, Unocal, the US led consortium, failed to undertake construction work on the ADB backed project.

As per the framework agreement signed during the Ashkhabad Summit on 11 December 2010, the envisaged route of the gas pipeline is from Turkmen city of Dauletabad gas fields to Fazilaka, India via Herat-Kandahar (Afghanistan) and Quetta, Pakistan. The designated capacity of the gas is expected to be 33 billion cubic metres per year with estimated cost of $8 billion. According to initial estimates, "India and Pakistan would each stand to receive around 38 million cubic meters of gas (42% each) out of the 90 million cubic meters shipped daily," with the rest going to Afghanistan. For Pakistan it also means transit fees and employment opportunity.[53] Instability in Afghanistan and Pakistan are the major reasons why the project remains on paper, apart from price and availability of the Turkmen Gas.

Pakistan has also immensely benefitted financially from the "Frontline status" two times. When Pakistan became frontline state, the US provided $3.2 billion in 1980 to be followed by another 4.2 billion in 1986.[54] Another estimate says that the US provided $3 billion during 1980s to the rebels, and Saudi Arabia gave nearly $4 billion, this excluding that given by private individuals or charitable organizations.[55] The CIA, "with Saudi finances as well as Pakistani logistical support, managed the raising, training, equipping, paying and sending into battle against the Red Army in Afghanistan of a mercenary army of Islamist volunteers."[56] In the second "frontline status state, the US aid to Pakistan from 2001 to 2008 is estimated to be US$11.2 billion, the bulk of which has gone to security assistance either through military aid or reimbursements.[57] The Post Chagai nuclear sanctions were lifted, thus permitting a 5-year, US$3 billion aid programme (including military), besides granting funds for counter-terrorism. Pakistan also became eligible for purchase advanced fighter jets and received compensation for the non-delivery of an earlier consignment of F-16s;a training programme for military officers suspended during the 1990s was revived; in addition to US$3 billion in debt rescheduling; and debt relief from IMF to the tune of US$9 billion.[58]

Getting Away with N-Proliferation

The Afghan intervention also advanced Pakistan's interests unintentionally. In 1979-90 Pakistan's nuclear weapon programme, albeit clandestine, got a boost when the US had to lift sanctions preventing aid to it imposed under Glenn Symington Amendment on the eve of Soviet intervention.[59] Not only did it overlook Solarz Amendment preventing aid to countries clandestinely acquiring nuclear commodities from US for use in nuclear explosives, the American President, under Pressler Amendment continued to certify year after year from 1985 to 1989 that Pakistan did not possess a nuclear device.[60] As Soviets withdrew from Afghanistan, in 1990, sanctions were reimposed on Pakistan, with the American President refusing to certify that it did not possess nuclear explosive device.

Again post 9/11 not only did its clandestine programme got a legitimacy when US ended sanctions slapped post-Chagai nuclear explosion, the United States also looked the other way as Pakistan conducted unabashed nuclear proliferation. Write Levy and Scott, "But the consensus in Washington was that what mattered more than prosecuting the guilty was saving Pakistan's vulnerability (and valuable) president."[61] Khan's role in proliferation related activities, especially to Libya, North Korea, Egypt, Saudi Arabia, has been well documented.[62] The state got away with putting the entire blame on "the father of the Pakistani Bomb," namely A Q Khan, notwithstanding the common knowledge about who has the finger on the nuclear trigger in Pakistan and closely guarded the clandestinely acquired programme is.[63]

The western sources raise concern, "that most of Pakistan's nuclear sites are close to or even within areas dominated by Pakistani Taliban militants and home to Al-Qaeda."[64] Listed in support of such assertions are attacks on nuclear missile storage facility at Sargodha on 1 November 2007; on Pakistan's nuclear airbase at Kamra by a suicide bomber 10 December 2007; and armament complexes at the Wah cantonment on 20 August 2008 attack.[65] The reason for the fears is rooted in the collusion between those who have access and the militants for they share an anti-US sentiment.

Central Asia

Pakistan's fears, argues Fair, "of Indian encirclement are not limited to Delhi's presence in Afghanistan. India's relations with Iran, rapprochement with China, and access to Central Asian states (including two bases in Tajikistan), animate Pakistan's concerns that it is being surrounded by hostile states or states friendly to India."[66]

Pakistan's desire to have good relations a la forming an Islamic brotherhood did not succeed. Nor did its "Muslim security belt stretching from Turkey to Pakistan with Central Asia as the 'buckle,' to provide both 'strategic depth' and needed allies in her policy struggles over Afghanistan and Kashmir," materialize.[67] Pakistan's objectives to establishing trade links with the landlocked Central Asian nations in order to give them access to the Arabian Sea port of Gwadar required a cooperative Afghanistan given its geographical position. Another Pakistani interest has been the potential 1,040 mile gas pipeline from Turkmenistan. Rizwan Zeb says, "Later Islamabad's support to the Taliban, which the CARs opposed and perceived as a threat to their national security, created further problems, which became the primary reason why Pakistan's *bid for observer status in the SCO was rejected.*"[68]

Post September 11, Pakistan has found a new ally in Central Asia and a strong supporter for its membership in the SCO. Uzbekistan seems ready to move past the Pakistani Government's former support for radical Islamic groups in Central Asia. Uzbekistan is interested in gaining accesses to Pakistan's major Indian Ocean ports of Karachi and Gwadar. Despite this latest goodwill, the specter of Islamic radicals who fled Uzbekistan and sought refuge in Pakistan remains a "delicate issue."[69]

Iran

Enjoying an early bonhomie with Iran from the days of CENTO and RCD (now evolved into ECO) and receiving support on Kashmir, 1965 and 1971wars, Afghanistan today perhaps is the roadblock of its relationship. While usually downplaying their differences, irritants in the relations are Pakistan's relations with the United States and Saudi Arabia; within Pakistan, Iran plays a role in the sectarian conflict, backing Shias against majority Sunnis, and both countries suspect the other's involvement in insurgencies in their Baluchistans (Sistan Baluchistan in case of Iran). In Afghanistan the prime objective of Iran is to reduce influence of United States and Saudi Arabia and Sunni Islam in its neighbourhood. It is here that it has had a clash of interest with Pakistan. Iran's objectives in Afghanistan are clear: to create economic influence a la reconstruction, reduce US influence, retain buffer zone of Herat and check drug trafficking. Things became worse as the initial rapprochement between Iran and US after the former strongly condemned 9/11 attacks and participated in Bonn conference ended a la Bush including Iran in his 2002 "axis of evil" speech.

As Soviets intervened in Afghanistan, Iran, engaged in hostage crisis, was tilting towards Soviet Union. Its reaction thus was confined to verbal criticism and demand for withdrawal of Soviet forces, notwithstanding the refugee inflow (incidentally were later trained in Iran[70]). Iran's role was further reduced as it got embattled with Iraq. As the war ended, Iran apart from ending isolation and helping Soviets check US influence, sought to ensure stability on its borders with Afghanistan "as it was rebuilding its own shattered economy, to support the establishment of a Tehran-friendly government in Kabul, *to reduce the influence of Pakistan* and especially Saudi Arabia in Afghanistan, and to transform itself into a critical trade and energy bridge between Central Asia, Afghanistan, and the Persian Gulf."[71] Post withdrawal civil war saw Iran consolidating Darri speaking non-Pushtun minorities as well as consolidating Shia groups in the form of Hizb-e-Wahadat as also hobnobbing with Jamaat-i-Islami parties in Tajikistan and Afghanistan. Within Afghanistan the polarization was clear: Pakistan, Saudi Arabia on one side and Iran on the other.[72]

As Taliban rose to power, support was also given to, besides Hizb-e-Wahadat, to Massoud and Dostum.[73] It was this Taliban which indulged in ruthless killings of Hazaras in its Pakistan-backed battle for Mazar-e-Sharif which was heavily contested by Northern Alliance and the kidnapping and subsequent killing of eight Iranian diplomats in September1998, despite amassing of troops on border by Iran. The Taliban then ran through of Iranian cultural centre in Mazar-e Sharif, setting the library ablaze, and violently crushing an uprising in Herat in May of 1999, reducing amount of life-giving water flowing from the Helmand river to Iran.

Apart from pledging assistance at Kabul and London conference, Iran has given Afghanistan $43 million to improve a 125-kilometer "Golden transit Route," linking the Dougharoun region in Iran to Heart, inaugurated by Karzai in 2005. Besides the construction of a 176-kilometer railroad linking it to Heart, Iran has also provided loans and grants to Tajikistan for the construction of a 5 kilometer transit route Anzab tunnel to connect Iran, through Herat, Mazar-e-Sharif, and Tajikistan, to China; it is upgrading a tax-free trade route, linking the Oman-based port of Chabahar to the southwestern border post of Malik in Afghanistan, and to Kandahar and Kabul, which once completed, would greatly diminish the economic importance of the Karachi-Kandahar road, Afghanistan's only current roadway to international markets. It is upgrading bridges over Helmand and Parian rivers on the Iran-Afghanistan border.[74]

The irritant in bilateral relations are, apart from the international troops whose presence is resented by Iran, 2 million refugees of which

900,000 were properly identified; refugees returned to their homeland after the fall of the Taliban, but a significant number returned to Iran. And Turkmenistan-Afghanistan-Pakistan pipeline is an alternative to its own proposed $7 billion, 2,600 kilometer Iran-Pakistan pipeline. Iran wields considerable influence in the "buffer" Herat where Ismail Khan promoted its interests, notwithstanding shifting him from Governor (also withdrawing the title of Emir) to insipid ministry in the Centre. Pakistan is also peeved at India building a port in Chabahar in Iran, which among other things, would solve its connectivity problems and facilitate transport of Indian goods to Afghanistan, in the process bypassing Pakistan completely.[75] Pakistan had long been suspicious of Iranian influence in Afghanistan, but has been making efforts recently to improve relations with Tehran. In February Pakistan claimed to have helped in the capture of Jundollah Sunni rebel group leader Abdolmalek Rigi, who Iran had said was based in its Baluchistan province.[76] Pakistan is also worried about India–Iran defense agreement signed in 2003 which includes warship repair facilities to be constructed at Chahbahar and maintenance and up gradation of Iran's Mig-29s, T-72and anti-tank guide missiles.[77]

Conclusion

9/11 may have changed Pakistan's tactical policy but not its strategic interests in Afghanistan. Implications of its moves have been serious. Pakistan seems to be buying time, procrastinating direct discussions, or follow up with action. Its immediate stake is preventing Indian influence, and the bogey of Indian interference from its consulates in Afghanistan particularly in strife torn Baluchistan. The American withdrawal will give it space, but whether it will reduce pressure on forces, is difficult to say. It would therefore seek to maintain influence by encouraging pro-Pakistan regime, certainly not pro-India regime. Its cultivation/non-action against Afghan Taliban is therefore with an eye to future. In fact Pakistan may well accept scaling down of US troops since it cannot obtain any concessions from Afghanistan as long the US is present, backing the regime.

Manzur Ijaz warns Pakistan against using Pushtun card. "Instead of seeking control over Kabul through a crude Pashtun force, religious or otherwise, Pakistan will have to consolidate and modernise its own Pashtun belt, bordering Afghanistan. If FATA and other backward Pashtun areas have better educational institutions and industrial infrastructure, Pakistan can better compete with India in providing goods and services because of geographical proximity and ethnic similarities."[78]

Seeing Pakistan's drift to support Taliban, the United States may well use Iran to balance Pakistan in Afghanistan. Such a shift could be seen when Iran was, for the first time, invited to join international talks on Afghanistan in Rome; besides the US looked the other way when details of Iran's cash payments to Afghan President Hamid Karzai emerged; and as US-Iran back channel talks continue, it has as a gesture listed the anti-Iranian Jundallah as a terrorist organization.[79]

One can safely conclude with Zafar Hilaly who writes "let us not obsess about India, let us obsess about what is good for us. While it is true that India has built deep inroads within the Northern Alliance and can be counted on to use its influence against us, our interests cannot be confined to containing India alone. Our interests also extend to building vital oil and gas pipelines connected to Central Asia's vast reservoir as well as developing our overland infrastructure for trade and commerce with China, especially with its western regions that border Pakistan."[80]

Notes and References

1. Ayaz Amir, "Let us stop flattering India So Much," *The News*, 24 December 2010, http://www.thenews.com.pk/TodaysPrintDetail.aspx?ID=21826&Cat=9
2. Larry P. Goodsen, *Afghanistan's Endless War: State Failure, Regional Politics and the Rise of Taliban* (Seattle: University of Washington Press, 2001), 60.
3. Ahmed Rashid, *Descent into Chaos* (New Delhi: Allen Lane, 2008), 38–39.
4. Peter Marsden, *Afghanistan: Minorities, Conflict, and the Search for Peace* (London: Minority Rights Group International, 2001), 6.
5. Hizb-i-Islami had 75 per cent Pashtun members; Hekmatyar himself was Kharruti Pashtun. Goodsen, *Afghanistan's Endless War*, 61.
6. Ahmed Rashid, *Taliban: Islam, Oil, and the New Great Game in Central Asia* (New York: I.B. Tauris, 2001), 201–02. It was recognized by Pakistan, UAE and Saudi Arabia as early as 1995.
7. Anthony Davies, "How the Taliban Became a Military Force," in *Fundamentalism Reborn*, William Maley (ed.) (New York: New York

University Press 2010), 43-64; Dennis Kux, *The United States and Pakistan, 1947-2000: Disenchanted Allies* (Baltimore: John Hopkins 2000), 335.

8. Kamal Matinuddin, *The Taliban Phenomenon, Afghanistan 1994—1997* (Karachi: Oxford University Press,1999), 20-24.
9. Amer Rizwan," South Asian Security Complex and Pakistan-United States Relations Post 9/11," *IPRI Journal,* 10/2 (Summer 2010): 47.
10. Oliver Roy, "Why War is Going On In Afghanistan: The Afghan Crisis in Perspective," *Journal of International Affairs,* 2000http://www.sam.gov.tr/perceptions/Volume5/Dec2000-Feb2001/VolumeVN4OLIVIERROY.pdf,
11. Marvin G Weinbaum and Jonathan B Harder, "Pakistan's Afghan policies and their Consequences," *Contemporary South Asia,* 16/1 (March 2008), 26.
12. Mohsen M. Milani, "Iran's Policy Towards Afghanistan," *Middle East Journal,* 60/2 (Spring 2006), 239.
13. Christine Fair, "Time for Sober Realism: Renegotiating US Relations with Pakistan," *The Washington Quarterly* (April 2009), 151. According to Fair, there was "no transparent accounting of the actual number or kind of Pakistani troops arrayed, most of which are ordinarily garrisoned in this theater."
14. Michael Cohen, "No Win Policy for Afghanistan," *Dissent,* 57/2 (Spring 2010), 8.
15. Rizwan Zeb, "War Against Terror: Lessons for Pakistan," unpublished paper, 3-4. Cited in Rifaat Hussain, "Pakistan's Relations with Pakistan and Afghanistan: Continuity and Change," *Strategic Studies*, http://www.issi.org.pk/ss_Detail.php?dataId=227#
16. Ahmed Rashid, *Descent into Chaos*, 121. However, he says, "After U.S. forces searched these Soviet-era airfields it became clear that no such bunkers existed."
17. Marwin Weinbaum, "Afghanistan and its Neighbour: an ever dangerous neighbourhood," USIP, Special Report 162 (June 2006), 5.
18. Hilary Synnott, "What is Happening in Pakistan?" *Survival,* 51/1, 65.
19. Ahmed Rashid, *Descent into Chaos*, 110.
20. Matt Waldman, "Dangerous Liaisons with the Afghan Taliban: The Feasibility and Risks of Negotiations," USIP Special Report 256 (October 2010), 12.
21. Text of Musharaf's speech, *Washington Post online*, 19 September 2001, http://www.washingtonpost.com/wp-srv/nation/specials/attacked/transcripts/pakistantext_091901.html
22. "The Taliban was opposed to this project and launched frequent attacks on the construction workers in an attempt to force the winding up of

the work. A total of six Indians, including a Border Roads Organization driver and four ITBP soldiers, and 129 Afghans were killed in these attacks." *Press Trust of India*, 22 January 2009, "India hands over Zaranj-Delaram highway to Afghanistan," http://timesofindia.indiatimes.com/India/India_hands_over_Zaranj-Delaram_highway_to_Afghanistan/rssarticleshow/4016669.cms

23. *India and Afghanistan: A Development Partnership*, External Publicity Division, Ministry of External Affairs, New Delhi, 2009. The publication gives details of all the ongoing and completed Indian projects in Afghanistan.
24. Robert D Kaplan," Behind the Indian Embassy Bombing," *Atlantic Magazine*, August 2008, http://www.theatlantic.com/magazine/archive/2008/08/behind-the-indian-embassy-bombing/6949/
25. Raja Karthikeya Gundu and Teresita C. Schaffer "India and Pakistan in Afghanistan: Hostile Sports," *South Asia Monitor*, no. 17, Centre for Strategic and International Studies (August 2008).
26. Marvin G Weinbaum and Jonathan B Harder, "Pakistan's Afghan Policies and their Consequences," *Contemporary South Asia,* 16/1 (March 2008): 35.
27. Barnett R. Rubin and Abubakar Siddique, "Resolving the Pakistan-Afghanistan Stalemate," *Special Report*, USIP United States Institute for Peace, Washington DC, October 2006, 10.
28. Meirav Mishali-Ram, "Afghanistan: A Legacy of Violence? Internal and External Factors of the Enduring Violent Conflict," *Comparative Studies of South Asia, Africa and the Middle East,* 28/3 (2008), 478.
29. Selig S Harrison, "'Pashtunistan': The Challenge to Pakistan and Afghanistan," *IDEAS* (Newsletter of Pushtun Peace Forum, Canada), 1/1 (2008), 8.
30. Mohammad Taqi, "Ajmal Khattak: The Revolutionary Dervish," *The Daily Times*, 15 February 2010, http://www.dailytimes.com.pk/default.asp?page=2010%5C02%5C15%5Cstory_15-2-2010_pg3_5
31. Adeel Khan, "Pukhtun Nationalism: From Separation to Integration," *Asian Ethnicity,* 14/1 (February 2003), 67–83. Khyber Pukhtunkhwah or NWFP became part of Pakistan through a referendum in July 1947which they boycotted as they wanted the option to be either an independent Pushtunistan or joining with Afghanistan instead of accession to India or Pakistan. The Muslim League voted in the referendum, for joining Pakistan. KKM was banned in 1948, Khan imprisoned.
32. Joshua T. White, *Pakistan's Islamist Frontier: Islamic Politics and U.S. Policy in Pakistan North West Frontier*, Center on Faith and International Affairs at the Institute for Global Engagement, USA

(November 2008), 96, available at http://www.cfia.org/go/frontier, cited in Nasreen, 1099.

33. Harrison, "'Pashtunistan'," 12.
34. In March 1955, mobs even attacked Pakistan's embassy in Kabul, ransacking the Pakistani consulates in Jalalabad and Kandahar.
35. Rubin and Siddique, "Resolving the Pakistan-Afghanistan Stalemate," 9.
36. Nasreen Ghufran, "Pushtun Nationalism and the spread of Insurgency in The North West Frontier Province of Pakistan," *Asian Survey*, 1093.
37. Harrison, 'Pashtunistan',"12.
38. "An opinion poll carried out by the U.S. State Department in 2007, for example, found that most Hazaras, Pashtuns, Tajiks, and Uzbeks did not view ethnicity as a factor dividing them." Seth G. Jones, "The Rise of Afghanistan's Insurgency State Failure and Jihad," *International Security,* 32/4 (Spring 2008), 11-12.
39. Ghufran, "Pushtun Nationalism," 1108.
40. Maqbool Ahmad Bhatty, "Coping with Afghanistan Challenges," *The Dawn*, 26 July 2003, http://archives.dawn.com/2003/07/26/op.htm
41. Weinbaum and Harder," Pakistan's Afghan Policies and their Consequences," 34.
42. Jon Lunn and Ben Smith," The Af-Pak Policy and Pushtuns," Research Paper 10/45, http://www.unhcr.org/refworld/pdfid/4c21c6062.pdf p. 8.
43. *The Durand Line: History, Consequences, and Future*, conference report organized by the American Institute of Afghanistan Studies and the Hollings Center for International Dialogue Istanbul, Turkey, July 2007 http://www.hollingscenter.org/reports/current/2007-7-Durand Line.pdf
44. This was stated by Mr. Masud Khan, the spokesman of Pakistan for Foreign Affairs, a news briefing on 25 July 2003. *The Dawn*, 26 July 2003, http://www.dawn.com/2003/07/26/top1.htm
45. Rashid, *Descent Into Chaos*, 287.
46. Rashid, *Descent Into Chaos*, 268.
47. Roy, "Why War is Going On In Afghanistan."
48. "Mr Karzai Can't Have it Both Ways," *Daily Times*, 12 March 2006, www.dailytimes.com.pk/default.asp?page=2006%5C03%5C12%5Cstory_12-3-2006_pg3_1
49. Rashid, *Descent into Chaos*, 249.
50. Gundu and Schaffer, "India and Pakistan in Afghanistan," 2.
51. "Pakistan allowed exports to Central Asia through Afghanistan," *The News*, 19 July 2010. http://www.thenews.com.pk/blog/blog_details.asp?id=739
52. Rubin and Siddique, "Resolving the Pakistan-Afghanistan Stalemate," 17–18.

53. Raja Muhammad Khan, "Economic significance of TAPI," *The News*, 21 December 2010, http://www.thenews.com.pk/TodaysPrintDetail.aspx?ID=21431&Cat=2
54. Hussain Haqqani, *Pakistan: Between Military and Mosque*, Carnegie Endowment for International Peace, 2005, 88.
55. Peter L. Bergen, *Holy War, Inc.* (New York: Free Press, 2001), 68; Rashid, *Taliban*, 197.
56. John K Cooley, *Unholy Wars: Afghanistan, America and International Terrorism* (London: Pluto Press, 1999), 2.
57. "Security-related assistance, including reimbursements, arms sales, and internal security assistance, ran $8.1 billion. The remaining $3.1 billion was invested in development programs." C. Christine Fair, Keith Crane, Christopher S. Chivvis, Samir Puri, Michael Spirtas, *Pakistan: Can the United States Secure an Insecure State?* (Santa Monica: Rand Corporation, 2010), 157. The figures have been taken from Kronstadt "*Direct Overt U.S. Aid and Military Reimbursements to Pakistan, FY2002–FY2010*," Washington, D.C, Congressional Research Service, 7 August 2008.
58. K Alan Kronstadt, "Pakistan–US relations," *CRS Report to the Congress*, 6 June 2007, 44. Craig Cohen, *A Perilous Course: US strategy and assistance to Pakistan*, Center for Strategic and International Studies, 2007, 61.
59. For acquisition of Pakistan's nuclear weapon capability, see Herbert Krosney and Steve Weissman, *Islamic Bomb* (New York: Times Book, 1981).
60. Rodney W. Jones and Mark G. Mc Donough, *Tracking Nuclear Proliferation: A Guide to Maps and Charts*, 1998, Carnegie Endowment for International Peace, 1998, 140.
61. "Whatever suited him," a senior British foreign office source said, "he would come up with his own framework for survival and we would help him get through it, as long as the dirty deals were wound up." It was a compromise struck in the world of realpolitik. Adrian Levy and Catherine Scott-Clark, *Deception*, (New Delhi: Penguin, 2007), 355.
62. Thomas C. Reed and Danny B. Stillman, *The Nuclear Express* (Minneapolis, MN: MBI Publishing Company 2010), 261-68.
63. In October 2003, Richard Armitage flew to Islamabad to meet Musharraf. The White House agenda was to keep the general onside. A drama was conceived that drew from Musharraf a promise to shut down Pakistan's nuclear black market in return for winning US support for his unelected regime. It was agreed that A.Q. Khan would be arrested, along with a dozen of his fellow scientists, but Pakistan would keep hold of them, allowing the West to pose limitless questions via

ISI interrogators but leaving the country/'s military elite in the clear. Levy and Scott-Clark, *Deception*, 8.

64. Accordingly nuclear weapon infrastructure is located around region around Islamabad and Rawalpindi—sites such as Wah, Fatehjang, Golra Sharif, Kahuta, Sihala, Isa Khel Charma, Tarwanah, and Taxila.
65. Shaun Gregory, "The Terrorist Threat to Pakistan's Nuclear Weapons," *CTC Sentinel,* 2/7 (2009): 2-3.
66. C. Christine Fair, "Pakistan's Democracy: The Army's Quarry," *Asian Security,* 5/1 (2009): 80.
67. Jefferson Turner, "What is Driving India's and Pakistan's Interest in Joining the Shanghai Cooperation Organization?" *Strategic Insights,* 4/8 (August 2005). http://www.nps.edu/Academics/centers/ccc/publications/Online Journal/2005/Aug/turnerAug05.html
68. Rizwan Zeb, "Pakistan and the Shanghai Cooperation Organization," *China and Eurasia Forum Quarterly,* 4/4 (2006), 55.
69. "Uzbekistani, Pakistani Presidents Discuss Counterterrorism Cooperation," Tashkent Uzbek Television First Channel (in Uzbek), 6 March 2005, FBIS Document ID: CEP20050307000151; "Pakistan's Musharraf Meets Uzbekistan's Karimov, Sign Anti-Terror Agreement," Tashkent Uzbek Radio 1 (in Uzbek), 6 March 2005, FBIS Document ID: CEP20050307000011; and "FYI—Musharraf Says Pakistan, Uzbekistan To Cooperate Against Terrorist Groups," Tashkent Uzbek Television First Channel (in Uzbek), 6 March 2005, FBIS Document ID: CEP20050306000079, cited in Turner, "What is Driving India's and Pakistan's Interest?" http://www.nps.edu/Academics/centers/ccc/publications/OnlineJournal/2005/Aug/turnerAug05.html
70. John K. Cooley, *Unholy Wars: Afghanistan, America and International Terrorism* (London: Pluto Press, 2000), 83-84.
71. Mohsen M. Milani, "Iran's Policy Towards Afghanistan," *Middle East Journal,* 60/2 (Spring 2006), 240.
72. Rasul Bakhsh Rais, "Afghanistan and the Regional Powers," *Asian Survey,* 33/9 (September 1993), 905–22.
73. Amin Saikal, "The Rabbani Government, 1992-96," in, *Fundamentalism reborn? Afghanistan and the Taliban*, William Maley (ed.) (London: C. Hurst and Co., 1998), 41.
74. Mohsen M. Milani, "Iran's Policy Towards Afghanistan," *Middle East Journal,* 60/2 (Spring 2006), 251-2.
75. Gundu and Schaffer "India and Pakistan in Afghanistan," 2.
76. "Pakistan: winning over Tehran and Kabul," Reuters, 13 March 2010, http://blogs.reuters.com/pakistan/2010/03/13/pakistan-winning-over-tehran-and-kabul/

77. Ijaz Khan, *Pakistan's Strategic Culture and Foreign Policy Making: A Study of Afghanistan's Policy Change* (New York: Nova Science Publishers, 2007), 74. According to Ijaz Khan, "From Pakistan's perspective, the most significant provisions the one providing for granting India the use of bases in Iran in case of war between India and Pakistan".
78. Manzur Ejaz, "Washington Diary: Competing in Afghanistan," *Daily Times*, 12 August 2009, http://www.dailytimes.com.pk/default.asp?page=2009%5C08%5C12%5Cstory_12-8-2009_pg3_3
79. Shibil Siddiqui, "Balancing Pakistan Iran and Afghanistan," *The Express Tribune*, 7 November 2010. http://tribune.com.pk/story/73375/balancing-pakistan-iran-and-afghanistan/
80. Zafar Hilaly, "Time to Settle," *The Daily Times*, 24 December 2010, http://www.dailytimes.com.pk/default.asp?page=2010\12\24\story_24-12-2010_pg3_2

15

Afghanistan: The Peace Process and the Role of the *Quetta Shura*

Mariam Safi

Western countries are ostensibly eager to keep Mullah Muhammad Omar, the Amir-ul-Momineen (Commander of the Faithful) of the Taliban insurgency out of peace talks with the Afghan government. Is this a realistic approach, or at the very least, a viable strategy? Looking at the structure of the insurgency it seems highly ambitious to assume that elements within the insurgency will circumvent its Amir and join the negotiation table to end the long and tragic violence that has paralyzed the socio-economic and political development of Afghanistan for three decades. The Strengthening Peace Commission (PTS) established in 2003 and led by Hazrat Sebghatullah Mojaddedi claims to have disarmed 9,000 insurgents since its creation but in reality these numbers are questionable. The failure of PTS was largely a result of an incoherent reintegration strategy, lack of mechanisms for oversight and implementation and insufficient resources. This article will evaluate the insurgency's position on reconciliation and reintegration and identify possible hindrances and solutions as dictated in Mullah Omar's recent Eid sermons, in depth interviews with former members of the Taliban regime, Afghan media, and members of Kandahar's Provincial Council and southern District Shuras[1] (council of tribal elders) members. Exclusively, this analysis has drawn on interviews with the former Foreign Affairs Minister of the Taliban regime Mullah Wakil Ahmad Mutawakil, prominent Afghan journalist Mujahid Kakar, Kandahar Provincial Council Vice Chairman Aghalali Dastagiri, and tribal elders from the most volatile districts in Kandahar, such as Panjwayi, Dand and Daman districts.

The Afghan Peace Process

The July 2014 withdrawal deadline does not signify an end for the insurgency. The peace process aimed to facilitate NATO's withdrawal and the transition of security from foreign to national forces is not pragmatic unless reconciliation is pursued with Mullah Muhammad Omar and his top commanders in the *Quetta Shura*. This approach should be envisioned in accordance with dialogue tools that would set a simultaneous process of top-down and bottom-up mechanisms at reconciliation and reintegration. Regrettably, the international community does seem prepared to acknowledge that its 'war on terror' measures have failed to enthuse the Taliban to join the political process, disrupt, dismantle, and defeat Al-Qaeda, or root out the threat of militancy or garner Pakistan's unconditional support in fighting extremist elements. The transition from NATO to Afghan local forces is scheduled to begin in the later part of 2011 and will continue till 2014, at which point the security transition period is thought to conclude. Nonetheless, the sustainability of this approach remains vague and uncertain as the Afghan Government struggles to build confidence between the state and the insurgency while the international maintains its opposition to holding dialogue with the *Quetta Shura*. The peace process has become President Hamid Karzai's only tactical and strategic solution to attaining durable peace in Afghanistan. It is nine years too late, yet timely nonetheless. The Afghan people and the government are willing to coexist with insurgents as they sense that with the current deadlines imposed by NATO-led ISAF, the USA will eventually withdraw leaving them to the behest of the Taliban. Keeping this in mind, both Mullah Mutawakil and Mujahid Kakar agree that peace in Afghanistan is unattainable without pursuing reconciliation with the leadership of the insurgency and perhaps outlining a productive role for Pakistan.

More pointedly, perceptions gathered by the author in a recent visit to Kandahar in December 2010 shows that local influential figures, tribal elders and provincial council members are sceptical about the reconciliation and the new transition time-lines set by NATO at Lisbon in 20 November 2010. The security situation in Kandahar is gradually becoming stable since the US troop surge, cited Aghalali Dastagiri, member of the provincial council for Kandahar. Haji Karam Khan, the head of the ad hoc district Shura in Panjwayi district, shared a similar sentiment with Aghalali citing a reduction in Taliban presence in surrounding villages since NATO began its operations in Kandahar. However, Haji Karam Khan was quick to suggest that peace could not be sustained if concessions were not given to Pakistan to lure them into becoming an effective and transparent ally in the peace process. Other interviewed members of the district Shura also concurred that there was a lull in Taliban presence in the village of Panjwayi; however they too were cautious of being overtly confident about the recent military gains, arguing that a military approach would not suffice in ending their worries of another Taliban like-regime taking over Afghanistan. They suggested that a political solution was central to breaking the momentum of the insurgency, however none were optimistic about the manner in which reconciliation and reintegration was being pursued.

Mullah Omar must be included in Peace Talks

"The Taliban think they can win this war,"[2] asserts Kakar. "Currently all major urban centres are surrounded by the insurgency, it resembles that of Dr. Najibullah's period when the mujahedeen had encircled all major cities," cites Kakar, referring to the former Afghan president's short tenure after the fall of the Soviet regime. After the withdrawal of the Soviet Union, Najibullah tried tirelessly to extend his authority outside of Kabul, but was unsuccessful since the mujahedeen had gathered both local and outside support in the provinces surrounding Kabul. Consequently, in 1992, just 3 years after the Soviets left, the mujahedeen captured Kabul. Similarly, the present expansion of the insurgency in northern and western regions of Afghanistan has more or less circled most major urban centres. Thus after NATO's withdrawal, if an effective strategy for reconciliation and realistic transition time-line is not implemented, then President Karzai's government could witness the same fate as his predecessors.

Accordingly, this makes dialogue with the top strata of the insurgency that much more prudent particularly at this juncture seeing as how both the international community as well as the insurgents is not winning the war but not losing it either. The United States has been hesitant to solicit unconditional support for dialogue with members of the Taliban leadership council, the *Quetta Shura*, led by Mullah Muhammad Omar.[3] Reasons for this vary amongst NATO members, but the general justification from the US State Department has been the *Quetta Shura's* 'perceived' close links with Al-Qaeda and Pakistan's Inter-Services Intelligence (ISI). The US State Department holds the position that Mullah Omar is unable to play a "constructive role in Afghanistan's future because he is unlikely to renounce terrorism and remains attached at the hip to Al-Qaeda Chief, Osama Bin Laden."[4] Other reasons cited include Mullah Omar's close association with Pakistan's ISI, and the assumption that removing him from the peace process will drive a wedge in the upper ranks of the Taliban leadership. In reality, the only wedge this will be caused will be between the Afghan Government and the insurgency, as it will inevitably widen the levels of mistrust and suspicion between the two as the former tirelessly pursues reconciliation.

When asked about the prospects for reconciliation and reintegration with 'moderate' elements of the insurgency, Mullah Mutawakil argue that "reconciliation will not yield positive results if certain individuals are excluded."[5] Mutawakil asserts that the pessimism in his statement is linked to his thorough understanding of the insurgency's hierarchical structure. He states that the Taliban system is structured around local commanders, the *Quetta* and the *Peshawar Shura*, fixated around a single Amir. Hence, Mullah Omar must be recognized and given due consideration in the peace process if reconciliation is to be fruitful. He argued that the international community and Afghan Government must not neglect the fact that "Taliban are currently fighting a jihad against what they see as occupiers (US and NATO members) and in a jihad an Amir's role is critical, and insurgents would not take any decision independent of their Amir."[6] With this in mind, Mutawakil predicts that gaining access to foot-soldiers, or the prospects for reintegration, will be impossible without reconciling with the Amir in the Taliban hierarchy. Mutawakil warns that "if the Amir is distanced from the reconciliation process it would show that they (US) do not believe in reconciliation and that they are only supporting their [strict and narrow] agenda for reintegration."[7] Furthermore, the Taliban hierarchy has witnessed few instances of flexibility in membership or representation since 1996. For the most part, the leadership has shown more continuity then discontinuity during both the pre and post-2001 periods[8] depicting the acute strength and importance of the Taliban leadership and the unlikely chances of creating a wedge between the lower and upper ranks of the insurgency following the assumption that alleged 'foot-soldiers' would reintegrate without addressing the role of Mullah

Omar. This is representative of an obscure strategy and understanding of the Taliban hierarchy. The composition of its leadership, ideology, and political aims have not witnessed any acute changes since 2001 and NATO must not approach the issue of reconciliation narrowly by identifying the insurgency as a heterogeneous movement as it is very much a homogenous force despite new adaptations in tactics and scope.

Aghalali Dastagiri suggests a slightly different perspective on reconciliation. In a one-on-one meeting in his office in Kandahar city, Aghalali argues that reconciliation with those Taliban fighters who are willing to join mainstream Afghan society is acceptable. However "those Taliban who have blood on their hands should be punished" and not reconciled.[9] Aghalali resonates an important feeling, presently shared amongst various members of President Karzai's closest circles. It proves that there are elements within the Afghan Government who would also agree with the US and other NATO members that reconciliation with the stop strata of the Taliban insurgency should be questioned, or perhaps not pursued at all.

Nonetheless, justifications for excluding Mullah Omar from the peace talks are without credence. The current insurgency is religious based with several motivations but none that seek to wage *jihad* beyond Afghanistan's borders. There is sufficient evidence to show that the Taliban have not pursued ideological inclination, unlike Al-Qaeda, to show its intentions of participating in a global *jihad* or affiliating its objectives with those of Al-Qaeda. This becomes further obvious when looking at Taliban/Al-Qaeda relations in the late 1990s. Giving an account of Al-Qaeda and Taliban relations in the 1990s, former spokesman for the Taliban regime, Maulavi Qudratullah impresses the point, "…we [Taliban regime] did not invite Osama, we got him as a legacy."[10] The relationship between Mullah Omar and Osama bin Laden was founded on a "common Muslim identity and Pashtun tribal values of hospitality and honour"[11] and not the vision for global *jihad*. Moreover, Osama bin Laden's "provocative and antagonistic" ways had, at many instances, infuriated Mullah Omar to the point where Osama had to be reminded that the Emirate followed the orders of only one Amir, and that was explicitly not Al-Qaeda's. Mullah Omar's reaction to Osama's 1998 "World Islamic Front for Jihad against Jews and Crusaders" announcement was one such example of this. After Osama blatantly ignored repeated demands by the Taliban regime to refrain from activities that garnered

Afghanistan negative international attention, Mullah Omar was forced to order the closure of several Al-Qaeda training camps. Also, US intelligence reports in 2001 had defined the Taliban–Al-Qaeda relationship as being focused on short-term tactical gains rather than long-term policy. Many believed that the Taliban were only entertaining bin Laden to secure funds and fighters which were needed at that time to counter the Northern Alliance. It was this short-term tactical strategy which saw the Taliban hosting bin Laden in the mid-1990s. Many international experts have concluded that the relationship between the two in the pre and post-2001 era was primarily based on "pragmatic needs and personal alliances, rather than ideological coherence."[12]

On the other hand Pakistan has, and continues to exert, both direct and indirect influence over the Taliban's strategic decision making. Pakistan's ever increasing role and influence over the Taliban's autonomy has created contentions between the two. For instance, elements from the Pakistan Government, military and ISI are expected to sit in the *Quetta Shura*[13] and the reasons cited for this is Pakistan's aspirations to strengthen its strategic depth in Afghanistan. The primary focus of Pakistan's strategic depth lies in ensuring that its political and economic interests are taken care of and that expanding Indian influence is countered in the region. A meeting with the tribal elders of Panjwayi district in Kandahar province revealed that there was some truth to this notion. The regularly debated controversy over whether foreign *jihadist* fighters have been aiding the Taliban in Afghanistan seems to be a reality for Panjwayi residents. When Haji Karam Khan, head of Panjwayi district and Achakzai tribe was asked whether he thought the reconciliation initiative was progressing effectively his answer was short and blunt, "reconciliation will not work if Pakistan does not agree with it...even if an insurgent group would want to reconcile, Pakistan would not allow it to do so."[14] He went further and stated that to him and his tribesmen it was 'obvious' from whom the Taliban were getting their resources and support. When the author further probed, the tribal elders revealed that before the troop surge or operations began in Kandahar, they had witnessed many Pakistani, Arab and Chechen fighters operating alongside the Taliban in their district.

Similarly, Kakar also noted that it was irrelevant to discuss the prospects of either reconciliation or reintegration in Afghanistan, when the key to dialogue lay on the other side of the border. He stated that the key to peace in Afghanistan was "to put pressure on Pakistan since the Pakistani army and ISI make up a great degree of support for the Taliban." So the first step should be to prevent Pakistani support for the Taliban and then the next step is to start the dialogue process.[15] Pakistan's tribal border belt provides the Taliban with the only sanctuary available to them outside of Afghanistan. This coupled with funding channels that are virtually untraceable, training facilities and the flow of weaponry, essentially defines some of the recognized links between the ISI and the insurgency. However, Pakistan's support to the Taliban was never exempt of impeding demands from the insurgency which many Taliban members have begun to slowly see as an encroachment on the insurgency's operational autonomy. Pakistan's dualistic agenda towards Afghanistan has both former and current Taliban members questioning Pakistan's viable role in the reconciliation process. Matt Waldman, in describing the Taliban, states that many Taliban commanders have acknowledged that they "...were unhappy about perceived ISI influence over the movement especially at the leadership level."[16] Mutawakil, a former member of the Taliban regime, also expressed doubt over a possible mediating role for Pakistan after the London Conference summoned international support for the Afghan-led peace process. "They [Pakistan] should not be given an active role, for this will not produce positive results; it would be a mistake" asserted Mutawakil in an interview the author had conducted in February 2010.[17]

Mullah Omar's 2009 and 2010 Eid al-Fitr messages have also shown that the Taliban have no ambitions to follow transnational *jihadist* struggles. He instead stresses a desire for an Islamic system that embodies economic, security, legal, educational and judicial aspects. The Taliban leadership's specific reference is to the prevention of civilian casualties; promotion of Islamic system; respect for all individuals regardless of gender, political, racial and lingual discriminations; and a foreign policy that promotes mutual respect between regional neighbours, shows signs of flexibility on their behalf.[18] Moreover, Waldman argues that ISI pressures, growing troop presence, the assassination of numerous Taliban commanders, fatigued fighters, and growing local resentment are also grounds reason why Taliban commanders are beginning to lean towards a political settlement with the Afghan Government.

Furthermore, Mullah Omar's Eid statements can also be analysed to determine the changes that are taking place internally in the overall aim of the Taliban movement. Antonio Giustozzi, an international expert on Afghanistan, presents the most comprehensive outline of the differences between the old Taliban regime and the current insurgency, defining members of the current movement as 'Neo-Taliban.'[19] Giustozzi expresses that the Taliban regime [Taliban regime 96-01] varies from the Neo-Taliban in that, "...they (Taliban insurgency) seem to have absorbed from their foreign jihadist allies a more flexible and less orthodox attitude towards imported technologies and techniques."[20] The Taliban have adopted communication strategies that are far more effective than NATO-led ISAF's or the Afghan Government. This is particularly true seeing the number of websites, radio stations, magazines and other mediums of communication the Taliban have established which help broaden their scope and reach significantly. Furthermore, Ahmed Rashid marks that "Mullah Omar sounded more like a diplomat than an extremist" in his 2009 Eid statement which showed first signs of flexibility on the *Quetta Shura's* part.[21] Rashid recognizes that Omar's statement though continues to urge insurgents to fight the US, it also pledged "that a future Taliban regime could work towards building peace and non-interference from outside forces, and would pose no threat to neighbouring countries."[22]

Giustozzi also suggests that the Neo-Taliban is less of a homogenous hierarchal movement pointing to foot-soldiers as representing a new generation of 'autonomous' fighters.[23] However, befitting western perceptions of reintegration with so-called autonomous fighters, this belief neglects the Taliban's omnipresent heterogeneous characteristics. The insurgency, despite its structural changes still preserves its loyalty to its Amir-ul-Momineen, Mullah Omar, from whom these insurgents continue to get their directions. Moreover, the insurgency's two Shuras, the Quetta and the Peshawar Shura, continue to implement their Islamic ideologies through 'formal' shadow governments in 33 out of 34 provinces in Afghanistan. The *Quetta Shura* itself is represented by members of the old regime (Taliban era) who were predominantly from tribes based in Kandahar. Some of these members have now been either killed or arrested, and they include Mullah Muhammad Hassan, Mullah Jalil, Qudratullah Jamal, Mullah Akhtar Muhammad Mansur, Amir Khan Muttaqi [arrested], Abdulhai Mutema'en [arrested], Mullah Obaidullah, Mullah Beradar [arrested], Muavlai Abdul Kabir and Agha Jan.[24] In light of this, it becomes clear that the insurgents is not ideologically divided groups and still reflects the attitudes that were explicit during the Taliban regime. Therefore, without the Taliban leadership's sanction and oversight, reconciliation, or even at the very least, reintegration would be incomprehensible.

Moreover, it would be pertinent to look at the recent debacle over face-to-face talks between "the inner circle of President Hamid Karzai" and Mullah Beradar (a member of the *Quetta Shura* who was arrested by Pakistan in early 2010). It was claimed that Beradar was transported to Kabul to talk to Afghan officials.[25] This claim was later was found to be baseless; however this incident sheds some light on the discrepancies of the current reconciliation approach. Mujahid Kakar highlighted two facts that show the illegitimacy and ineffectiveness of the reconciliation process even if these claims were to be true. First, Kakar questions if peace talks had actually taken place how effective these talks would have been considering that Beradar was in the custody of the Pakistanis. He states that it would not have been difficult to transport Mullah Baradar who is in Pakistani custody to Kabul, "but how effective can he be as a mediator if he remains to be in custody."[26] Furthermore, "Mullah Beradar has already been replaced in the Quetta Shura by Mullah Abdul Qayum Zakir and Mullah Akhtar Muhammad Mansour, hence even if Baradar was the 'senior Taliban member', the US and Afghan government claimed to have talked to, there is still huge doubt over the kind of role he could have played" reasons Kakar.[27] Similarly, Mutawakil also expressed doubts over these reports, stating that without "an official and formal address," the Taliban are unlikely to agree to talks.[28]

Taliban Need an Address

Mullah Omar and Maulavi Abdul Kabir, member of the Leadership Council of the Islamic Emirate of Afghanistan and the Coordinating Chief of the Eastern Province, rejected the National Consultative Peace Jirga and the creation of High Peace Council that followed it. Mullah Omar referred to the jirga as a "spurious jirga"[29] and Maulavi Kabir described the High Peace Council, "as a one-sided entity, having been established to protect their unilateral goals and interests."[30] These comments should not be interpreted as the Taliban's disregard for the peace process but should indicate reasons for their rejection. Neither reaction represent an outright rejection of the mandate of the HPC;

instead they highlight a level of frustration and resentment the Taliban harbour in the light of the constraints prescribed onto them, in what is supposed to be a negotiation process.

Mullah Mutawakil echoed Maulavi Kabir's projections over the HPC. When asked what he perceived as hindrances to the Afghan peace process, Mutawakil cited the lack of an official address for the Taliban as the single most important impediment to the peace process. He described this as a "technical issue" which should be addressed without delay if the Taliban are to entrust faith, trust and legitimacy to the Afghan Government's efforts in integrating the insurgents into Afghan society and various levels of the government. He asserts that the Taliban need a political office which should be located in a foreign country "where media and diplomats alike can have access to Mullah Omar's representatives."[31] Consequently, Mutawakil suggests that the insurgency's existing political commission led by Mullah Mohammed Tayeb Agha should be institutionalized in either of the following two nations, Qatar or the United Arab Emirates.[32] These two nations were suggested because of their friendly relations with the Afghan Government, credibility amongst the Taliban and their experiences dealing with issues of militancy in their region. Conversely, Kakar construes that the mandate of the HPC is a mere repetition of the unsuccessful peace council that was established under Mojaddedi, "this has happened before but it did not work because the Taliban did not respond to it, at some level there might be contact with low level Taliban commanders but peace is not achievable in this way, as NATO and the Afghan government imagine it to work, because Taliban think they can win this war."[33]

There are other hindrances to the peace process that must be addressed to.

Afghan and international experts have been trying to promote the position that Mullah Omar and his commanders are in fact "fatigued and under increased military pressure" at the moment. Though we cannot misunderstand their fatigue for weakness seeing that the insurgency still retains its strength against foreign troops, we can however argue that after three decades of fighting, Mullah Omar is showing indications that he wants to put an end to this war. "We (Mullah Omar) can consider any option that could lead to the achievement of this goal (the goal of independence and an Islamic system)."[34] However, the Afghan conflict represents a labyrinth of paradoxes in which the peace process is just another mired process.

In addition to ignoring the importance of reconciliation, Mullah Mutawakil cites the removal of the UN sanction list, US bounties, and closure of Bagram prison as catalysts for the peace process. "Peace can only happen, when trust is developed, there is not trust in the current process," disclaims Mutawakil.

Furthermore, an important aspect of the negotiation process, lies is the surreptitious nature of these talks which have been regularly exposed by western media. The success of these talks depends a lot on its secretive nature and this should not be jeopardized by any official or media organ. Both Mutawakil and late Richard Holbrooke believed this statement to be true. Mutawakil laments that the peace process in Afghanistan is complex in that it involves many entities, such as the Afghan Government, NATO-led ISAF, and the US. He states that "as important as it is for the US and Taliban to dialogue, these discussions should be kept secret and behind closed doors." Holbrook, who denounced claims that talks had taken place with high level Taliban leaders lashed out at the media citing false reports of peace talks, "Confidential things must remain confidential in order to be confidential. And I believe in the confidentiality of serious discussions."[35]

The peace process is riddled with contradictions and this was one of the primary reasons why PTS failed to yield positive results in 2003. How can reconciliation take place with those insurgents who are still on UN sanction lists, or, have US bounties on them? How can we reconcile with the Taliban while simultaneously targeting, attacking, imprisoning and torturing insurgents? How can trust be built on fallen promises, misleading reports by western media and constant squabbling between the Afghan Government and its allies over how to proceed with negotiations? NATO-led ISAF's counter-insurgency campaign (COIN) is also affecting peace process, taking the position that the US troop surge which is currently engaged in Operation Dragon Strike in Kandahar will be enough to force the insurgency to the negotiation table. This, as Matt Waldman argues is questionable in strategy, "given the constraints of counter-insurgency operations, and Taliban sanctuary and support in Pakistan."[36] Conversely, tribal elders from Panjwayi expressed relief over operation Dragon Strike, anticipating "an eighty per cent decline in the presence of the Taliban,"[37] since NATO's efforts began in Panjwayi. Ninety five per cent of the local population prefers President Karzai over the insurgency because the Taliban have lost the hearts and minds of the local population with their draconian laws, killing of innocent civilians, extortion, and oppression of tribal elders, Shuras and women. However, tribal elders caution that a military solution will not root out the Taliban, unless a political strategy was simultaneously implemented. Furthermore, the insurgency has sufficient room for casualties, as one fallen commander is quickly replaced by a more "aggressive and vengeful" fighter.[38] The elders also argue that NATO led ISAF should build on the momentum it has gained in Kandahar. Reconciliation efforts could prove more fruitful when the insurgency has been weakened. Moreover, elders showed renewed hope and support for the Afghan National Army. They promoted the notion of transiting security to Afghan forces stating that a competent and strong ANA would guarantee security for locals in Kandahar and elsewhere in the country. This, to the elders, was at the cusp of the reconciliation initiative and operation Dragon Strike. Realizing that NATO's operations will cease by 2014, they explained that a few more months of strong military action against the insurgency in Kandahar and the promotion of better equipped ANA soldiers could bring stability and security to the province, giving both the Afghan government and international forces the victory they have failed to gain in the last nine years.

The Afghan Government and the international community have not fought one war in the last nine years, but nine wars each year, and this is due to the constant revisions in initiative, approach and strategy. However, the Afghan Government and international community can prevent its future from falling into a similar pattern of recycled initiatives by learning from its previous mistakes. Both must understand that reintegration is not possible without reconciliation taking precedence, or else it will suffer the same fate of its predecessors. Nonetheless, this has been particularly difficult when the international community, specifically the United States refuses collaborate with the Afghan Government in what is suppose to be an Afghan-led initiative. To encourage the Taliban to come to the negotiation table, certain preliminary efforts should be made by the Afghan Government and its allies. These efforts include (a) garnering western support in engaging the Taliban Leadership Council in the peace process, (b) provide the Taliban legitimacy by institutionalizing its commission, (c) define a role for Pakistan in the peace process, (d) remove sanctions list, (e) and close down Bagram Prison.

An analogy on Afghanistan shared with the author by Afghanistan's Ambassador to Spain, His Excellency, Masood Khalili, who is the only survivor of the suicide attack that claimed the life of Ahmad Shah Masood, illuminates the essence of what the current peace process represents for the Afghan people. Khalili says, "Afghanistan is like me, a body full of shrapnel, but a heart full of hope." Appropriately stated, Ambassador Khalili's analogy is reflected in President Karzai's peace initiative. Notwithstanding the challenges and constraints of the peace process, the Afghan Government and its peoples continue to have the hope and determination to pave the way forward and bring about a new day for this war-torn nation.

Notes and References

1. Shuras are illustrative of traditional dispute resolution (TDR) mechanisms operating in Afghanistan.
2. Mullah Wakil Ahmad Mutawakil, "No Peace Process without the Quetta Shura," personal interview, 28 October 2010.
3. "US Sees No Future for Mullah Omar in Afghanistan," *EarthTimes*, 14 October 2010. 10 Oct. 2010. <http://www.earthtimes.org/articles/news/348714, future-mullah-omar-afghanistan.html>.
4. "US Sees No Future for Mullah Omar in Afghanistan."
5. Interview with Mutawakil.
6. Interview with Mutawakil.
7. Interview with Mutawakil.
8. Thomas Ruttig, "How Tribal Are the Taleban? Afghanistan's Largest Insurgent Movement between Tribal and Islamist Ideology," Thematic Report, Afghanistan Analysts Network, April 2010, 3. Web. 11 Oct. 2010. <http://aan-afghanistan.com/index.asp?id=865>.
9. Aghalali Dastagiri, "No Peace Process without the Quetta Shura," personal interview, 5 November 2010.
10. Anne Stenersen, "Blood Brothers or a Marriage of Convenience? The Ideological Relationship between Al-Qaida and the Taliban," paper presented at the annual meeting of the ISA's 50th Annual Convention "Exploring the Past, Anticipating the Future," New York, USA, 15 February 2009, 6. 2010-23-11 <http://www.allacademic.com/meta/p312525_index.html>
11. Stenersen, "Blood Brothers or a Marriage of Convenience?"
12. Stenersen, "Blood Brothers or a Marriage of Convenience?" 3.
13. Matt Waldman, "The Sun in the Sky: The Relationship between

Pakistan's ISI and Afghan Insurgents," *Crisis States Discussion Papers* 18 (2010), 1-26.

14. Karam Khan, "No Peace Process without the Quetta Shura," personal interview, 6 November 2010.
15. Mujahid Kakar, "No Peace Process without the Quetta Shura," personal interview, 25 October 2010.
16. Matt Waldman, *Dangerous Liaisons with the Afghan Taliban: The Feasibility and Risks of Negotiations*, Report no. 256 (Washington: United States Institute of Peace, 2010), 3.
17. Mullah Wakil Ahmad Mutawakil, "The Taliban: Reconcilable or Irreconcilable?" personal interview, February 2010.
18. Message of Felicitation of the Esteemed Amir-ul-Momineen Mullah Mohammad Omar Mujahid on the eve of Eid-ul-Fitr," Alemrarah.co.cc., 8 September 2010. Web. 20 October 2010. <http://alemara.co.cc/>; interview with Maulavi Abdul Kabir, Member of the Leadership Council of the Islamic Emirate of Afghanistan and the Coordinating Chief of the Eastern Provinces, "Peace Talks in Conditions of the Presence of Foreign Forces Are Meaningless and Futile," Alemrarah.co.cc., 19 October 2010. Web. 20 Oct. 2010. <http://alemara.co.cc/>.
19. Ruttig, "How Tribal Are the Taleban?" 18.
20. Ruttig, "How Tribal Are the Taleban?" 18.
21. Ahmed Rashid, "A Deal with Taliban?" The New York Review Books, 27 January 2010. Web. 10 October 2010. <http://www.nybooks.com/articles/archives/2010/feb/25/a-deal-with-the-taliban/?page=1>
22. Rashid, "A Deal with Taliban?"
23. Ruttig, "How Tribal Are the Taleban?"
24. Rashid, "A Deal with Taliban?" 21.
25. Dexter Filkins, "Taliban Elite, Aided by NATO, Join Talks for Afghan Peace," New York Times, 19 October 2010. Web. 12 Oct. 2010. <http://www.nytimes.com/2010/10/20/world/asia/20afghan.html>
26. Interview with Kakar.
27. Interview with Kakar.
28. Interview with Mutawakil.
29. "Message of Felicitation of the Esteemed Amir-ul-Momineen Mullah Mohammad Omar Mujahid on the Eve of Eid-ul-Fitr."
30. Interview with Maulavi Abdul Kabir, "Peace Talks in Conditions of the Presence of Foreign Forces Are Meaningless and Futile."
31. Interview with Mutawakil.
32. Interview with Mutawakil.
33. Interview with Kakar.
34. Waldman, Dangerous Liaisons, 7.
35. "No High-level Talks between Afghan Government and Taliban–US

Envoy," Trend, 30 October 2010. Web. 30 October. 2010. <http://en.trend.az/regions/world/afghanistan/1774515.html>.

36. Waldman, *Dangerous Liaisons*, 7.
37. Tribal Elders, Panjwayi District, Kandahar Province, "No Peace Process without the Quetta Shura," personal interview, 10 November 2010.
38. Interview with Tribal Elders, Panjwayi District, Kandahar Province.

16

Negotiating with the Afghan Taliban: Paving the Way to Peace or Civil War?

Vishal Chandra

"You have the watches, we have the time."
A common Taliban refrain against western endeavour in Afghanistan

These are very uncertain times in the three-decade-old Afghan war. The expected withdrawal of bulk of western troops in the coming years amidst growing instability and confusion has provided a new context to the Afghan situation. It was not long ago when the US President Barack Obama had referred to the US-led mission in Afghanistan as a "war of necessity."[1] As the year 2014 approaches, divisions within the US establishment are growing over ways and means of dealing with the Afghan challenge. Except for the Taliban 'ideologues' and their Pakistani patrons, perhaps nobody seems to be clear of the future course of action. The Taliban and their diverse allies and sponsors have successfully stalemated and transformed the Afghan war to their advantage, leaving a vastly superior US-led western coalition scurrying for an 'honourable' exit strategy. No wonder, the Afghan war is regarded as unsustainable and un-winnable in much of the western world. The 100,000 plus American and NATO-led force seem to be engaged in a war with no end in sight. There has been a growing perception that the Afghan war cannot be won militarily and that there is a need to find a political settlement by way of direct negotiations with the leadership of the insurgent groups, especially the Taliban, operating from Pakistan.

The West is apparently far more preoccupied working towards an exit rather than being worried about the long-term strategic implications of losing the war. It would certainly be a turning point in the international politics if both the US, supposedly a super power, and the NATO, world's largest military alliance since World War II, are humbled on the Afghan soil in the first great battle of the twenty-first century. The western exit strategy broadly has three components: (i) developing Afghan National Security Forces (the ANSF), comprising of around 350,000 to 400,000 Afghan National Army (ANA) and Afghan National Police (ANP) put together; (ii) transfer of security responsibilities from the NATO-led force to the ANSF in a phased manner by 2014; and (iii) an Afghan-led and owned process of political reconciliation, especially aimed at the Taliban. This paper is a modest attempt to examine the viability of the reconciliation process as the West draws down troops from Afghanistan and uncertainty over the likely course of politics beyond 2014 intensifies.

Much Confusion

Everybody seems to be talking to everybody in Afghanistan these days, yet nobody is sure of who is talking to whom or the exact objectives of these talks. Those who until recently were dubbed as 'enemies of Afghanistan', are now being sought after for 'reconciliation'. Are Taliban 'brothers' as the Afghan president would sometime refer to them or are they the 'enemies of Afghanistan'? How 'national' is this so-called 'reconciliation' process, and what exactly would the 'reconciliation' with the Taliban mean? Would it come at the expense of gains made last one decade? Is it about 'reconciliation' or is it merely about striking 'deals' with the Taliban, and Taliban as a whole or with sections of the Taliban or certain Taliban individuals? Is Pakistan, a key source of instability and war in Afghanistan, a 'brother' or an 'enemy'? Furthermore, why would the Taliban leaders negotiate if the West is pulling out troops and the government in Kabul is not likely to survive for long thereafter?

At a more sociological and ideological level, the compatibility of the Taliban ideology with the inherent religious and social diversity of Afghan people and country is being questioned. Where are the reasons to believe that the Taliban are going to be any accommodative at the social, political, and the religious levels? Taliban have so far not shown any flexibility or moderation in their ideological beliefs and political objectives. Will they regard shias (who comprise a sizeable minority, nearly 19 per cent of the population) as Muslims;

and are they going to allow people to practice their religion and follow their social norms as per their own traditions and beliefs? Will they give up their demand for an 'emirate' or will Afghanistan continue to be a 'republic'? From the developmental point of view, Taliban do not have much to offer in terms of building up the Afghan economy and state structures.

Related to this are the future of the democratic political system in Afghanistan and the nature of Afghan state—whether a unitary centralized state or a decentralized and a more federal political structure would suit the political landscape of Afghanistan. Who controls the 'reconciliation' process? Though it was supposed to have been an Afghan-led and owned process but that does not seem to be the case. Who will be the guarantor for the deal with the Taliban? Who would ensure that the parties to the deal stick to the things agreed upon? What if the Taliban later violate the deal and capture Kabul? Given the Taliban track record and especially the role of Pakistan in thwarting all past attempts for political reconciliation, the current US initiatives are bound to raise suspicions about the overall intentions of both towards a negotiated political settlement of the Afghan conflict.

It is generally argued that without addressing some of these concerns, there is no point pursuing reconciliation with the Taliban as this is more likely to take the situation back to 1990s. If the Taliban have to be brought back into power, then what was the whole objective of the US invasion of Afghanistan after 9/11? In the current context, it is difficult to believe that the Taliban would renounce their ties with Al-Qaeda or any other extremist ideology and embrace democracy and that too when they are ascendant.

Growing Divide

The Afghan perception about the current reconciliation process is obviously divided in view of a range of historical, political and ideological factors. The divide between the Pashtuns and non-Pashtuns, or between north and south, is palpable. However, at the same time, it would be wrong to assume that there is complete consensus within the Pashtun communities on ways and means of reconciling with the Taliban. The degree of support among the Pashtuns may vary from tribe to tribe and region to region depending upon the nature of their relations with Kabul and the intra-Pashtun dynamics. There is no organized anti-Taliban Pashtun resistance force or clear articulation of the Pashtun approach to the idea of reconciliation with the Taliban.

The support or opposition to the idea of reconciliation with the Taliban depends on three factors: (i) perception about Afghan Government's abilities; (ii) Taliban intentions and their ultimate ideological objectives; and (iii) whether the return of the Taliban to power jeopardizes or strengthens the position of factions vying for political domination in anticipation of western drawdown by 2014. In a way, the politics of reconciliation is basically part of the larger power politics being played out along ethnic lines since 1990s. Several attempts have been made since Soviet withdrawal in 1989 to bring competing Afghan factions together, including the Taliban and the United Front in the late 1990s, but without any success. Apart from external interference, the inability of the Afghans to come to terms with new social and political realities after the Soviet withdrawal had played a significant role in continuing the civil war through the 1990s. The old power structures, elites, and the institutions that were completely altered and destroyed during the war in 1980s were replaced with a range of newly empowered political elites and power stakeholders, especially among the non-Pashtun groups. Afghanistan is yet to reconcile to a major transformation brought about by the decades old war by way of overthrowing the old ruling class and systems and the emergence of diverse localised power-brokers with no ability to provide national leadership and governance. Absence of a functional Afghan state with effective national institutions for decades together has reinforced sub-national identities and politics with almost no scope and hope for the emergence of a strong national leadership in the near future.

Talking of reconciliation with externally-backed powerful Pashtun militant groupings at a time when the Afghan Government is weak and the western forces are drawing down, is bound to evoke a sense of political and social insecurity and possible marginalization among other Afghan groupings in the new political arrangement. On the other hand, the biggest challenge before the government in Kabul is to strengthen its position in order to ensure its survival as the West seeks to end its combat mission by 2014. Kabul is not left with too many options but to try and negotiate deals with the Taliban leaders even if it has grave consequences.

Future Challenges

In the next two to three years, following issues are likely to shape the future course of Afghan conflict:

Strategic Partnership Agreement/Status of Force Agreement

Not much is known about the fate of the Status of Force Agreement (SoFA) or the Strategic Partnership Agreement being negotiated between Washington and Kabul. It is suppose to define the nature of western presence and role of the US forces in the country beyond 2014. Differences over certain operational and authority issues, and the possible fallout of the prolonged American presence both at the national and the larger regional level, seems to be holding the Agreement back for now. The US and most of the European countries contributing troops are facing severe crisis due to economic recession and are reluctant to make long-term financial commitments to Afghanistan. However, the Agreement is deemed necessary for the survival of the government in Kabul and the strengthening of the Afghan army and police. The US has given clear indications that the withdrawal of conventional forces and end of active combat operations by 2014 would not mean the withdrawal of Special Forces or end of training and mentoring mission for the Afghan National Security Forces (ANSF).

What after Karzai?

The leadership question assumes significance in view of western withdrawal and growing Taliban influence. It is not definite at the moment whether elections could be held on time in 2014 or not. This gives rise to the question: what if elections do not take place or even if elections are held, how much credibility would it have as vast parts of the country may by then be simply out of control? Nothing can be stated with any certainty at this point in time about the next line of leadership or what modus operandi would be followed to avoid political vacuum in case elections do not take place. Establishing a caretaker or an interim government is not going to be an easy process. Rising uncertainty is making domestic politics more competitive as alignments and re-alignments take place in an effort to cobble an alternative political arrangement. This could be both an opportunity for cooperation as well as conflict. Building consensus on post-Karzai leadership among disparate Afghan factions is going to be a challenge.

Though Karzai has announced that he would not be seeking a third-term, which would also require amendment in the Afghan Constitution, it is still early to be commenting on his role in years beyond 2014.

At the larger regional level, it may bring US and Pakistan together or may further divide them, depending on the outcome of the ongoing efforts for reconciliation with the Afghan Taliban. Pakistan is likely to push for the inclusion and strong representation of Taliban elements into the new political set up. Possibility of greater friction between the US and Pakistan on the future leadership of Afghanistan cannot be ruled out. All of this may lead to greater anarchy or even a new round of civil war in parts of the country.

Strength of the Afghan National Security Forces (ANSF)

One of the vital components of the western exit strategy is phased transition of security to the Afghan army and police by 2014. The process is already under way even as serious doubts are being expressed about the preparedness of the ANSF. This is perhaps one of the weakest aspects of the western exit strategy. NATO military officials involved in the training of the Afghan army have time and again warned that the army will not be in a position to assume full security responsibilities by 2014. The army, despite phenomenal growth in its numerical strength since the Obama Administration decided to shift the focus from Iraq to Afghanistan in 2009, is far from being an effective deterrent to the Taliban-Haqqani onslaught. The army would need long-term external support in terms of both funding and mentoring in order to sustain and grow as an effective national force.

However, compared to other institutions, the Afghan army despite continuing logistical deficiencies and socio-political challenges is said to be doing relatively well. If the army is able to survive the turbulence and uncertainties of the Afghan conflict and war, it is likely to play a significant role in shaping the future of Afghanistan after 2014–15. However, in the immediate term, the biggest challenge before the army would be to hold itself together in the face of growing political fragmentation, social polarization and donor fatigue. There is already a view that the strength of the ANSF may be downsized depending on the level of western commitment after 2014. The future of the ANSF is thus far from assured.

Short-term Prognosis

As the US/NATO forces withdraw from parts of the country, the Taliban will establish absolute control over large parts of southern and eastern Afghanistan and push for greater control over the Kabul region and parts of northern and western Afghanistan. Given the growing Taliban activism in the north, social tension between Pashtuns and non-Pashtuns are likely to run high in years to come. Resurrection of the former United Front (or the Northern Alliance) may not be possible though armed opposition groups in the north may begin receiving direct external support. However, a full come back of Taliban to power in Kabul is still a distant possibility as 30–40,000 US troops stationed in joint Afghan-US military facilities across the country would continue to conduct special operations against Afghan insurgent commanders on either side of the Durand line. The conflict is likely to remain stalemated. Factional commanders would continue to consolidate their position in anticipation of political vacuum after 2014.

New political formations are likely to emerge as alternatives to Karzai by 2014–15. It would be increasingly difficult for Karzai and the post-Karzai leadership to balance between the rising prowess of the Taliban and the opposition groups from north. Whether Karzai and the factions from north would show greater inter-dependence in times to come is difficult to ascertain. However, it may be increasingly difficult to hold presidential as well as parliamentary elections by 2014–15 and hectic diplomatic efforts would be required to decide on the future leadership as the country plunges into anarchy and chaos. The UN and western interlocutors, as they scout for next line of leadership in Kabul, would have to face challenges similar to the Bonn I (27 November –5 December 2001). There could be a strong demand for incorporating Taliban elements in the new political structure, which may not be acceptable to the leadership from the north. There would also be a demand for change in constitution to devolve greater powers to the provinces, reducing the presidential powers by creating the post of prime minister, allowing revival of party system by amending electoral laws, etc.

The US decision to maintain certain force levels well after 2014 could throw up a new regional dynamic as the US struggles for a 'reset' in its ties with countries opposed to her presence. Meanwhile, regional countries are left with no option but to wait for the next line of leadership to emerge in Kabul. At the same time, various Afghan factions and the neighbouring countries could be aligning themselves as Pakistan remains intransigent on the issue of ceasing its support for extremist militant organizations. The continuing US-Iran standoff may also impact on the overall US presence in Afghanistan. Growing political uncertainty raises the level of proxy politics as factions seek to consolidate their position, further complicating the political future of Afghanistan.

Potential Civil War Scenario

In the given situation, a carefully tailored negotiation strategy could at best serve a limited tactical purpose in the short-term. It is least likely to pave way for a long-term national reconciliation in Afghanistan. Prospects of defection or division within the Taliban are ruled out unless West remains strategically involved in the Pakistan-Afghanistan region for many more years. Negotiating while pulling out forces is not likely to yield any concrete results, and would instead work to the advantage of Taliban and Pakistani military establishment. Both would simply be buying time given their perception that the West is left with no option but to retreat. Unless there is some clarity about the objectives and the nature and level of future US engagement in the region, prospects of even tactical reconciliation would remain bleak. Kabul does not have the institutional capacity to bear with the challenges and potential adverse consequences of sharing power with a much stronger opponent. Worse, if one were to go by the 2014 time line, both US and Kabul do not have enough time at hand to pursue a sustained result-oriented dialogue with the Taliban and their patrons.

Four fundamental questions are critical to the assessment of the current reconciliation process: (i) Are Taliban willing for a negotiated political settlement? (ii) Is the current reconciliation process unifying or dividing the country? (iii) Would the current reconciliation process strengthen or weaken the political process that began after 2001 and help revive a functional modern Afghan state? (iv) Finally, would it help restore a sustainable internal balance of power whereby various Afghan factions, while reconciling with each other's political space, would work towards a unified Afghan state? The answer to the above questions is too well-known to be elaborated here. Even if there is a section/elements within the Taliban which could be willing to engage

Kabul or the US, Pakistan's military establishment would remain averse to the idea of any direct negotiations between the two. On the other hand, a Pakistan-brokered peace deal may not be acceptable to the Afghans. If the Taliban emerge stronger and survive the western intervention, then the reconciliation would not be as much about how much Kabul is willing to accommodate the Taliban, but how much the Taliban would be willing to co-opt the other groups.[2]

In fact, the current process cannot be regarded as a 'reconciliation' process as it is more about negotiating tactical political 'deals' with the Taliban which would come at the expense of the elected government in Kabul and whatever little or more gains have been made in the last one decade in terms of establishing an inclusive political system in Afghanistan. It was back in 2004–05 when Karzai had first offered amnesty to the Taliban and Hezb cadres, and has since taken several unsuccessful initiatives to reach out to the Taliban. It may be argued that after three decades of war, there is a need to take a long-term view of the idea of reconciliation. A national Afghan-led reconciliation process has to have a strong social component to it as well. Reconciliation at the societal level too would be required if it is to work at the political level.

Though the so-called international community had widely endorsed the need for an Afghan-led and owned peace process during the January 2010 London Conference on Afghanistan, the assassination of Chairman Burhanuddin Rabbani of the Afghan High Peace Council was a clear disapproval of the role of current Afghan Government by the Pakistan-backed Afghan insurgent leadership. The supposedly secret meetings held between the US interlocutors and purported Taliban representatives in Germany and Qatar, and developments thereafter, have brought to fore the politics of inclusion and exclusion over the role of divergent stakeholders in the negotiation process. It has undermined the authority of the current Afghan Government, and may be indicative of the future US strategy to work out a completely new political arrangement after the end of Karzai's presidential term in 2014. Until then, much would also depend on the outcome of the US presidential elections due at the end of this year and the contours of the US strategic partnership agreement with Kabul if it comes through before 2014. Meanwhile, prospect of an Afghan-led negotiation strategy is likely to get further diluted as the politics in and around Afghanistan becomes competitive and uncertain.

From the western point of view, the whole idea of opening negotiations with the Taliban is to ensure a reasonably trouble-free pull out of its conventional forces. This is least likely to happen if one were to draw lessons from Afghanistan's past. Retreating US/NATO troops would not be spared of violent attacks and continuing casualties unless a sufficiently self-reliant and strong Afghan Government is in place in Kabul. Taliban have so far fully exploited the weaknesses in the US-led war and the fault lines within the western coalition to transform the conflict to their advantage. It is not clear as to how Taliban is expected to respond to the idea of US reportedly maintaining special operations capabilities and expanded covert intelligence network in Afghanistan after 2014. Here, it would be interesting to note what Mullah Omar had stated prior to US launching the Operation Enduring Freedom:

> I am considering two promises. One is the promise of God, the other is that of Bush. The promise of God is that my land is vast. If you start a journey on God's path, you can reside anywhere on this earth and will be protected... The promise of Bush is that there is no place on earth where you can hide that I cannot find you. We will see which one of these two promises is fulfilled.[3]

The fact that the current political system is not acceptable to the Taliban and a Taliban-dominated government would not be acceptable to the other Afghan groups, both politically and socially, has the potential to push Afghanistan into a full scale civil war. Perhaps, Afghanistan may have to go through yet another round of civil war before a workable political equilibrium is restored with or without the US support. This is all the more likely as national or pan-Afghan leadership or a strong singular authority ruling from Kabul is not likely to emerge anytime soon. Much is clearly still to come before the political scenario in Afghanistan gets clearer.

Note: Some of the inferences drawn in the paper are based on author's personal interactions with a cross-section of Afghan people during his visits to Afghanistan. Views expressed here are personal.

Notes and References

1. "Text of Obama's Address to Veterans," *The New York Times,* 17 August 2009, at http://www.nytimes.com/2009/08/18/us/politics/18obama.text.html?ref=politics&pagewanted=all
2. This point was made by a former Indian Ambassador to Afghanistan during an International Seminar on Afghanistan organized by the Maulana Abul Kalam Azad Institute of Asian Studies (Kolkata) at Jamia Millia Islamia, New Delhi, in February 2012.
3. "Mullah Omar—in his own words," *The Guardian*, 26 September 2001, at http://www.guardian.co.uk/world/2001/sep/26/afghanistan.features11

Regional Concerns

17

Central Asia as a New Transit Way for NATO to Afghanistan

Vafo Niyatbekov

Afghanistan is situated in the strategic location of the region. Its geopolitical position allows it to influence developments both in Central Asia and other countries like Pakistan, India, China, Iran, etc. The advantageous geographical location of Afghanistan appears to be very favourable to the world and other regional powers. The location of YOKE which borders with both Iran—a potential source of oil for the USA—and China, the main competitor for the USA in the region, thus makes the actual presence of international military commitment in the country significant and plays a strategic role for the USA. A continued presence of American military presence and its commitment in Afghanistan require reliable routes to deliver the personnel and ammunition.

Navy Vice Admiral Alan S. Thompson, who directs the Defense Logistics Agency, in the beginning of 2009 called support for operations in landlocked Afghanistan "the most difficult logistics assignment we have faced since World War II." The military's fuel needs are prodigious. According to the Government Accountability Office (GAO), about 300,000 gallons of jet fuel are delivered to Afghanistan each day, in addition to diesel, motor and aircraft gasoline. A typical Marine Corps combat brigade requires almost 500,000 gallons of fuel per day, according to a recent study by Deloitte Analysis, a research group. Each of the more than 100 forward operating bases in Afghanistan requires a daily minimum of 300 gallons of diesel fuel, the study said. According to the GAO report, in June 2008 alone, 6.2 million gallons of fuel went for air and ground operations, while 917,000 gallons went for base support activities including lighting, running computers, and heating or cooling. The

US military remains heavily dependent upon supplies traveling roads in the south from Pakistan to Afghanistan.[1]

The issue of reliable transportation route for delivery of cargo to Afghanistan has recently raised a significant concern. The main transit arrangements of American cargo as well as NATO military forces go through Pakistan, although it is not that reliable. In the end of 2008, Pakistan stopped the provision of supplies of international contingent of NATO in Afghanistan through its territory. According to the sources in Pakistan Government, temporary shut down of supply route for multinational forces in Afghanistan was caused by anti-terrorist campaign that had started previously with support of military air forces, artillery and tanks nearby in the strategic region of Khyber on the border area between Afghanistan and Pakistan. During the last months of 2008 more and more columns of trucks carrying supplies from Karachi to Afghanistan for cantoned military men and their allies were attacked by Taliban forces and fighters of Al-Qaeda. As a result of such attacks, there were victims and significant material damage.

Government official of north western border region of Pakistan, Tariq Hayat imposed a curfew during the anti-terrorist campaign on the most important roadways through which military cargo passed. "The road is temporary closed till the elimination of all terrorists from Khyber area" said Tariq Hayat.[2] Pentagon reported that 44 trucks and 220,000 gallons of fuel were lost due to attacks or other events in June 2008 alone according to the GAO.

Up to 75 per cent of all of the supplies for Afghanistan based NATO forces come to Karachi port. Most of these reach Peshawar and then to Kabul through Khyber pass. The second route goes to Karachi through Quetta then to Kandahar. Part of Afghan belt-road connecting Kabul and Kandahar is always in danger.[3] Four serious attacks of American and NATO convoys that happened in Pakistan urged international forces to conclude a transit agreement with former Soviet Union republics that border with Afghanistan in the north.

The process of diversification of transportation routes of cargo delivery itself started on 29 June 2004 in Istanbul during the summit of 26 NATO countries where the NATO-Russia Council meeting of ministers of foreign affairs took place and problems between partners were raised although the solutions were postponed till the next meeting on another level. In concurrence with Russia initially transit corridors were to provide military activities of anti-Taliban coalition and beginning from last autumn for NATO activities in Afghanistan.[4]

At that moment NATO air planes were allowed to deliver cargo and armament along the net of air corridors connecting military bases of NATO and the USA. The net had several directions: North area "Gansi" airbase of US, 30 km to the north from Bishkek through Lugovoe (Kazakhstan); then to the south of the Aral sea; then from the Kazakh gulf through Kaspii to Nasosnaya (Azerbaijan), Vaziani (Georgia); and split there into south-eastern airbase Incirlik (Turkey) and through Gudauta (Georgia) to Kostanica (Romania); another directions: from the airbase in Tajikistan (French Air Force dislocation), and Kokaidy airbases (airbases of Germany), the corridors would connect in the sky above Khanabad and Chirchik airbases and connect with joint corridor over the southern zones of the Aral seaboard.

In 2008, NATO concluded an agreement with Moscow that allows using Russian railways and motor ways to deliver cargo embarked for coalition troops in Afghanistan.[5] On 3 April 2008 in Bucharest the NATO summit was dedicated to perspectives of peaceful and stable development in Afghanistan, where the President of Uzbekistan Islam Karimov addressed to transform from contact-group 6+2 which stipulates the participation of neighbouring countries of Afghanistan (China, Uzbekistan, Pakistan, Iran, Turkmenistan and Tajikistan) plus the USA and Russia to contact group 6+3 bearing in mind an essential participation of the NATO representative in this negotiation process. The President of Uzbekistan also stated that Uzbekistan stood ready to discuss and sign with NATO the agreement on providing for corridor and transit through its territory to deliver the non-military cargo through the border junction Termez-Khayraton, as well as create a trans-Afghan trade corridor. It is worth mentioning that Uzbekistan has previously eliminated American military commitment from its territory and that step was considered by western countries as a sign of external political change.

Looking in general at the situation in Central Asian republics, it may be mentioned that Central Asia has been transformed from peripheral region to a region which occupies important position in the political agenda of Eurasia. One of the main factors that have determined its new political role is the potential of transportation complex and mainly its transit component. Central Asia holds quite an enormous transportation and communication network and is at the junction of Euro-Asian railways. It has access to the Persian Gulf through Iran, through Afghanistan and Pakistan to the Indian Ocean, through China to Asia-Pacific region. The region possesses quite a great potential to participate in present dynamically formatting international transit. The current development explains the ambition of Central Asia countries to provide effective realization of existing potential.

The Central Asian transit of cargo to Afghanistan firstly depends on Russian Federation. In general, Washington is satisfied with transit to Afghanistan through Russian Federation. American authorities are happy to see the realization of agreement with Moscow on air transit of military cargo for NATO military in Afghanistan. The participation of Russian Federation itself in transit process of military cargo is considered to be a significant contribution into NATO efforts in providing security and stability in Afghanistan.

Special attention should be paid to railway transit. In the beginning of 2010 NATO gained a possibility to deliver non-military cargo to Afghanistan through Russia. It was realized on 27 January 2010. NATO General Secretary Anders Fogh Rasmussen had signed an agreement on railway transit with Minister of Foreign Affairs of Kazakhstan Kanat Saudabayev. It was reported on official web site of NATO. A similar agreement with Russian Federation was signed in 2008. In order to let cargo (especially humanitarian) pass through Russia, there was a need of agreement from Kazakhstan and Central Asian countries. The new route was supposed to complement the existing route through Pakistan.[6]

Although cooperation between NATO and Russia terminated after military activities in South Ossetia in August 2008, it took the whole of 2009 to mend ties between Russia and NATO. On 26 January, the first meeting of Russia-NATO council at the level of Chiefs of Defence took place since Russia-Georgia conflict. In summer 2010, NATO commenced a development of experimental European routes. On 19 June, the first NATO shipment reached Klaipeda port. The shipment arrived from German port but then was transported by Lithuanian railway. The cargo was to be transported through Lithuania to Latvia, then via Russia, Kazakhstan, and Uzbekistan to Afghanistan. Around 5000 containers of NATO go through Russia in one year.[7]

The intergovernmental agreement between Moscow and Washington permits 4,500 flights and 50,000 tons of military cargo per year through Russian airspace which includes armament, military equipment, military stores and personnel. According to the agreement, aircrafts carrying military cargo must land in the territory of Russia, whereas Russia has a right to inspect the aircraft boards. Washington is against that. Moscow opposes the use of military transportation aircrafts insisted by Bruxelles, and maintain the cargo should be transported by charter flights.[8] But such mode of transportation is not working to the full extent.

Pakistan reopened Afghan border crossing to NATO and the USA on 11 October 2010. Authorities of Pakistan banned NATO supply convoys in the beginning of October after attack from American helicopters that led to the deaths of two Pakistani soldiers. Both representatives of NATO and Pakistani military officials were engaged in 'negotiations' or 'joint investigation' in Afghanistan, where it was stated that the soldiers were firing warning shots in attempt to warn the helicopters of their presence but American helicopter crew mistook them for Taliban. While the border was closed, Taliban destroyed around 30 containers of fuel of NATO and US military. The last attack resulted in 13 destroyed containers of fuel. Pakistani transportation companies are used for transportation of fuel and other cargo in Afghanistan.[9] The renewal of NATO transit has many advantages but the new reliable opportunity of transportation through Central Asia should be considered as well.

Formation of transportation services and involvement of international transit cargo traffic in Central Asia is the significant issue of economic, political and social life. The competitive advantages and geographical position of the region can greatly contribute into improvement of current economical situation in the region. Quite a number of factors and conditions can be mentioned in this context, which determines potential of transportation services in the region. Those can be summarized as the following.

1. Geo-economical: geographical position against global economical centres mentioned above;
2. Geopolitical: stability of international relations and security of transportation corridors;
3. Infrastructural: high capacity of transportation network and point of interactivity of transportation modes;
4. Technological: use of technologies and logistics services for rugged regions.

Traditionally Russia plays an important role in economical life of Central Asia, and recently has taken an active part in foreign economic policies in the territory of CIS countries, especially in Central Asia. A part of it is the participation of Russia in development of transportation corridors in the region which is closely related to further access to South Asia through Afghanistan. Along with that, realizing the significance of transportation-transit factor, Central Asian republics conduct an active policy in the sphere of transportation as well. Since independence, each country of the region aims to overcome disparity in their traditional transportation systems by concentrating on intercontinental routes to gain diversified access to the world markets and ocean ports.

Tajikistan mostly concentrates on development of direct transportation and transit between the regions of the country. The project on the reconstruction of the Dushanbe-Khudjand roadway to the borders of Uzbekistan has commenced. The realization of the project will allow year-round over ground transportation between the northern part of Tajikistan and the rest of the country. Roadway reconstruction project on the regional level is held in the frame of intergovernmental agreement on Asian motorways and is meant to be the part of the corridor which starts in Russia, goes across Kazakhstan, Uzbekistan, Tajikistan, Afghanistan and Iran accessing seaports.[10]

The Republic of Tajikistan also contributes into development of near-border territories. During the last 4 years, 2 bridges connecting two countries have been put in commission. Those cross the Tajik–Afghan border in the regions of Ishkashim, Darvaz, Payandj and Khorog city. Frontier markets have opened in the territory of frontier control crossing point on Tajik side; those promote development of localities on both sides of the border. The next project of transportation services development will bring some certain economical dividends.

The projects on renewal of railways revived after elimination of Taliban in Afghanistan in 2001. Iran was one of the first to start the realization of projects. Khaf (Iran)–Herat (Afghanistan) railway was finished in 2008. It was totally funded by the Iranian side and the main economical effect was expected from exporting cargo from Herat and western province of Afghanistan to the regional and world markets. In May 2007, the President of the Republic of Tajikistan Emomali Rakhmon proposed to build the railway to Iran. The railway was supposed to pass through Kolkhozabad, Nizhniy Pyandzh (Tajikistan), Kunduz, Mazar-i-Sharif, Herat (Afghanistan), Mashhad (Iran).

In the middle of 2010, Ministers of Foreign Affairs of Iran and Tajikistan, Manuchehr Mottaki and Khamrokhon Zarifi signed an agreement on preparation of techno-economical rationale of the railway building that would connect Tajikistan with Iran through the territory of Afghanistan. It was proposed that the railway would connect China, Kyrgyzstan and Afghanistan with Iran and then through the Iranian port of Chabakhar with other parts of the world.

Earlier in the beginning of 2008, after the meeting of the President of Tajikistan Emomali Rakhmon with the Minister of Foreign Affairs of Afghanistan Ranghin Dadfar Spanta the latter stated that China intended to build a railway to Afghanistan and further to Pakistan. "The Afghan side suggests that the route cross the territory of Tajikistan," said the minister and mentioned the cost of the project would be $8 billion.

Looking at the transportation projects of three countries (Iran, Tajikistan and Afghanistan) it is worth mentioning the general dynamics of approach of three countries. That process had its reflections in politics as well. In July 2006 the leaders of three countries had a meeting in Dushanbe. At present the current tendency is more of geopolitical rather than historical nature. In general, this meeting can be seen as an attempt of two leaders (of Iran and Tajikistan) to create an alternative idea as opposed to the idea of *pantukrism* ideology, which does not correspond to the national interests of Teheran and Dushanbe.

Tajikistan should become a geopolitical centre of the whole Central Asian geopolitical tellurocratia strategy. The republic plays a central role here; moreover its territory can become a geopolitical laboratory with two impulses—the Islamic impulse of Indo-European Eurasian south and Russian geopolitical impulse going from heartland from the north. Thus another line should be drawn—Moscow-Dushanbe-Kabul-Teheran where the unique geopolitical reality could be formed.[11] All four countries have displayed an active political interaction and it is seen in the diplomatic relations between these countries, except Afghanistan due to existing crisis in the country itself.

There is another project of the building of railway services through the Republic of Tajikistan joining Kashgar (China) and Herat (Afghanistan). Under terms of the project, the length of the railway would be almost 2000 km, 392 km of them passing through Tajikistan. Techno-economical expertise will be provided by Iran with Iranian

Government allocating $1 million. It is estimated by Tajik experts that the railway will cost the country $3.5 billion. The Kashgar-Herat railway will have three branches: two of them will run across Turkmenian railway and another one across the Uzbek line. Asian Bank for Development has allocated $2.5 millions to Afghanistan for preparation of techno-economical justification in its territory. The length of railway on the territory of Afghanistan wills be1, 105 km whereas in Kyrgyzstan it will be 196 km. The experts from China are preparing the techno-economical justification in Kyrgyzstan. From Kashghar (China) to Kyrgyzstan, the total route length of the railway will be 215 km.

Conclusion

Considering transport communications of the Central Asia and Republic of Tajikistan in particular have certain value in continental and inter-regional transportation of goods that is defined by sets factors. But a major factor is location of the region between the world economic centres. Thus the positive in dynamics of these processes is contributed by the large countries and regions which are contiguous with the Central Asia and promote the geo-economic interests. The economic analysis shows that in some cases overland connections can provide viable alternative to sea transportations, essentially raise transport availability of the countries through which they pass, and incur considerable growth of transportations, especially container.

Today the Republic of Tajikistan has considerable appeal as transit territory, offering optimum conditions of passage of goods. Transport communications passing into the country through Republic of Uzbekistan and Republic of Kyrgyzstan and provide alternative routes. This can be followed up through Afghanistan and Pakistan also. Transport arteries crossing through the Republic of Tajikistan allows considering the republic in the near future as the centre of transit traffic.

Notes and References

1. Пакистанские коридоры смерти//http://www.artofwar.net.ru/profiles/sergei_skripnik_andrei_greshnov_p/view_book/pakistanskie_koridory_smerti

2. http://www.izvestia.ru/news/20/news195197/index.html
3. Пакистанские коридоры смерти//http://www.artofwar.net.ru/profiles/sergei_skripnik_andrei_greshnov_p/view_book/pakistanskie_koridory_smerti
4. Кузарь В. НАТО в зеркале заднего вида // Красная звезда. 2004. 30 июня.
5. Кузарь В. НАТО в зеркале заднего вида.
6. http://www.lenta.ru
7. http://news.mail.ru/politics/3162997
8. http://news.mail.ru/politics/3162997
9. http://www. CNN/InterRight/dawn.com
10. Транспортные коммуникации ЦА: варианты максимального использования их потенциала// http://www.cps.uz/rus/analitics/publications/transportnie_kommunikaii_a_varianti_ maksimalnogo _ispolzovaniya_ix_poteniala.mgr
11. Дугин А. Основы геополитики. Геополитическое будущее России.—М.: Арктогея, 1997.—С. 354-357.

18

Problems and Perspectives in Countering Militant Threats in Afghanistan: Their Impact on Neighbours

Oybek Makhmudov

This article looks at the problems and perspectives in countering the threat of religious militant groups in Afghanistan and analysing their impact on neighbour countries. Regional organizations operating in Afghanistan lack expertise to effectively counter international militant activities. Every organization tries to solve its own national interests. The last OSCE summit in Astana showed that it was more populist events (more than $30 million spent in the summit) which would enhance Kazakhstan ambition and position, through Russia lobbying, rather than trying to solve real security problems in Kyrgyzstan and Afghanistan that were given greater importance. In addition the meeting concentrated more on solving issues of internal threats than external. This is because at present Russia would like to secure her interests in Central Asia, and concentrate more on Afghanistan without involving the region. NATO also has problems in countering terror activities in Afghanistan, as they are mostly implemented according to western perceptions, without taking into account the specifics of traditions, history, mentality, geography, culture, in this country and region. That is why it is necessary to implement the 6+3 initiatives of multi regional security organizations, including neighbour countries, in efficiently solving militant conflicts in Afghanistan.

In addition regional organizations from 1999 to the present could not block the penetration of religious militants groups from Afghanistan to South Kyrgyzstan and Tadjikistan. The regional security structures failed in adequately preventing to the threats of well organized militants' tactics of guerrilla warfare. The militants, armed with light weapons and night vision goggles, are prepared for longer armed struggle. The dispersal of small arms from Afghanistan has contributed to militants activities in the Central Asian region. Afghanistan provided a permanent source of a variety of weapons. The huge quantities of small arms, ranging from assault rifles to hand grenades, were supplied from Afghanistan to the militants in Central Asian countries. After the Soviet retreat from Afghanistan, the Soviet army left quantities of weapons including AK-47 that began to be used regularly in confrontation between the Taliban and the Northern Alliance and were also exported to Pakistan. The gun is now produced in Pakistan at very low price. For example, small arms and shotguns are sold for $40 and AK-47s for $70 at the Khyber Pass Armaments Company on the Grand Trunk Road.

In addition between the years 1986 and 1989, the US channeled around 1,000 Stingers to the mujahedeen. The flow of small arms to Afghanistan did not end even after the Soviet forces left the country in 1989. Before the Russian troops left, the US increased its arms supplies to Afghanistan to ensure that the Soviet decision to leave would hold. The US provided the mujahedeen with Stingers and Milan anti-tank missiles, and continued to support the Afghan guerrillas in their fight against the pro-Soviet regime. Besides leaving behind large stockpiles of small arms after its forces had withdrawn, the Soviet Union, in turn, launched an intensive series of arms and ammunition supplies to Kabul. At this stage of the armed conflict, Pakistan continued to act as a conduit for weapons transfers from various supporters of the mujahedeen. However, due to severe tensions and disagreements between the main mujahedeen groups based in the Peshawar, by the end of the 1980s, the military and financial aid from the mujahedeen was regularly directly channeled to tribal leaders and military commanders inside Afghanistan.

It has been estimated that roughly one half of the small arms currently circulating within Afghanistan arrived there during the cold war years, most of them from countries involved in the Afghan conflict. For example, the United States delivered at least 400,000 Kalashnikov assault rifles to the Afghan guerrillas in cooperation with the Pakistani ISI. In addition, at the beginning of the 1990s, the ISI still had access to around 3 million Kalashnikov originating from the pipeline operations. The small arms accumulation in Afghanistan came from three main sources: the stocks of foreign governments, small-scale arms manufacturers in the region, and black-market suppliers.

The small arms in Afghanistan is sold for cash; bartered for teak wood, hostages, heroin, or religious artifacts; or countertraded for grain and oil. The deals are transacted by smugglers sending gold to South Asian countries, trafficking in counterfeit computers to Russia, or shipping toxic waste to Somalia. The ships with the arms are probably registered in a flag-of-convenience country boasting commercial secrecy, low registration fees, and the opportunity for rapid name and ownership changes. The payments can move through a series of coded western bank accounts in the name of a global network of ghost companies and are protected by the banking and corporate secrecy laws of one or several of the many financial havens around the world.

The primary threat present inside Central Asian countries is the presence of religious militants groups believed to have links with the Taliban and Al-Qaeda. These groups are thought to have become particularly activate after military operations against the Taliban and Al-Qaeda in Afghanistan and in Pakistan.

The main threats in Central Asia consist in lack control of uranium resources in Kyrgyzstan and Kazakhstan that the international militants groups could get hold of. The threat of militant groups in getting of radioactive materials in the Kyrgyzstan became a serious thing, especially in case of the illicit smuggling incidents in Central Asian drug routes (in the south of Kyrgyzstan in Mayluu-Suu tailings are located) which could be used for smuggling radioactive materials.[1]

The lack of guards at the uranium sites could pose a serious proliferation threat from acquisition by militant groups, depending upon the level of radioactivity in materials that have been abandoned. Many militants groups operate in the territory of the Kyrgyzstan, including Al-Qaeda and others as IMT, Eastern Turkestan Islamic Movement, and Hizb-ut-Tahrir, which are major threats to regional stability. Analysts point to the fact that terrorist groups are being forced from the Afghanistan-Pakistan border areas and are "actively pursuing their agenda in Central Asia following the intensified attacks by the ISAF in Afghanistan and Pakistan."[2] In July 2009, Kyrgyz authorities arrested 18 people accused of assisting international militant groups. Most of those detained had been trained in Afghanistan. Hizb ut-Tahrir has a significant presence in the Kyrgyzstan; it might collaborate with Al-Qaeda. According Ariel Cohen, "Hizb ut-Tahrir takeover of any Central Asian state could provide the global radical Islamist movement with a geographic base and access to the expertise and technology to manufacture weapons of mass destruction."[3]

Another threat has emerged from the lack air security regarding preventing supply of arms to Afghanistan from planes flying illegally from Belgium, Ukraine or South Africa to traffic weapons originating in Eastern Europe and delivering them to clients from Africa to Afghanistan.

The growing civilian casualties caused by US and ISAF air strikes in Afghanistan and Pakistan poses a major challenge for the international forces and its allies in the terror counter operations. The attacks and the casualty estimates available to date focus largely on the areas where direct military clashes have taken place involving US, NATO, ISAF and ANA/ANP in countering Taliban and other militant groups. These are also the areas where most air strikes are concentrated. The UN maps show that Taliban and other militants have influence over a major part of Afghanistan rather than the 11-13 per cent area that is the focus of actual fighting. It quotes the UN Secretary General as noting that roughly 175 of the country's 400 districts (around 44 per cent) is at times outside government control.

All this factors lead to the following problems:

1. Absence own regional security system in Central Asian republics, security generally guided by Russian and American considerations;
2. Lack of operational modalities in regional military forces and failure at the planning and implementations stages to properly coordinate the deployment and operational activities of the armed forces between the various power ministries;
3. Domination of the political ambitions in admitting countering strategies;
4. Lack of finance for arming local armed forces and especially in Afghanistan.

A comparison between militant groups and state armed forces in Afghanistan and region will bring out the real picture.

The Taliban commanders use their finance resources as vital tools in recruitment to their troops. According to estimates, the average soldier is paid between $100-150 per month, while cell commanders are paid considerably more, approximately $350 per month. The Taliban fighters are often deployed for only short temporary service. Taliban commanders often use a call-up system by which young men in areas under Taliban control are called up to report for short several day operations. Additionally, the Taliban offers from $10 to 20 per day for attacks on western forces, and $15 to launch a single mortar round into nearby coalition military bases, and $1,000 for the head of a government worker or a foreigner.[4]

The majority of foreign fighters are recruited from Pakistan's madrasas, refugee camps in Baluchistan, and reportedly as far east as Miram Shah in Pakistan's FATA. During ISAF operation in Helmand's southern Garmser district in spring of 2008 it enhanced the foreign fighter facilitation network. In this operation, around 150 foreign fighters were killed in just one week's period. According to reports there were more than 500 fighters in the district, most of them foreign. Coalition forces in Helmand have even "syndicates" of militants moving back and forth across the Helmand-Pakistan border, including Pakistanis, and elements of Al-Qaeda. The major source of Taliban funding is a *zakat* collected from villagers in areas under Taliban control. The exact tax assessment varies from area to area, though in some places the *ushr* or a ten per cent is collected. The tax is linked to agricultural production of crops like wheat and fruits, as well as illegal crops like opium, and is often paid once or twice yearly following major harvests. Most Taliban fighters are farmers and Taliban campaigns are timed to allow the Taliban to harvest their opium fields every spring. The Taliban have historically charged opium farmers an *ushr* on opium at harvest time. Furthermore narcotics traffickers who buy opium directly from farmers must pay the Taliban a tax, as well as truckers who pay a per-kilogram transit tariff. But the Taliban also provide protection for traffickers. In exchange for a fee, Taliban fighters have been known to forcefully defend narcotics processing labs and refineries that manufacture opium into heroin. The donations from supporters in Pakistan and the Gulf states are a further source of revenue for the insurgency activities.

The Taliban benefited from the discontent caused by banning of poppy cultivation in Helmand and Kandahar. In Helmand, the Taliban were welcomed into farming communities that were often the target of government-led eradication forces. In the last years, the eradication campaigns came under intense attack from Taliban forces, and eradication could not be completed in towns along the Arghandab river, especially because the Canadian military refused to support counter-narcotics units.

In contrast, local armed forces are not so well trained as the militant fighters. That is why they could not carry on combat operations in mountains terrain of Afghanistan and Tajikistan. Also Afghan forces lack equipment and communication systems in the field. The uniforms and body armour remain widely mismatched and very poorly distributed. Most police personnel are issued at least one uniform that is traded out for warmer/cooler uniforms depending on the season. The composition of this equipment varies between American, Russian and Chinese military grade equipment to 3rd party equipment that provides no real protection. ISAF and NATO forces usually carrying actions in day time, but from 2009 the Taliban fighters began conducting night time patrols and raids in some areas of Kandahar city, occasionally engaging ANP units with small arms fire, and Taliban patrols have been known to visit houses at night and forcefully demand food and supplies.[5] The Taliban's nighttime patrols increase people's fear of its activities. While the Pakistani state has had trouble dealing with insurgents, the Afghan security forces are still considerably weaker than their counterparts across the border. It is entirely plausible that as NATO troop levels come down, militants will find Afghanistan to be the regional weak link. Afghan and Pakistani Taliban factions, along with Baloch separatists, and perhaps other militant groups in the South Asia region, may come to find safe havens within Afghanistan's territory if a power vacuum is left by the withdrawal of foreign troops.

Thus, if the Afghan military is deterred from engaging in extensive cross-border operations by its stronger neighbour, Pakistan will not face similar constraints in violating Afghan territory. If Pakistani militants come to find strongholds in a weak Afghan state, Pakistan may be tempted to strike.

In global levels strong confrontations exist with Euro-Atlantic and Eurasian regional security organizations' as NATO, OSCE, CSTO and SCO in countering security and terrorism issues and targeting information. It results the limited transnational military cooperation rendering ineffectual any efforts to pursue fleeing insurgents, or containing the conflict.

For external actors, the unstable situation in Afghanistan creates favourable opportunities in controlling energy resources in region by the armed forces. NATO might also provide security for infrastructure in energy producing states. NATO views most energy producing countries as unstable, as in Middle East. Therefore they propagate that Central Asian countries will need in military assistance to secure their energy supplies. Although Russia and China are attempting to work together within the SCO to balance their influence in Central Asia, Russia plays a dominant role within the CSTO. The CSTO is mostly a tool to keep the Central Asian states under control. Russia wants to prevent the Central Asian states from selling their natural gas to the Europe without going through Russia, since in this case Russia's pipeline monopoly would be threatened and the states in the region would become more independent.

Russia wishes to keep all energy exports from the territory of the former Soviet Union under its control. The current conflict over the closing of Manas Air Force Base in Kyrgyzstan reveals the means by which funds and influence are being struggled over in Central Asia. In this case, Russia pledges to pay more than US, but results were ineffective. The economic capability of western countries is much more powerful and real than Russians. While the Central Asian leaders enjoy certain advantages in this 'Great Game', there is a lack of outside pressure which is needed to implement important political and economic reforms. Russia's objective to weaken American influence in the region and to permanently secure its own role as a regional power has failed. Anyway Central Asian countries are not any more interested in having a single dominant actor in the region. However for reviving the dominance in region, Russia has tried to augment the rapid forces of Collective Security Treaty Organizations as military tools for imposing its perspectives on national states during internal and external tensions in the region. The emerging strategic landscape of the region has not only affected the interests of the traditional actors as US and Russia, but also the national interests of neighboring countries, as Afghanistan, China, Iran, Pakistan, Turkey, as well as those like the European Union, India, Japan. The current greater game involves more than ten players. Most of them use the combinations of geo-economics with geostrategic tactics. This mixture of changing world politics suggests that the new Great Game for the influence and control of heartland resources is far more complex than was in the nineteenth century when there was competitive colonization of the region by the England and Russia.[6]

Now US and Russia negatively accept the increasing Chinese influence on whole of Central Asia. China is pursuing the long-term goal of becoming the most important actor in the region. While the Russian strategy is mostly based on the development of military cooperation with the Central Asian states, China is concentrating on economic cooperation. Russia's resurging military might in the region could also influence decision-makers and producers in the Caspian and Central Asia. In this situation, the United States, Europe and China represent other external players with considerable military capabilities which could shape the security of the region and the energy routes which run through these volatile territories. The existing contradictions between Russia and China (migrations, trade, etc.) are of lesser impact to the main challenge of increasing American presence in the region. Thus Russia and China have been cooperating to reduce US influence in the region and, as they accrue more Central Asian energy assets, will have more points with which to prevent US encroachment into their spaces of influence. For Russia one major purpose in mitigating the US and NATO influence in the region is because these are viewed as challenging to Russia's reviving importance and presence in the region. In Russian geopolitical assessments calculations, the Central Asian region is valuable in projecting its power status as a competitor with the US and the EU.

China and India's perceived need to secure access to energy supplies will make these countries more global rather than just regional powers, while Europe and Russia's co-dependency is likely to be strengthened. A growing energy demand will promote geopolitical and energy competition among great powers that, in turn will reinforce their perceived energy insecurity.

The best solution in sustainability of Central Asian countries and Afghanistan may be found in the following measures:

1. Gradually mitigating raw resource dependency on other countries to developing alternative sources of energy and intellectual resources;
2. Preventing privatizations of strategic energy fields by the foreign companies.

To establish energy security supplies it is extremely necessary to safeguard the vulnerable land trade routes and infrastructures in the region. In this issues China and India must be integrated in securing the global energy supply chain, including Central Asian routes, since as large consumers they are equally interested in stable supplies. It would be of grave significance for old and new players for seizing energy resources of region.

Therefore the foreign actors should accept the national specifics and interests of Central Asian countries and Afghanistan before implementing any strategies and mediation. And external actors should involve Central Asian countries more in meeting on nontraditional security challenges, particularly climate protection, disarmament, energy and raw material supplies, the commercialization of renewable energy resources.

Mid-term Scenarios in Afghanistan and Beyond

The ongoing armed conflicts in Afghanistan could spread to Pakistan that is destabilizing the neighbouring South Asian and Central Asian countries.

Operationally, there is some evidence of Al-Qaeda working with the Afghan Taliban. Al-Qaeda itself does not do real operations in Afghanistan; it is not in the position to do so. The most it can hope to be is a kind of force multiplier for the other entities that are already there. In that context it has been ready to provide some support and assistance to Afghan Taliban units in weapons training and providing some material assistance. Also, some of the foreign fighters are experienced fighters and know quite a lot about military tactics. So there has been, at the tactical level, certain of amount of cooperation. In Pakistan there are links between the Al-Qaeda, the Tariki Taliban and the Pakistan Taliban, because the Al-Qaeda leadership are in the tribal areas and they have not just come there in 2001. The Al-Qaeda has gradually and effectively created local alliances through intermarriage and business relationships in South Asia and tried to penetrate Central Asia.

The major threat at present will be come from Al-Qaeda. This group has the necessary funds, people and experience to be able to conduct terrorist activity in every part of the world. There is serious concern that Al-Qaeda may decide for expand of its activity to Central Asia, and will be able to realize it in midterm perspectives.

Certain factors provide grounds for concern that Al-Qaeda may expand its activity to Central Asia.

1. The loss, or risk of losing, safe shelters by Al-Qaeda in western and north-western Pakistan as a result of intensified activity by Pakistani and US troops in that area, and friction between tribes and individual armed groups. In this context,

the black holes emerging in Tajikistan and Kyrgyzstan could at least partly provide an alternative temporary or permanent shelter to some Al-Qaeda militants or their families. A similar situation has already arisen in the past (with the IMT in Tajikistan), and it cannot be ruled out that it also exists now (it is suspected that Mullah Abdullah, the Tajik commander linked to Al-Qaeda, and his supporters returned to Tajikistan in spring 2009).

2. The militants groups in Afghanistan could defeat the Government of Afghanistan in relatively short order and re-establish the state that hosted Al-Qaeda and provided a useful base for transnational terror groups to train and plot against secular regimes. These international militants groups then turn their attention to incumbent the regime in Pakistan and undermining the stability in whole Central Asia.
3. During next few months there are probabilities in realizing militant's activities in Central Asia from Afghanistan. These activities would be implementing by the groups located in Afghan territories. They are from various international militant groups that move from Afghanistan to Central Asia, who are responsible for implementing specific tasks (participation in battles, organization of terror activities). These militants group would be the most trained and prepared. Another groups as "Tajiks" would come from Tajikistan territories and their objectives include destabilization in the Sogd Region of Tajikistan for complete loss of control of secular regime over the territory of the neighbouring countries.

The suicide bombings in London, Moscow, Madrid, Tajikistan, Kabul and insurgency movements in Europe and escalating of religious conflicts in Middle East should bring about a change to the views of foreign actors and global organizations in admitting common strategies for countering terrorism. Therefore only with joint efforts of the regions will it be possible to mitigate threats from the militants groups. In addition the rich geo-cultural and geo-religious potentials of the Balkan, Central Asia and South Asian regions should be taken into account to effectively counter and prevent proliferation of religious militant tendencies.

Notes and References

1. UNODC, Regional Office for Central Asia, www.dbroca.uz/gallery/thumbnails.php? album=8
2. R. Muzalevsky, "Kyrgyz Operation against IMU Reveals Growing Terrorist Threat," 1 July 2009, www.cacianalyst.org/?q=node/5144.
3. Ariel Cohen, "Hizb ut-Tahrir: An Emerging Threat to U.S. Interests in Central Asia," The Heritage Foundation, 30 May 2003, www.heritage.org/Research/Russia and Eurasia/BG1656.cfm.
4. Samuel Chan, "Sentinels of Afghan Democracy: The Afghan National Army," *Military Review* (January-February 2009), 13.
5. Steve Rennie, "Locals live in fear of Taliban," *Canadian Press*, 4 January 2009; Gloria Galloway, "Taliban Ratchet up fear in Kandahar City," *The Globe and Mail*, 26 September 2009.
6. Mehdi P. Amineh, *Globalization, Geopolitics and Energy Security in Central Eurasia and the Caspian Region* (The Hague: Clingendael International Energy Program 2003), 209.

19

Indian Interests and Strategic Stakes in Afghanistan

Anwesha Ghosh

India shares ancient and civilizational ties with Afghanistan. Cultural linkages and strategic aspects across South Asia make it imperative for India to seek bilaterally beneficial relationship with Afghanistan. However the ties between the two countries were briefly halted during the period when Taliban was in power in Kabul. In the three decades of King Zahir Shah's rule and later on when Nazibullah's government was in power in Afghanistan till the advent of Taliban, India had major presence there, providing assistance in fields of education, medical, engineering and defense. After Najibullah's violent killing by the Taliban in 1996 and the deterioration of security conditions there, India had to make an exit from Afghanistan. Unlike Saudi Arabia, Pakistan and UAE, India never recognized Taliban's assumption of power in 1996.

Strategically sandwiched during the Great Game, Afghanistan has never managed to emerge out of the plague of external interference.[1] The 11 September terrorist attack on the United States and the subsequent responses has been to a large extent responsible for the change of strategic calculations of many countries towards Afghanistan and the region at large. 9/11 brought to surface a number of trends that were less visible earlier. Perception of threat and sense of national insecurity reached its height at that time which made a country like India feel like she was on the front line of America's war on terror. Age old historical ties between the two countries, India's experiences with the Taliban regime and their supporters, the strategic challenges that the nexus poses and India's own security perceptions are some of the factors that have shaped India's policy towards Afghanistan. This paper attempts to analyse determinants of India's interest, her role in Afghanistan's reconstruction endeavor, challenges faced in the context of her past experiences and also her strategic stakes in Afghanistan. The argument of the paper is that India's interest and stakes in the country is legitimate and should be considered from a broader geopolitical context. Even after the US withdrawal it is likely that India as a rising regional power would make her presence felt through her development initiative and exercise her capabilities, willingness and legitimacy for a long-term engagement in Afghanistan.

The Indian Concern

Geographically Afghanistan can be seen as a 'hyphen' between Central Asian and South Asian security environments. It was crafted as a buffer zone and not as a nation-state, with the aim of separating dominant regional powers. Today it is more of a connector state between the surrounding security zones than separator. It draws together various security-related issues like narco-terrorism with an Islamist background and spills them over to all bordering regions. Indian interest in Afghanistan cannot be separated from larger foreign policy imperatives. Security, as mentioned, is one of the important areas of India's interest in Afghanistan. With the disintegration of the Soviet Union, Afghanistan became the epicenter of contest for influence and power politics and after the Soviet withdrawal, without much surprise the land became the victim of contestation for control. Each regional country tried to establish its influence and the result was clashes of interest which contributed in making situation within Afghanistan even more explosive. In the post cold war era, main concern of many nation states have been emergence of non-state actors having transborder linkages and heavily armed as a major security threat.[2] State patronage of such groups only worsens the situation. Even before American invasion in 2001, India was convinced that the Taliban regime and Al-Qaeda's access to Central Asia and the potential *jihadi* violence in the Indian state of Jammu and Kashmir (with Pakistan's support) constituted a serious security threat. It was nervous about the fallout of a Taliban success on the internal security situation in Jammu and Kashmir where a number of Afghan veterans from different parts of the world had increased dramatically.[3] The nexus between Taliban, Al-Qaeda and militant groups that target India like Lashkar-e-Taiba (LeT) and Jaish-e-Mohammad (JeM) is obvious and therefore India had to be concerned about this unwanted development. There have been instances when Al-Qaeda had openly declared India as one of its targets. Scholars have argued that the testing time for India came in 1999 when Pakistan, backed by Taliban/Al-Qaeda regime entered the Kargil region of Jammu and Kashmir with a view to internationalize the issue.[4] The 2001 terrorist attack on Indian Parliament was also believed to be the handiwork of the Afghan mercenaries having connection with Pakistani Intelligence agencies.[5] The hijacking of IC814 to Kandahar is one of the instances which indicated a close relation between JeM and the Taliban-Al-Qaeda coalition.[6]

There were reports of various training camps established in Afghanistan were training of various groups that were operating in Kashmir was being carried out.[7] In fact after the withdrawal of the Soviets from Afghanistan the covert war was replicated in Kashmir. The ideology disseminated by these groups has dangerous significance for peace and stability in the region. The ISI was involved in supplying arms to the terrorist organizations and colluding in the drug trade. But what was most alarming was the nexus among the Pakistani military/ISI and Afghanistan's Taliban regime and its Al-Qaeda mentors in sponsoring terrorism in not merely Jammu and Kashmir but also all over India. India from the very beginning had viewed Taliban as a source of imbalance unlike some of the countries of the region. India along with Russia, Iran and some central Asian countries cooperated to ascertain that Taliban influence does not fan out across Afghanistan. They supported the Northern Alliance to counter the Taliban after their rise to power. India would naturally not like to be again put in a disadvantageous position as it was during the Taliban regime.

India's main interest has been to develop deep relations with the people of Afghanistan with whom it has shared century old historical ties. Therefore India has concentrated on developmental initiatives that would assist it to establish a chord with common man in the areas that is dominated by Pashtuns with whom it had age old ties. At the same time Afghanistan would provide an access to some of the countries of Central Asia to secure its trade links and diversify its energy sources.

India's Engagement in Afghanistan

India's assistance activities and development partnership with Afghanistan covers *four* broad areas, namely, humanitarian assistance, major infrastructural projects, small and community based development projects and education and capacity building initiatives.

India is the sixth largest donor and the largest OECD donor to Afghanistan. Humanitarian assistance includes food assistance, sending of winter clothing, gifting of vehicles for mass transport as well as for Afghan National Army among other things. She has medical missions in Kabul, Kandahar and Herat but following the Kabul attack and worsening security situation some of the medical missions were closed but those missions have been resumed now. Over three hundred thousand patients have been treated by these medical missions and have been provided with free medicines.[8] Major infrastructural projects undertaken by India in the country includes building the parliament building, transport and communication network. The Border Road Organization has completed building the 218 kilometre Delaram-Zaranj road links to facilitate movement of goods and services from Afghanistan to the Iranian border and onwards, to Chahbahar Port. This would give Afghanistan another outlet to the nearby port and this would also facilitate India's trade with Afghanistan and Iran.

India is committed to development and infrastructure projects in various sectors in Afghanistan. She is helping Afghanistan to build Salma dam power project in Herat province. India has built a transmission 220 KV line from Pul-e-Khumri to Kabul to provide it with 24 hours electricity supply under North-East Power System project. Apart from this India is providing $100 million under food assistance for school feeding programme to be administered through the World Food Programme. It is constructing hospital in Kabul, reconstructing Habiba school, have dug 26 tube wells in North-West Afghanistan; it has built telephone exchanges in 11 provinces connecting to Kabul, it is expanding National TV network by providing uplink from Kabul and downlinks in all 34 provinces. 84 small projects are under different stages of implementation in 19 provinces of Afghanistan. A road, built by an Indian company with aid from the Asian Development Bank (ADB), connects Kandahar with Spin Boldak. Total aid of India for developmental activities in Afghanistan at present stands at $1.3 billion. India has sent about four thousand Indian workers in Afghanistan who are now protected by Indian paramilitary and police forces. In terms of soft power, India's assets like music, movies and television shows in Afghanistan are remarkably popular; these also contribute positively in bringing two countries closer. A unique characteristic of India's assistance is that most of its projects are grounded on Afghanistan's requirement than what India thinks would be good for Afghanistan.

Several visits that took place after 2001, gave a new lease of life to the bilateral relations between the two countries. Both the countries signed bilateral preferential trade agreement in 2003 when Karzai visited India. This gives tariff concession to Afghan goods. India hopes her investment in the Iranian port at Chahbahar will allow her to gain trading access to Afghanistan, bypassing Pakistan. Pakistan currently allows Afghanistan transit right for its exports to India but does not allow Indian goods to move to Afghanistan. During Prime Minister Manmohan Singh's visit to Kabul in 2005, Indian Prime Minister assured Karzai of New Delhi's continued cooperation and assistance in stabilizing the county's security and democracy. India pledged to construct the parliament house at $ 200 million. In April 2006, Karzai made his fourth visit to India since he became the Afghan leader in 2001. At this occasion he led a 110-strong delegation made up of cabinet ministers, members of the Afghan National Assembly and business people.[9] These high level visits have led to better understanding between two countries.

Post 9/11 Indian Perspective

The post 9/11 American invasion of Afghanistan had remarkable "empowering" effects at the domestic, regional and international domain in addition to its geo-political and strategic ramifications favourable to India.[10] Impact of the US led war following post 9/11 attack was significantly felt by India at different levels. Domestically, the extremist elements within Indian Muslim population who till then glorified and identified with *jihadist* ideas in the name of God got a huge blow. Apart from popular resentment religious extremism was questioned everywhere. India gained strategic mileage and attained an upper hand in Afghanistan when following the US led war in Afghanistan ties between India and Afghanistan grew stronger much to Pakistan's annoyance. Pakistan's "Strategic Depth" was pretty much at loss after American invasion and India's support to Northern Alliance. Apart from that, it was this occasion when it was seen that India actually achieved a strategic leverage in the whole region including Central Asia and Iran. A significant improvement could be visible in the bilateral relations between US and India. For the first time in their history, the US administration indicated that the world's largest democracy, situated next to China, next to Pakistan-Afghanistan, West Asia and Central Asia, is needed as a stabilizer in the region.[11] After 9/11 India insisted that her position against the Taliban regime, Al-Qaeda and Pakistan as key boosters of international terrorism was justified and thus India increased diplomatic campaigns to persuade US to put pressure on Pakistan to stop its cross border terrorism in Kashmir. US responded since it was aware that Pakistan occupied Kashmir was being used to serve as reservoirs for anti-US *jihadis*. India opted for closer military and strategic cooperation with Washington and forwarded active support to America's global war against terrorism.

In a sense, India's post 9/11 policy seems to have paid some dividends thereby helped New Delhi to regain much of its lost ground. For India, Afghanistan is also a potential route for access to Central Asian energy. India as an observer in the Shanghai Co-operation Organization has been pursuing better relation with Central Asian countries for energy cooperation. New Delhi seeks friendly allies in the neighborhood which can provide a gateway to energy rich Central Asian States such as Turkmenistan and Kazakhstan. India-Afghanistan relation got further boost when all top leaders including Indian educated Hamid Karzai visited India with the aim of reactivating ties with India. Afghan Expert J. Alexander Their says "India is looking to ensure that other countries in the region favour or at least are neutral on its conflict with Pakistan." Afghanistan on the other hand, he says, looks to India as "a potential counterweight in its relationship with Pakistan."[12]

Pakistan's Response

The Taliban were propped up by Pakistan in early 1990s to attain strategic depth, quell sub-nationalist aspirations plaguing the country, negate resurgence of the Durand line dispute, and bleed India in Kashmir from the bases in Afghanistan. Today, Afghanistan is clearly a part of the dominant conflict in South Asia "Afghanistan ... in many ways has replaced Kashmir as the main arena of the still-unsolved struggle between Pakistan and India."[13] From Pakistan's perspective, its own support for the Taliban government was essentially helpful in two ways. Firstly, it relieved the pressure arising from Afghan-Pakistani border dispute and Pashtun nationalism and secondly, it helped her gain long sought "strategic depth" vis-à-vis India. Though there are arguments in favour of the refugee crisis that was unleashed on Pakistan by Soviet invasion of Afghanistan and the subsequent civil war as strong factors behind such a move. However in the post 9/11 era, Pakistan suffered heavy losses on every conceivable field after the exit of Taliban and entry of Karzai administration, whose foreign policy agenda is pro-Indian and at least rhetorically fixed on conflicts in its relationship with Pakistan.[14] Unstable Afghanistan could mean refugee influx into Pakistan, into Pashtun-dominated FATA and NWFP yet Pakistan's interests are so very much linked with Afghanistan's instability that it opposed Indian involvement in Afghanistan from the very beginning. It is not surprising therefore, that Pakistan sees India's growing influence in Afghanistan as a threat. Pakistan could not afford a situation when the devil of Durand line and other issues will be raised. Conversely, the Indian Government's sustained support for perceptibly anti-Pakistani forces in Afghanistan has been interpreted as "strategic encirclement" by Pakistan.[15] After India opened consulates in Herat, Mazar-e-Sharif, Jalalabad, and Kandahar, Pakistan charged that these consulates provide cover for Indian intelligence agencies to run covert operations against Pakistan, as well as foment separatism in Pakistan's Balochistan province. Former Pakistan President Pervez Musharraf charged India of trying to create an "anti-Pakistan Afghanistan" contending that New Delhi is using its consulates in Places like Jalalabad and Kandahar to formant trouble in his country.[16]

Pakistan is also not comfortable with the strengthening of Indo-US bilateral relations. Promotion of democracy is an area where interests of two countries coincide. India strongly believes that US withdrawal before the attainment of stability in Afghanistan will lead to greater chaos. Pakistan for obvious reasons does not reflect similar sentiments on the same issue. Pakistan also remains skeptical of India's Central Asian strategy within a context of a stabilized Afghanistan.

The Emerging Trends

India has watched with caution when the Obama administration proclaimed an 18 month deadline for his Afghan "surge". This can be seen a wakeup call to the countries in the region who will pay the highest price for continuing instability in Afghanistan. Unlike other neighbours of Afghanistan, India strongly believes that US withdrawal without stabilizing Afghanistan will lead to a greater chaos.

Afghanistan's geopolitical relevance for India arises primarily from its security concerns vis-à-vis Pakistan. New Delhi would not like to see a repetition of the post Soviet withdrawal scenario of 1989. For India, it is essential that the fundamentalist Taliban regime, even one that is willing to make tactical peace with the West does not take root again. Given the fast moving dynamics in Afghanistan and especially after January 2010 London Conference when she appeared isolated over its insistence that there is no "good" versus "bad" Taliban, talks in western capitals about differentiating between the "bad" and "good" Taliban in order to make deal with the latter not just horrifies India. From her experiences and close proximity India knows that any Taliban faction, good or bad, will sooner or later revert to its extreme doctrinaire way of looking at the world.[17] India insists that Afghanistan can never be secure as long as Pakistan continues to be a safe haven for Islamic *jihadi* groups.

US commitment to Afghan war has been criticized. At a very critical juncture the war got diverted to Iraq which led to the strengthening of Taliban. Moreover the announcement of withdrawal was not accompanied by a fall back strategy and is believed to have given a wrong signal to the Taliban who interpreted it as defeat. Taliban is yet to contemplate a compromise which will facilitate their becoming part of the government. Relation between Afghanistan and US has deteriorated significantly after Karzai's second term as President over issues of corruption and heavy rigging that took place during re-election. It is unlikely that Mulla Omar and other hardcore elements would agree to retract from violence and play a second fiddle to any government in Kabul. US have qualified its statement of troop withdrawal now. The current position is that such withdrawal would be conditioned upon the situation as it develops on ground.

An increasing number of Indian analysts are convinced that the US cannot really "exit" from Afghanistan by 2011 or even 2014, no matter what the stated position of Obama policy is. There is an emerging consensus in private Indian circles around a most likely Afghan scenario—at least 50,000 ISAF forces will stay in Afghanistan for more time to protect major population centres so that even if western alliance cedes much of the countryside to various Taliban factions, it will prevent all out civil war by leaving the governance of provinces to local warlords and that drones and air power will play the role of final arbiter.[18] Even though the situation may not reach as it was in the early nineties, Afghanistan would remain under international glare. It is not clear whether this would lead to enduring peace.

India's role in Afghanistan has been recognized by the world community. For example in a recent statement the US State Department spokesman C. J. Crowley said, "We have worked hard across the region to try to move countries beyond a zero-sum mentality. Pakistan has an interest in what happens in Afghanistan. So does India. And likewise, going in the other direction, Afghanistan has an interest in what goes on in countries that border it, whether it's Pakistan and India on one side or Iran on the other."[19] Shashank Joshi recently made a strong case in *The Guardian* that now is the time to build on India's considerable soft power presence in Afghanistan, which consists of development aid, cultural ties and symbolic projects such as the building of the new parliament building in Kabul, and combine it with an increased hard power posture.[20]

National Security Advisor of India Shri Shiv Shankar Menon visited Kabul in March after a terror attack in Kabul which killed 7 Indians. Similar incidents have taken place many a times before to thwart India's developmental work as there is a perception that it would add to India's influence in the region. This incident has triggered an urgent security reassessment of the massive Indian programme in Afghanistan and for the first time forced the Indian Government to seriously rethink about the projects and the associated risks it is willing to take in a post 2011 scenario. In fact there is an increasing chorus of senior voices within Indian security community which view India "should stop frittering its resources on what is for the foreseeable future a hopeless cause—Afghanistan."[21] However the public opinion in India is yet not against India's involvement in Afghanistan and believes India being a strong neighbor can help Afghanistan in many ways by leveraging its own experiences in building social, educational and political institutions.

Conclusion

India is the largest regional donor and remains central to process of regionalism in South Asia given its superiority compared to rest of the states. India's involvement in the country indicates her willingness and preparedness to become more involved in the attempt to reconstruct and stabilize Afghanistan. An atmosphere of mistrust is presiding in the country which often gives the indication of a zero sum game. India's interest in Afghanistan does not run parallel to any other country in the region as it directly hits on India's security and stability.

Nevertheless India as the main provider of security in its troubled neighbourhood can only be a long-term prospect if she first deals with her own domestic instabilities and problems stemming out of underdevelopment. The battle against Taliban and Al-Qaeda is still heavily reliant on US and NATO efforts and it is obvious that India won't be able to replace the international security forces any time soon. The idea is rather that while the international forces try to maintain military control and rebuild the Afghan National Security Force, the regional actors should work towards creating a situation where a heavy presence of security forces is no longer necessary. This would be possible if India can build a new trust, ease anxieties and find a way for Pakistan to share in some of the benefits arising from relative stability of Afghanistan.

Notes and References

1. Mondira Dutta (ed.), Emerging Afghanistan in the Third Millennium (New Delhi: Pentagon Press 2009), 375-91.
2. Smruti Pattanaik, "Indian Interest in Afghanistan: Opportunities and Challenges," in *Stabilizing Afghanistan: Regional Perspectives and Prospects*, Maqsudul Hasan Nuri, Muhammad Munir and Aftab Hussain (eds.) (Islamabad: Islamabad Policy Research Institute 2011).
3. Ahmed Rashid, "The Taliban: Exporting Extremism." *Foreign Affairs,* 78/6 (November/December 1999), 22-23.
4. Riyaz Punjabi, "Kargil Aggression: The Continuum of a Strategy," *Journal of Peace Studies,* 6/3 (1999): 3-8.
5. Pattanaik, "Indian Interest in Afghanistan."
6. Ahmed Rashid, *Decent into Chaos* (London: Allen Lane, 2008), 112-17.
7. K. Warikoo, "Afghanistan Factor in Kashmir Crisis," in *Afghanistan: The challenge*, K. Warikoo (ed.) (New Delhi: Pentagon Press, 2007), 200-01.
8. "India to resume Medical Mission work in Afghanistan," *The Times of India*, 20 July 2010.
9. Jagmohan Meher (ed.), *Afghanistan: Dynamics of Survival* (New Delhi: Kalpaz Publication, 2008), 208-12.

10. Meher (ed.), *Afghanistan*, 208-12.
11. See Chidanand Rajghatta, "India, US sign 10 year defence agreement," *The Times of India*, 30 June 2005.
12. Jayasree Bajoria, "India-Afghanistan Relations," Council on Foreign Relations. http://www.cfr.org/publication/17474/indiaafghanistan_relations.html (accessed on 11 December 2010)
13 Barnett R. Rubin and Ahmad Rashid, "From Great Game to Grand Bargain: Ending Chaos in Afghanistan," *Foreign Affairs*, 87/6, 30-34.
14. Barnett R. Rubin and Abubakar Siddique, "Resolving the Pakistan-Afghanistan Stalemate," *United States Institute of Peace Special Report* 176 (2006).
15. Rubin and Rashid, "From Great Game to Grand Bargain."
16. See newspaper report "Musharraf questions India's role in Afghanistan," 10 November 2010. http://www.rediff.com/news/report/india-creating-anti-pak-afghanistan-says-musharraf/20101110.htm (website accessed on 12 December 2010)
17. Subhash Agarwal, "India's role in post-2011 Afghanistan—Can Canada & India collaborate?" *Canada-Asia Agenda*, 8 (28 April 2010).
18. Agarwal, "India's role in post-2011 Afghanistan."
19. "Stable Pakistan is not a threat to India: US," *Daily Times*, 29 July 2010.
20. Eric Randolph, "India's Afghanistan Dilemma," *The Guardian*, 5 January 2010.
21 Sushant Sareen, "AfPak and India's Strategic Innocence," Institute of Defense Studies and Analysis, Report, 2 April 2010.

20

Afghanistan's Thirty Years War: End Game in Kabul?

Krishnan Srinivasan

Foreign interventions were habitual during the process of Afghan nation-formation in the nineteenth and twentieth centuries, and were usually resisted, and did not contribute to the welfare of the Afghans, who harbour a well-known and well-merited aversion to foreigners. The present Afghan war has been going on for more than thirty years and during those years, several million Afghans were killed, and more than ten million have fled, leaving 28 million in the country. Almost all the great powers have tested their military might there, promises of peace and democracy degenerated into more war and devastation, and uncountable fruitless operations resulted in more bloodshed, hatred, horror, and an upward spiral in drug production.

The Taliban ruled Afghanistan from 1996 to 2001, and are best remembered for barbaric Islamist practices and the wanton destruction of the Buddha monoliths at Bamiyan. From 2001 onwards, under unanimous UN Security Council resolutions, an International Security Assistance Force was set up, initially to protect the government of Hamid Karzai, and then to eliminate Al-Qaeda and combat insurgents. 100,000 US troops are in ISAF and 40,000 from 48 other countries in what is already the longest military exercise in US history. Yet, there is no international consensus on the limits or objectives of intervention, and it seems the Americans themselves hardly know why they are there. They assert they have no quarrel with the Afghans; it is only the Al-Qaeda that is the enemy. Speaking to me at the time of ISAF's creation, Jaap de Hoop Schaffer, NATO secretary general, envisaged early withdrawal when democracy and rule of law were established in Afghanistan. That type of nation-building did not succeed in Kosovo or Albania or Bosnia in Europe. How was it ever possible in Afghanistan?

Afghanistan is portrayed as the most acute security problem in the world, and the Taliban as a threat to regional and global peace. Is terror contained because ISAF/NATO is in Afghanistan? The answer depends on what defines the Taliban. Today, people everywhere have heard of these Afghan 'students', but to describe their objectives, apart from the defeat of foreigners in their country, is problematic. Despite the presence of ISAF, 65 per cent of Afghanistan is under Taliban sway. The Talibs are now vastly different from the pre-2001 variety, being younger, more skilled at propaganda, and closer to Al-Qaeda, Wahabis and Salafis. They have better tactics, use guerilla methods and are entrenched even in urban areas. They obtain widespread Afghan respect because they are seen as fully opposed to foreigners. Karzai himself describes the Talibs as 'disenfranchised brothers', thereby confusing the people and his army.

The Karzai Government's control continuously shrinks in the face of the Taliban and security deteriorates every year. Al-Qaeda has been disrupted by the US offensive but the Taliban are far from defeated or degraded, due to their safe havens in Pakistan. Calling Pakistan the "epicenter" of global terrorism, Admiral Mullen, Chairman, US Joint Chiefs of Staff, has said that America cannot succeed in Afghanistan unless terrorist safe havens in Pakistan are shut down. So the prime obstacle to removing the threat of terror is clearly identified.

ISAF's aim to disrupt, dismantle and defeat Al-Qaeda and its principal backers, the Taliban, has had to be modified more realistically. This year, according to President Obama, the US will start transferring out of Afghanistan and 2014 is the timeline to shift authority to Kabul. The goal is to secure agreement with the Taliban because the Afghan army and police cannot possibly cope with internal and external threats unless the level of threat is reduced. This exit strategy is only about exit and not strategy, according to Henry Kissinger.

Afghanistan must prepare for the reality of US military withdrawal. There is wide disapproval of the Afghan campaign in the USA and all NATO countries, making it politically impossible to stay on. The US military budget, at this time of economic strife, is higher than rest of the world combined, and the ratio between the highest and the average incomes in America is an unacceptable 120:1.

US troops may remain in Kandahar and former Soviet-era bases, not for the sake of Afghanistan, but to maintain surveillance over Pakistan's nuclear facilities that are vulnerable to terrorists. Washington will never make any public pronouncement on this, unless it is obliged to by domestic political considerations.

There is some progress in Afghanistan; it is not a medieval or broken state. There have been advances since 2001 in respect of the media and civil society; roads, rail and power. Six million children go to school, of which 38 per cent are girls. In 2001, only 1 million went to school and they were all boys. There is primary health centres in 2/3rds of the country as opposed to 10 per cent in 2001. But there are setbacks in economy and security, rule of law, corruption and narcotics, and human rights abuses are perpetrated both by government and the insurgents. Reconstruction in Afghanistan needs prolonged engagement with the West and the UN since it will need huge funding. The US says it is committed in the long term to Afghanistan's development agenda but, as by far the largest donor, its aid has too closely been tied to counterinsurgency strategies, with the blurring of humanitarian and military objectives.

In politics too, there have been serious errors. Greater external controls over the governance process have weakened moves for Afghan self-government. The Afghans have a tradition of decentralized authority, whereas the USA stresses a strong centre though simultaneously undermines it by dealing direct with warlords and local power groups. Sub-governance is probably the right answer, but all Afghans will oppose American think-tank proposals of balkanization into quasi-sovereign provinces or seven administrative units that correspond roughly to ethno-political divisions. There is a culture of corruption at all levels, with ISAF itself guilty of paying protection money to local warlords. Counter-narcotics policies are not succeeding, and NGOs are acting like parallel authorities. Polity is a hybrid between the traditional and modern, and the debate goes on about a presidential or parliamentary system, and the role of shuras and jirgas in any future dispensation. Despite the problems in determining legitimacy, the West will have to relax its control over outcomes. Elections have failed to produce an Afghan voice, and the traditional forms of consensus-building like the shura and jirga have also not succeeded.

In the search for a solution, various regional approaches have been mooted, especially since diverse ethnicities in Afghanistan need reconciliation. The ethno-linguistic complexities are immense, with Pashtun, Uzbek, Tajik and Hazara majorities living outside the country and the minority within Afghanistan. The neighbours act out competing and conflicting interests, to say nothing of outsiders like Saudi Arabia with its profound and malignant links with the Taliban. Pakistan wants to exclude any Indian influence in what it regards as its backyard; Iran cannot accept Shias being treated as apostates by Wahabis; China fears Uighur contamination by extremism; Central Asia fears narcotics and terrorism. The US refuses to involve Iran, while any armed action against Iran by USA or Israel will hugely increase radicalism in the Middle East and Central Asia with unpredictable consequences. Pakistan can be a deal-maker or deal-breaker, but a Pakistani brokered peace will not be acceptable to its neighbours or to all the Afghans.

There is no such thing as a card-carrying Taliban. *Pashtuns* and *Talibs* are not synonymous and the Taliban are not monolithic. The Talibs are in at least three formations—Mullah Omar's *Quetta Shura*, Haqqani in North Waziristan (strong Arab element and attached to Pakistan's ISI) and the Pakistani Taliban. Each Taliban group has a different leadership with different agendas. The Taliban are therefore more of a 'movement' intending to defeat ISAF/NATO and re-claim Afghanistan. Ethnicity and Islam are not cementing factors. Hekmatyar, the mujaheed of anti-Soviet vintage, is a constant spoiler, and the Taliban will not cohere after any settlement and once the NATO troops withdraw.

Despite all this, moves for a settlement are constantly afoot. Karzai is moving closer to regarding Pakistan as essential for his continuation, and Rabbani, a former Afghan president, is acting as his intermediary with the *Quetta Shura*, though the US does not want Mullah Omar in the peace and reconciliation process. The process is highly opaque between all the various players. There are whispers of future talks, perhaps in the Gulf, perhaps in Turkey. The broad principles could comprise: no partition, no single outside power to be dominant, no hand-over to Pakistan, no reversion to the *status quo*, no imposed neutrality, the Afghans to own the process, and Afghanistan's independence and sovereignty to be guaranteed by Pakistan.

It is unlikely that any talks will be fruitful unless there is a prior end to combat operations, and in addition to insurgents, any negotiation must include formal and informal power holders, and should ideally include obligations to human rights and accountability, though enforcement will be impossible. But there is a saying in Afghanistan: "In principle, no compromise; in compromise, no principle." And that, finally, is likely to be the untidy and unsatisfactory outcome.

Contributors

Binoda Kumar Mishra, Fellow, MAKAIAS.

Shanthie Mariet D'Souza, Visiting Research Fellow, ISAS, National University of Singapore.

Vladimir Boyko, Director of the Centre for Regional Studies (Russia and the East), Altai State Pedagogical Academy, Russia.

Aunohita Mojumdar, Freelance Journalist, Kabul.

Maqsudul Hasan Nuri, Acting President, Islamabad Policy Research Institute (IPRI), Islamabad, Pakistan.

Shahmahmood Sayed Miakhel, Country Director, Afghanistan, USIP.

Jagmohan Meher, Associate Professor, Department of Political Science, National Defence Academy, Pune.

Jamal Rehman, Advisor to the Chief of Staff of Office of the President of the Islamic Republic of Afghanistan on Foreign and Cultural affairs, Kabul.

Zubair Popalzai, BBC Monitoring, London, U.K

Gulshan Sachdeva, Associate Professor, Centre for European Studies, School of International Studies, Jawaharlal Nehru University.

Sayed Mohammad Shah, Senior Policy & Communications Officer, Afghan Research and Evaluation Unit, Kabul.

Abdul Rehman Ulfat Mahmoodi, UNDP.

Sanaullah Tasal, USIP, Kabul.

Savita Pande, Professor, Jawaharlal Nehru University, New Delhi.

Mariam Safi, Head of Research, Centre for Conflict and Peace Studies, Kabul.

Vishal Chandra, IDSA, New Delhi.

Vafo Niyatbekov, Senior Specialist, Department of External Policy and

Economic Development, Strategic Research Centre, President of the Republic of Tajikistan, Tajikistan.

Oybek Makhmudov, Uzbekistan, , Senior Lecturer, Institute of Retraining Teachers, Ministry of Public Education, Uzbekistan.

Anwesha Ghosh, Fellow, Institute of Foreign Policy Studies, University of Calcutta, Kolkata.

Krishnan Srinivasan, Former Foreign Secretary and Fellow, MAKAIAS, Kolkata.

Index